TORTURE .
TORTUROUS V]

Transcending Definitions of Torture

Victoria Canning

BRISTOL
UNIVERSITY
PRESS

First published in Great Britain in 2023 by

Bristol University Press
University of Bristol
1–9 Old Park Hill
Bristol
BS2 8BB
UK
t: +44 (0)117 374 6645
e: bup-info@bristol.ac.uk

Details of international sales and distribution partners are available at bristoluniversitypress.co.uk

British Library Cataloguing in Publication Data
A catalogue record for this book is available from the British Library

ISBN 978-1-5292-1842-8 hardcover
ISBN 978-1-5292-1843-5 paperback
ISBN 978-1-5292-1844-2 ePub
ISBN 978-1-5292-1845-9 ePdf

Cover design: Liam Roberts Design
Front cover image: istock/KonArt
Bristol University Press uses environmentally responsible print partners.
Printed and bound in Great Britain by CMP, Poole.

Dedicated to those who survive;

in memory of those who do not.

Contents

List of Figures and Tables   vi
About the Author   vii
Acknowledgements   viii
Outline of Book   x

Introduction: Why 'Torture and Torturous Violence'?   1

1   Outlining the Definitional Boundaries of 'Torture'   13
2   'Wandering Throughout Lives': Outlining Forms and Impacts   38
     of Torture
3   'I Wouldn't Call it Torture': Conceptualizing Torturous Violence 59
4   Sexualized Torture and Sexually Torturous Violence   75
5   Experiential Epistemologies: Embedding the Lived   101
     Experience of Women Survivors
6   Unsilencing   119
7   Addressing and Responding to Torture and Torturous Violence   144

Notes   164
References   167
Index   181

List of Figures and Tables

Figures

1.1   Defining torture   15

6.1   Forms of silencing   122

Tables

1.1   Developments of definitional boundaries of torture   18

2.1   Problems which may develop in the aftermath of torture, as   52
defined by the United Nations Convention Against Torture or
Other Cruel, Inhuman or Degrading Treatment or Punishment

7.1   Recommendations from key practitioners   159

About the Author

Victoria Canning is Associate Professor of Criminology at the University of Bristol. Her research and activist interests lie in gendered harms, zemiology, state power and violence, torture and specifically in trajectories of violence. She is currently Head of the Centre for the Study of Poverty and Social Justice, associate director in Border Criminologies at Oxford University, and trustee of Statewatch. Vicky has published and edited various books and articles, including *Gendered Harm and Structural Violence in the British Asylum System* (2017), *From Social Harm to Zemiology* (2021, with Steve Tombs) and *Stealing Time: Migration, Temporalities and State Violence* (2021, with Monish Bhatia). She is co-creator of the Right to Remain Asylum Navigation Board (with Lisa Matthews) and acted as academic consultant on the BAFTA award winning series *Exodus: Our Journey to Europe.*

Acknowledgements

As with every book, this has been a long process of discussion, research, reflection and debate. Although any errors are of course mine, the whole text has involved so much from many people – not least the survivors of violence and women seeking asylum who gave insight into the realities of violence and violation. Moreover, those who work at the fore of responding to torture and torturous violence are often overlooked in wider research and scholarly writings. This means that the very people who hear disclosures, watch structural and political shifts in state and organizational responses, and even see the wider sociopolitical implications of persecution, war, failed states, repression and conflict, are not central to some academic discussions. They also often see conflict and torturous violence in places that we like to pretend it isn't: the home, families and other everyday social institutions.

First thanks go to Antonia, Asma, Faiza, Jazmine, Mahira and Nour for spending time building oral histories. Endless thanks also to Migrant Artists Mutual Aid, and particularly Jen, Amina, Shani, Elizabeth and Anstey.

Huge thanks to all practitioners who engaged with this project and took time to discuss complex issues and ideas. Special thanks to Lisa Matthews and Michael Collins at Right to Remain – developing the Asylum Navigation Board (Canning and Matthews, 2020) and the podcasts and community engagements that went with it was one of the few times where serious work could be made more light-hearted – thanks both, and to Calverts for their ways of making ideas work for people seeking asylum.

Most of the projects for this text were in partnership with the Danish Institute Against Torture who have given space and time over almost a decade. Many thanks to everyone involved, in particular Marie Høgh Thøgersen, Tomas Max Martin, Rasmus Grue Christensen.

He will think this overly sentimental, but my main thanks go to Andrew M. Jefferson. Ten years ago, we met at the European Group conference in Chambery, where he flippantly suggested I might be interested in coming to DIGNITY to see what work was done there. Since then, AJ has supported in so many ways to engage with people and ideas even when I disagreed – always a learning curve. So many thanks, and to Lotte, Marie and Joshua for sharing time, home and sometimes Writer's Tears over the years.

Thanks to my family – in Northern Ireland, Mum, Dad, Sami, Stevie and Lisa, Ryan and Kylie, Mags, Den, Nanny, Vi, Saz, Paula and all the kids. Thanks to the Faloona sisters, and Crawf, June and Bobbi B. We lost Veronica just before this book was published – thank you, V, for reminding us what kindness looks like.

At home in Liverpool, I'm forever grateful to Drew, Cara, Zemi and Atticus – especially Drew! Thanks always.

In alphabetical order, many more thanks to: Dalia Abdelhady, Bridget Anderson, Monish Bhatia, Michala Clante Bendixen, Oscar Berglund, colleagues at BUP, Policy Press and Newgen, in particular Rebecca Tomlinson, Freya Trand, Angela Gage, Julia Mortimer and Helen Flitton, Helen Churchill, Border Criminologies, Mary Bosworth, Bristol Refugee Rights, Jon Burnett, Ergün Cakal, Alice Cutler, Esther Dermott, DIGNITY – the Danish Institute Against Torture, Andrew Douglas, Liz Douglas, Francesca Esposito, European Group for the Study of Deviance and Social Control, Andriani Fili, Daniel Jiménez Franco, Jacqui Gabb, Liv Stoltz Gaborit, Harm and Evidence Research Collaborative, Paddy Hillyard, Rhianne Jones, Martin Joormann, Alaa Kassab, Robert H. King and the Angola 3, Annika Lindberg, Lisa Matthews, Migrant Artists Mutual Aid, Migration Mobilities Bristol, Sanja Milivojevic, Emmett Minor, Ida Nafstad, Oasis CPH, Christina Pantazis, Georgios Papanicolaou, Amina Rafique, Refugee Women Connect, Darius Rejali, RFSL Newcomers Malmö, Right to Remain, Hannah Ryan, Simone Santorso, Hanna Scott, Nando Sigona, Katja Simončič, Ann Singleton, SPS undergraduate, postgraduate and research administration support, in particular Freddy, Hannah, Nikki, Evey and Isis, Kay Standing, Elizabeth Stanley, Statewatch, Swedish Red Cross Centre for Persons Affected by War and Torture in Malmö, Steve Tombs, Trampoline House Copenhagen, Philomene Uwamaliya, Jennifer Verson, Tony Ward, Frances Webber, Nicole Westmarland and Criva, Karam Yahya.

Outline of Book

Torture and Torturous Violence seeks to highlight the limitations in the adherence to, and prevalence of, narrow definitions of torture. Narrow definitions can prevent us from considering other forms of violence as torturous, even when the techniques of abuse – physically and psychologically – are the same and have similar or identical impacts as torture.

This book argues that, by recognizing the torturous nature of many forms of violence, we can collectively challenge the silence which allows for cyclical abuses to continue, and that create barriers to support. If and when we explore experiences of violence from a 'torturous' lens, we can most certainly dispel the myth that brutality is confined to areas of conflict or 'failed' states, but may be present in marriages and partnerships, or institutions and schools – spaces where power and powerlessness can manifest if it is allowed to. Indeed, as the text argues, torture and tortuous violence are issues for all of us, which benefit from collective recognition that its nature is pervasive, but never inevitable.

Torture and Torturous Violence is a call for practitioners, activists and scholars working on narrow definitions to reflect more fully on what the author terms *orthodox legalism*, and take more seriously the *experiential epistemologies* that can be examined and developed through the perspectives of survivors, and the practitioners who work to support survival.

Introduction: Why 'Torture and Torturous Violence'?

Introduction

Torture is simultaneously a silenced entity and an overused term – something we often shy away from in serious discussion, but a word we might use flippantly. It is not uncommon to use the term 'torture' to describe mild displeasures: sitting through a poorly written play, listening to a song we don't like, spending time with an odious relative. Meanwhile, debates about what *torture actually is* continue across the social and political sciences, law courts and military tribunals. In the aftermath of 9/11 in particular, whether violations should be deemed *torture* or *cruel and inhuman treatment* or indeed – as the Bush administration rolled out as a means to 'interrogate' potential terrorists – Enhanced Interrogation Techniques (EITs), continue. Meanwhile, violations which may amount to torture continue globally – daily and routinely.

This book stems from a long period of grappling with this concept: torture. Since the mid-2000s I have worked with and researched various forms of violence – some over long periods of time, others (such as childhood abuse) over shorter periods. Research and activism have focused on sexualized violence, trafficking, domestic abuse, conflict-related rape, and torture with women seeking asylum in Northern Europe. There have been many times that I have spoken with women who have survived various and often multiple abuses, never to refer to them as torture. And yet the forms of violence they are subject to, as this book will highlight, are no less impactful in their inflictions of harm than those which we might recognize as torture.

The crux of this disentanglement came during a conversation with a colleague who was visiting the Danish Institute Against Torture, an organization which has been a partner for three of my projects. As we discussed their long-term research efforts and books, and debated what is or may not be considered torture, he highlighted a 'torture' he had not come across earlier: the shooting of kneecaps in Libya. The application of the term in this context certainly evoked my interest. Growing up in Northern Ireland during and after the conflict, shooting someone in the knees (almost exclusively enacted and experienced by men) was simply called 'kneecapping'. It is an exercise by which a violator of (usually) paramilitary rules or norms is taken to an area – not even always remote – and shot in the kneecaps. If what they have done is viewed as mildly problematic, the knees will be shot from the front, usually causing surface level injuries (although deaths are recorded due to bleed outs). If the transgression is viewed as more serious, they may be shot from the back, causing longer-term damage through a kind of explosive rupture. As my father told us, in the 1970s this was 'worse' as a drill was used in place of a gun, and was termed 'Black and Deckering' (named after the brand of machinery).

Kneecapping was not (and still is not) uncommon. If you speak to people from Northern Ireland who lived through conflict and even up until now, you are likely to find someone who knows someone who has been kneecapped or, indeed, who has been the person administering the kneecapping. In college, a fellow student was reported to have written his name in his own blood after being kneecapped. My grandmother was once left to call an ambulance when a young man stumbled into her daughter's shop, covered in blood after his own kneecapping. Moreover, it is commonplace that kneecapping is organized and agreed in advance, whereby someone will be given an appointment with the underlying realization that a no show will leave two options: move to another country, or more brutal violence will occur.

To return to the point, the reference to kneecapping as torture was one that I had never considered before. The fact that my colleague had focused on Libya was the more obvious issue: Libya and Ireland had a long-standing illegalized arms trade during conflict, so it seemed reasonable that tactics of violence – like trade – travels. Later conversations with another colleague researching the history of Catalan resistance[1] found similar correlations, a deep historical relationship with movements in Northern Ireland.[2] However, the more the application of the term torture was considered in this context, the more it made sense. Had the kneecapping we knew of in Northern Ireland been administered by state officials in, for example, detention, it would have been an easy term to apply.

In short, and as this book will argue, how we define torture remains – consciously or not – broadly dependent on narrow legal definitions. Beyond the previous example, this is clear from torture narratives, books, legal texts and the empirical work drawn on in this text. This is understandable: torture, like other human rights violations, offers us one of the few ways in which we can pinpoint, examine and indeed address state accountability in the infliction of specific forms of violence. With so few tools at our disposal to address state crimes and harms, diluting the definitions that are explored in what follows, which centralize state actions, comes with its own perils. However, so too do we struggle with addressing forms of violence which amount to torture in everyday settings, not least domestic and sexualized violence. As this book outlines, women I have worked with in activist and research terms have relayed experiences of so-called 'false imprisonment', repeated strangulation (for some, to the point of passing out), scalding, rape and constant and unpredictable emotional and/or physical abuse. If what they have experienced had been inflicted by a state actor in a place other than home or their community, we would call it torture. And yet none of them did. This serves to remind us of the gendered implications of upholding narrow definitions – as we will see in Chapters 2 and 3, in particular, when torture texts consider the term, they are mostly considering men's experiences of torture without even referring to the gendered underpinnings of this in their work. It is predominately men who are tortured in custody, and so recognized as survivors of torture when mandates adhere to the United Nations Convention Against Torture or Other Cruel, Inhuman or Degrading Treatment or Punishment (UNCAT; United Nations, 1984). This is not to say that anything should detract from this reality, or recognition of the endemic violations of men in these spaces historically and contemporarily. What it *does* emphasize, however, is that the implications of this are that women often face further challenges in having their experiences recognized as being as *impactful as torture* in the aftermath of abuses with the same or similar sustained harms outside of the boundaries of UNCAT.

It is this disjuncture, this silencing, with which this book aims to work. In doing so I do not seek to undermine the significance of international definitions, nor to undermine the feminist arguments that came long before mine, and which situate torture in the everyday (see Copelon, 1994; 2004; MacKinnon, 2006). During the month leading up to submission of this book, I met with approximately 100 practitioners working in torture responses to consider the complications of doing so. Some advocated a complete move away from definitions based on law. Some argued discussions on torture can only ever be in relation to the law. Some said that in terms of their everyday practice, the law was completely irrelevant to supporting survivors or even bringing forward justice.

Instead of trying to formulate a response to all of these positionalities, I hope to provide analysis of debates and present empirical data that lends itself to creating ways to speak about forms of violence which amount to torture in the infliction of pain, but which are seldom recognized as such. The objective is to maintain the importance of state accountability in one sense (Green and Ward, 2004; McGlynn, 2008), but also centralize the point that many forms of violence in the everyday are not recognized fully in their impact and intensity. It does so specifically in Chapter 3 by unpacking a term I highlighted in the *British Journal of Criminology* in 2016 and wish to extend more fully as this book moves on, to focus on *torturous violence*.

Outlining key legal definitions of torture

A number of conventions are pertinent to discussing torture. UNCAT (1984) is most commonly recognized as the international backbone to understanding what is meant by the term 'torture'. According to the Convention, torture is:

> [A]ny act by which severe pain or suffering, whether physical or mental, is intentionally inflicted on a person for such purposes as obtaining from *him* or a third person information or a confession, punishing *him* for an act *he* or a third person has committed or is suspected of having committed, or intimidating or coercing *him* or a third person, or for any reason based on discrimination of any kind, when such pain or suffering is inflicted by or at the instigation of or with the consent or acquiescence of a public official or other person acting in an official capacity. It does not include pain or suffering arising only from, inherent in or incidental to lawful sanctions. (United Nations, 1984: Article 1; emphasis added)

That said, there is not always agreement on the grounds that constitute torture, especially in terms of recognizing women's experiences of violence and terror outside of state mandates, which definitions of torture – like this one – usually rely upon (United Nations, 1984; Green and Ward, 2004; MacKinnon, 2006; Kelly, 2012). For example, whether sexualized violence should be seen as a form of torture generally – in view of its impacts, potential for pain infliction, and inherent capacity to degrade and humiliate, tends to be contested. The UN Convention's emphasis on the involvement of a state official is often central to definitions and understandings, as it allows for the classification of state crime (Green and Ward, 2004), an issue particularly pertinent to critical criminology in terms of advocating accountability for crimes committed by the powerful. However, feminists such as Kastrup and Arcel (2004), Copelon (1994; 2004) and MacKinnon (2006) emphasize the physical and psychological pain inflicted, as well as the emotional and psychosocial impacts of sexualized violence. These point to relatively commonplace violence that women are disproportionately subjected to by men in the form of rape and sexualized abuse. Torture, as it stands in the UN Convention, arguably does not adequately recognize or represent women's experiences of sexualized violence paramount to torturous violence.

Some regional conventions do offer broader definitions, such as Article 2 of the Inter-American Convention to Prevent and Punish Torture, and Article 3 of the European Convention on Human Rights (see Smith, 2004a, 2004b for a fuller discussion). However, the UN Convention will be a central focus in parts of this book since the organizations involved in the empirical research used it as their primary mandate, although this dependence shifted as organizations increasingly recognized the gendered implications of narrow definitions – as this book will highlight. As the 2010s progressed, the UN began to address more systemically the issues of sexualized violence, domestic violence, and sexualized violence in war, conflict and civil unrest. This is not surprising, given that international consciousness was raised repeatedly in global contexts across the 1990s in particular and thus built on this evidence and UN Security Council Resolutions (such as from Rwanda, Former Yugoslavia, Sierra Leone, Democratic Republic of Congo, Bolivia, Iraq, Syria and Afghanistan). However, the extent to which these recognitions actually influence dominant torture discourses remains to be seen, and this point forms the central facet of the following chapters.

Addressing the complexities of torture and torturous violence

There is growing recognition that torture, as defined in domestic and international laws, can be a narrow lens to view and understand the same or similar forms of violence but that are not technically definable as torture per se. In particular, feminists such as MacKinnon (2006) and Arcel (2003) have highlighted that the endemic nature of violence against women can have similar sustained patterns of psychological and/or physical abuses and yet are not necessarily categorized as such. Moreover, when torture is discussed in academic literature, it is often in the context of ethical debates (Biswas and Zalloua, 2011), terrorism (Greenberg and Dratel, 2005; Jones, 2014) or by questioning whether torture is ever legitimate – such as the renowned (and highly critiqued) 'ticking time bomb' scenario whereby the options are to torture for information, or allow countless 'innocents' to die (Dershowitz, 2004).

Torture and Torturous Violence seeks to explore these debates, and move towards a deeper empirical and conceptual analysis of violence more broadly that does not necessarily include the act by state actors (or their corporate underdogs) with torturous intent. Although it will address these, drawing in particular on the work of Darius Rejali (2007; 2011) and Penny Green and Tony Ward (2004), the book expands these discussions to more fully understand what we might recognize as *torture* and offer a viable concept of *torturous violence*. It aims to shift focus from *who* inflicts torturous violence and *why*, to the *forms of violence* enacted and the *impacts* of them.

Methods and methodologies

The research basis of this book draws on projects spanning almost 15 years, firstly a study of the impacts of conflict-related rape as a PhD candidate (2008–2011) from an intersectional feminist perspective. As projects

5

developed, this perspective gradually infusing this with zemiology – the disciplinary study of social harm (Canning and Tombs, 2021). As a discipline, zemiology seeks to study and engage with harms – emotional, relational, psychological, physical, cultural and more – at micro, macro and meso levels, and beyond the confines of law or criminal justice, instead encompassing experiences of harm and connecting these with wider structural, institutional and sociopolitical contexts.

The empirical data included in this text develop from three specific projects. The first is a qualitative project exploring institutional approaches to sexualized torture in collaboration with the Danish Institute Against Torture (funded by Liverpool John Moores University, 2013–2014, a world leading organization working in psychotraumatological responses to torture). This entailed 19 in-depth interviews with psychotraumatologists, psychologists and lawyers working with survivors of torture in Denmark. The second is a qualitative and activist academic exploration of harm in Northern European asylum systems, specifically Britain, Denmark and Sweden (funded by the Economic and Social Research Council, 2016–2018). This incorporated 74 in-depth semi-structured interviews with psychologists, support workers, detention custody officers, lawyers, advocacy workers and other such practitioners working with people seeking asylum in the three case study countries (Britain: n=23; Denmark: n=21; Sweden: n=30). The objective was to explore state and organizational responses to women seeking asylum, and investigate women's experiences of the asylum process in relation to harmful practices which may have gendered consequences. Participants were recruited through purposive sampling initially directed at relevant institutions and organizations working with people seeking asylum in state and non-governmental organization (NGO) capacities, and snowball sampling within organizations once some contacts had been established. This has been supplemented with over 500 hours of ethnographic activist research with women seeking asylum during this period, as well as in-depth oral histories with six women seeking asylum, all of whose perspectives and experiences will be centralized in Chapter 5.

The third and most recent is a study entitled 'Unsilencing Sexualised Torture' (funded by the British Academy, 2020–2022). This seeks to identify forms of torture through a narrative oriented inquiry, coded from a categorical-content perspective of academic, governmental and NGO literature (Hiles and Cermak, 2008; Einolf, 2018a). It includes in-depth interviews with 20 leading practitioners including psychologists, psychotraumatologists and international lawyers to identify and examine how practitioners understand torture, and examples of best practice in response that can be developed to address sexualized violence which may amount to torturous violence. This has been supplemented with ideation and discussion workshops to explore strategies for best practice, addressing gendered complexities of support, and unsilencing sexualized torture with people working specifically in the fields of torture rehabilitation, traumatology and/or sexualized violence support, where appropriate (see also Fabri, 2011 on best practice).

As the book progresses, as well as oral histories with women, significant use is made of the perspectives of practitioners working in this field. The reasons for this focus are threefold. Firstly, people working with survivors of torture and/or sexualized violence often have insight into patterns of violence, long-term impacts of abuses, and experience of strengths and limitations of response strategies. Some of the participants included here have more than 40 years of international experience of working with survivors, and subsequently a wealth of insight into the longer-term trajectories of support, intervention and torture prevention. On the other side of this coin, some have only a few years of working in this field. With this comes important insight into the contemporary landscape of responses to torture and, in my experience, the normalization of structurally violent funding cuts affecting practice and provision. Secondly, those working with migrant survivors of torture offer a unique window into an international landscape of forced migration and its impacts on individuals, as well as the shifts in refugee demographics accessing support – and, indeed, not accessing support. This often mirrors wars and conflicts on an international scale. For example, in formative studies some of the most prevalent nationalities accessing post-torture support included Bosnian and Kosovan survivors; later Iraqi and Afghan; and more recently Syrian. This not only tells us about the wider conflict-related context, but that accessing support is more culturally normalized, since the length of time people are resident in a host country before entering post-torture therapies has been reducing. Thirdly, and importantly, those working with people seeking asylum are at the forefront of witnessing the impacts of exacerbated border restrictions and the harms they increasingly cause. This will be drawn out in more depth as the text moves forward, but it is significant in exposing that more precarious routes are increasing exposure to trauma for migrants; and that on a structural level, the web-like architectures of asylum systems not only compound earlier trauma, but inflict their own forms of trauma in the process.

A key objective throughout these projects has been to open debates on how we understand torture, and the implications of maintaining a somewhat narrow definition, such as those in the aforementioned conventions. It addresses the value and challenges inherent to widening the definition to more accurately represent the experiences of survivors of violence that is not currently recognized as torture. These are not simplistic debates: as Green and Ward aptly point out, if moves are made away from narrow definitions pertaining to state crimes, then the potential for state accountability is lessened, and the recognition of power that states and state actors can hold is undermined (Green and Ward, 2004). That said, given that the threshold for torture is arguably high, torture is not always recognizable or named as such, and subsequently convictions for torture are generally attributable only to extreme cases, if at all.

Without such discussions, however, organizations led by narrow definitions of torture can experience barriers to providing support to survivors of violence which could otherwise be considered to amount to torture. This includes survivors of sexualized and domestic violence, reinforcing gendered assumptions of torture as something inflicted mostly on men in, for example, prison and other state institutions. This is often true of formally recognized torture — that it is often men held in prison or in military institutions as dissenters, rebels and terrorists, such as in Myanmar, Iran and Guantanamo Bay. This in itself is gendered, but as with race and Whiteness, men and masculinity do not always register as being gendered in interview discourses. However, I will highlight examples of violence experienced by women I have undertaken oral histories with who are survivors of violence which might otherwise be recognized as torture, had the circumstances of their subjection mirrored those defined by narrow laws. This includes, but is not limited to, sustained domestic physical and psychological torment; multiple perpetrator rape; burning; beating; threat to kill; false imprisonment; as well as rape by smugglers, partners and family members.

A note on positionality and debates on the legitimacy of torture

Although it will not be a central aspect of this book, it is worth referencing that much of the more recent literature around torture centres on the debates over the legitimacy of its use. As Michelle Farrell outlines in depth, torture is not confined to academia, but plays out in the public imagination. Bolstered by media representations that convey fantastical notions of the ticking time bomb scenario, endless debates ensued, legitimizing the actual debates around, and policy for, the use of torture (Farrell, 2013). Many of these debates stem directly from the aftermath of 9/11, and the ensuing years of 'enhanced interrogation' led by the Bush administration in the 'war against terror'. In brief, as a means to legitimize the use of torture in Iraq, Afghanistan and other 'black sites' maintained for the use of imprisoning suspected terrorists, various well-known legal and political actors sought to promote various forms of torture as legitimate modes of interrogation, in particular waterboarding and 'clean' tortures such as force-feeding and forced standing. Some of the most prominent voices included, for example, renowned lawyer Alan Dershowitz and former US vice president Dick Cheney.

It is arguable that discussions around torture became somewhat stunted in academic circles, primarily due to the focus on the 'is torture ever legitimate' debate. Beyond feminist circles, rather than questioning what is meant by 'torture', the legal definition is predominantly accepted, and discussion focused heavily on EITs. By all accounts, this has been fruitful and significantly enhances our knowledge on the 'behind the scenes' of the occupation of Iraq and allied roles in Afghanistan. However, as Athey outlines, 'The torture debate has in no way really separated torture from the alibi of interrogation or considered torture's other ends, and the archetypal view further anchors our thinking to this alibi' (Athey, 2011: 133). By outlining perspectives of torture and torturous violence, you are invited to engage in critiquing, agreeing with or even rejecting this anchor.

I outline this here in part for those who come to debates around torture afresh and to be upfront on positionality: my own stance is that, no, torture is never legitimate. Firstly, as Rejali has highlighted in depth (Rejali, 2011), all evidence suggests that torture does not work even in its limited endeavour of obtaining information or confession. Instead, it creates an expansive machinery of targeting people and retrieving false information where information can be found otherwise. This point was more recently corroborated by Daniel Jones in relation to the Central Intelligence Agency's justification of EITs. Across 20 cases, including Abu Zubaydah (now in Guantanamo Bay) and José Padilla (currently in ADX Florence), Jones et al found that – against Central Intelligence Agency (CIA) claims – all 20 had been identified before the use of EITs (Jones, 2019). Torture, then, is not relegated only to the epistemological realm of questionable ethics and morality, but to the reality that it is an ineffective methodology.

Secondly, and drawing from a Kantian and somewhat liberal legal rights perspective on torture, as with the erasure of any rights, the erasure of the right to freedom from torture is a legal precedent we all do well to avoid.

However, and to emphasize why this discussion is addressed here before we even really begin, there have been times in the research process where interviewees and other participants have found ways to legitimize the use or potential use of torture. This usually begins with a scenario not unlike those discussed here – the (imagined, hypothetical) need to save innocent lives from an impending terrorist threat. The imagined therefore becomes part of the conscious. Moreover, this has extended for some to the othering of 'criminals'. There have been interviewees who exceptionalize the position of refugees convicted of crimes – 'crimmigrants', to use Juliet Stumpf's term (2006, see also Aliverti, 2012). Freja, a legal expert on torture working with survivors in Northern Europe, gives us an example of this:

'It's like the discussion about non-refoulement. Can we send people back who have been told, "You can't get asylum. You've committed a crime", or whatever, "You have to go back", and they say, "We can't go back because we're gonna be tortured", which makes sense … what are we gonna do? Most of the population are like, "It's not really our problem", so in a sense, if we don't have a solution and we just keep saying, "We can't send them back", in a way, we've become a bit naïve.' (Interview, 2021)

In this extract, the process of non-refoulement – a fundamental principle in international law which works to prevent the removal of people seeking asylum being sent to countries where they are at risk of persecution, in this example, torture – is overridden in the public imagination when the person has a criminal conviction. Torture gradually becomes more feasible under varying scenarios, in this case crimmigration is influencing the palatability of torture on return to one's country of origin. Importantly, that adhering to non-refoulement is perceived as "a bit naïve" is challenged by a key point raised in this book: that it is naïve to think torture or persecution is "not really our problem". As we will come to see, particularly when the *glocalization of torture* is introduced (Chapter 2), torture and indeed torturous violence is, in varying ways, everyone's problem.

Structure of this book

Torture and Torturous Violence is separated into seven chapters, all of which form a wider story and objective – transcending the definitional boundaries of torture. Chapter 1 outlines key legal definitions of torture, and critically evaluates recent and contemporary debates around torture and its uses. It draws on the work of Green and Ward (2004) in understanding torture as a state crime, and the contentions inherent to broadening this understanding. A central aspect is the introduction of three definitional responses to torture which are outlined here: orthodox legalism; legalist hybridity; and experiential epistemologies. We then move to look at torture and spatiality, torture as a social contract, and the expanding realms and definitions of torture.

Developing on from this, Chapter 2 outlines forms of violence documented by scholars, organizations and practitioners. These are unpacked across typologies and forms of violence, encompassing physical, psychological and 'clean' tortures, as well as introducing the *glocalization of torture* and strategies which appear to ensure that torture sits permanently in the psyche of the survivor. The second half draws together examples of the impacts of or problems stemming from torture, synopsizing lists by the Danish Institute Against Torture (DIGNITY, 2012), before exploring the depths of these impacts through practitioner reflections as a means to understand the complex cultural, temporal and relational implications that surviving torture can have on individuals, families and communities.

Having then situated key debates around torture and its impacts, Chapter 3 pinpoints specifically how *torturous violence* is constructed, and if and how it can be considered torture if inflicted outside of legal state defined norms. It is here that the gendered experiences of torture will be explored more intricately, considering intersectional forms of experience as well as indications of multiple forms or continuums (Kelly, 1988) of violence. In all, it draws together forms of torture that fit normative legal concepts, as well as torturous violence which goes beyond state-centric notions of torture.

Shifting from broad forms of torture and torturous violence, Chapter 4 focuses explicitly on sexualized forms of abuse. This is one form of violence which is often side-lined to 'feminist issues' or sits under the umbrella of conflict-related rape and sexualized violence. Although drawing from both of these avenues of thought, this chapter develops to consider forms of sexualized violence which is torturous in its infliction and impact, in conflict, during migration and indeed completely out of conflict environments. Drawing from practitioner perspectives and wider literature, it also incorporates the gendered nature of sexualized torturous violence, including against men and in domestic or personal environments.

Chapter 5 is the key chapter which moves us to look at complex, multifarious and intersectional experiences of conflict, detention, borders and violence as experienced by six refugee women. It is through the lens of these experiences that we can begin to move more fully towards understanding and conceptualizing *experiential epistemologies*, and explore ways in which legalistic notions of torture are limited in understanding and responding to torturous and sexually torturous violence. In particular, it will explore impacts of institutionalized violence, domestic and interpersonal abuses, so-called 'false imprisonment', and sexualized trafficking.

In Chapter 6, we disentangle evidence of silencing in the context of torture (Stanley, 2004; Kelly, 2012) and sexualized torturous violence in relation to stigma and shame, and evidence drawn from research which suggests silencing is pervasive in less obvious ways. Specifically, it seeks to consider some of the ways in which even those who are most vested in responding to torture – psychologists and psychotraumatologists – can replicate silencing of the issue by avoiding discussing it. Drawing from interviews with this group as well as earlier research (see Canning, 2019a; 2019b; 2021a), barriers can be erected by inadvertently *not* wishing to discuss sexualized violence, often as a means to avoid causing further harm or retraumatization. This discussion and evidence thus forms the foundations of the final chapter which goes on to consider what these implications are, and how they might be mitigated.

The concluding chapter of this book not only combines the key themes and arguments, but – drawing from interviews and ideation workshops – considers how we move forward in discussing, conceptualizing, addressing and responding to torture, torturous violence and sexualized forms of both these. Rather than simply suggesting examples of 'best practice', this chapter highlights the structural and sociopolitical constraints placed on practitioners which affect working conditions and – importantly – harmful policies and practices which affect survivors of many forms of violence in society more broadly, including in asylum systems, encampment and in the effects of under-resourcing of support services.

To reiterate, this book does not mean to undermine the value of the legal definitions of torture. Rather, it aims to expand the way we can see and think about violence that is as consequential and harmful as torture, but not always recognized as such. It does not aim to offer definitive accounts or analyses of torture, or to speak on behalf of survivors. Instead, take this text as a zemiological, intersectional feminist intervention to promote debate on the epistemological limitations of the torture concept, and the potential for building on the concept of torturous violence to better recognize, understand and address significant forms of violence that can be pervasive, devastating and endemically harmful in their infliction.

Outlining the Definitional Boundaries of 'Torture'

Introduction

Contemporary legal and academic frameworks around torture are predominately based in the UN Convention against Torture or Other Cruel, Inhuman or Degrading Treatment or Punishment (UNCAT; United Nations, 1984). Focus is therefore often placed on the intentional infliction of pain or suffering in the context of obtaining information, for the purposes of punishment, and/or with the involvement or consent of a state official, or sometimes working on behalf of a state. As such, torture is an instrument of state violence, one which is inflicted within sites of detention and confinement, and/or in relation to publicly political agendas. As UN Secretary General António Guterres recently noted, 'The prohibition of torture is absolute – under all circumstances. Yet this core principle is undermined every day in detention centres, prisons, police stations, psychiatric institutions and elsewhere' (Guterres, 2019). This statement, like many others, reiterates legalistic notions of torture as an infliction of suffering which relates almost exclusively to confinement. While this is of paramount importance in the context of state crime, there is significant scope for developing a gendered analysis of torture both within and beyond this sphere.

These discussions, debates and cases about what constitutes torture have serious sociopolitical consequences, as seen in the context of, for example, the Senate Intelligence Committee Report on Torture (Jones, 2014). However, the one common thread throughout much scholarship and literature is that it takes for granted normative definitions of torture, with little discussion of what torture is or what we mean when we use the term. As this chapter, and later chapters will highlight, over-dependence on this deterministic epistemological stance can be highly problematic. It arguably contributes to a form of silencing that overlooks more seemingly banal forms of violence which people may experience at the hands of the state in the everyday (Jensen and Rønsbo, 2014) or at the hands of violent partners and family within domestic spheres. It is this contention that Chapter 1 sets to outline and challenge. It does so by combining content analysis of various scholarly works, with discourse analysis of narratives of practitioners working with survivors of torture (who have been assessed as such – see appendices of Pérez-Sales [2017] for examples of this process) to introduce three definitional approaches: orthodox legalism; legalist hybridity; and experiential epistemologies.

'Torture': definitional developments and limitations

The standard legal definition of torture requires four key conditions to be present for torture to have occurred (see Figure 1.1).

In academic literature, reports and practitioner discourse, this somewhat narrow definition is regularly presented as sacrosanct, often without reference to how narrow it is and instead presented as epistemological fact. Torture, for many, is what this convention says: what is written defines how we come to see or 'know' torture. Whole texts and books are written with little contestation of this. For some, this is in itself important: since states are responsible for more deaths than any other human entity, it is indeed important that a tool such as UNCAT exists to keep the definition narrow, given the magnitude of violence states contemporarily and historically inflict within institutions, as well as in war and conflict more broadly (Green and Ward, 2004). Without this, the term *torture* risks being diluted and dispersed – further obscuring the implications of state inflicted or sanctioned abuses on people, in particular those held in captivity at their behest. It risks reducing accountability from state decisions and actions in a world where state violence already routinely goes unaccounted for.

This discourse, with minor deviations, creates the backbone of many of the most influential texts or author perspectives on torture. In *The Body in Pain*, Elaine Scarry emphasized that '[t]orture consists of a primary physical act, the infliction of pain, and a primary verbal act, the interrogation' (1985), before outlining ways in which these have been exercised across classical torture regimes, across the globe contemporarily and historically. In specifically clarifying what he means by 'torture', Darius Rejali – author of the ground-breaking book *Torture and Democracy* (2007) – states, '[b]y torture, I mean the systematic infliction of physical torment on detained helpless individuals by state officials for police purposes: that is, for confession, information, or intimidation', while acknowledging that 'no doubt one could slice torture in other ways' (Rejali, 2011: 26). Similar approaches are taken by many working in this field – Green and Ward (2004), Greenberg and Dratel (2005), Biswas and Zalloua (2011), Levinson (2004), and to an extent Pérez-Sales (2017) – with many more to draw from. Given the dominance of the UNCAT in

Figure 1.1: Defining torture

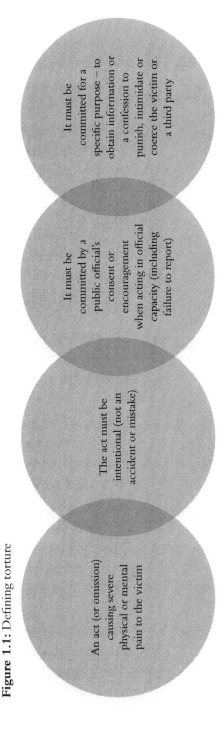

An act (or omission) causing severe physical or mental pain to the victim

The act must be intentional (not an accident or mistake)

It must be committed by a public official's consent or encouragement when acting in official capacity (including failure to report)

It must be committed for a specific purpose – to obtain information or a confession to punish, intimidate or coerce the victim or a third party

Source: Adapted from Convention against Torture and Other Cruel, Inhuman or Degrading Treatment or Punishment – see the Centre for the Study of Violence and Reconciliation (2014) for similar examples.

legal practice and public consciousness, and in particular the salience of a tool to identify and address state-inflicted violence of the magnitude and extent of torture, this approach makes sense. This epistemological supremacy influences practice in working with survivors of torture, while paradoxically being rejected by some in favour of survivors' own experiences of violence as the marker for defining what comes to be known and understood as 'torture'. Importantly, many texts completely and methodically overlook or exclude key debates raised by feminists on the need to recognize forms of violence beyond the state (as perpetrator) for narrow purposes (specifically interrogation) if we are to understand torture more holistically, and where power and powerlessness collide outside of these arenas.

For some, the definition of torture is narrowed further still. One such controversial approach to this lay with the Office for Legal Counsel in the United States, which argued that only acts 'of an extreme nature' could 'rise to the level of torture. ... Physical pain amounting to torture must be equivalent in intensity to the pain accompanying serious physical injury, such as organ failure, impairment of bodily function, or even death' (2003, in Levinson, 2004: 29). With this said, definitions of torture may be normatively connected to the Convention, but not exclusively so. In legal and academic realms, torture has increasingly been recognized more broadly, and importantly beyond the combination of the four facets of UNCAT, and yet it is this which most reports and academic texts continue to draw on, even if they do not specify so.

As Michelle Farrell depicts, various legal cases have influenced the ways in which torture has been engaged with, from the *Greek Case* (sometimes termed *Denmark v Greece*, 1969) whereby the European Commission of Human Rights reasoned that the term torture 'is often used to describe inhuman treatment, which has a purpose such as the obtaining of information or confessions, or the infliction of punishment, and is often an aggravated form of inhuman treatment' (in Farrell, 2013: 3; see also Evans, 2017). Although broader, this still inadvertently situates torture in the public political realm, between state actors (such as police officers) and people arrested or in custody, rather than, say, a woman in her home being subject to repeated beatings, threats and coercive control – however severe. To draw from Lisa Davis in this context, gender-based violence 'has historically been given a second-tier status, somehow not reaching the gravity of acts more commonly understood as torture' (2017: 317). Nor does the same scenario reflect the experiences of children living with abusive parents, a point I will raise in more depth in the following chapter.

Manfred Nowak and Elizabeth McArthur argued strongly for the recognition of power dynamics in the context of violence, in that powerlessness[1] creates a space for violent inflictions and that this is exacerbated in spaces of confinement, where unequal power relations are inherently manifest (Nowak, 2006). Specifically referring to the distinction between *torture* and *cruel, inhuman or degrading treatment* (CIDT), they had earlier stated:

> Outside a situation of detention and similar direct control, the prohibition of CIDT is subject to the proportionality principle. Only excessive use of police force constitutes CIDT. In a situation of detention or similar direct control, no proportionality test may be applied and the prohibition of torture and CIDT is absolute. Any use of physical or mental force against a detainee with the purpose of humiliation constitutes degrading treatment or punishment. Any infliction of severe pain or suffering for a specific purpose as expressed in Art. 1 CAT amounts to torture. (Nowak and McArthur, 2006: 147)

This has been extensively explored by Metin Başoğlu with colleagues over the past 30 years, and whose text *Torture and its Definition in International Law* outlines the controversies in the debate around defining torture, including the influence of feminist critique in the 1990s (see Başoğlu, 2017: xvii–xlii for a concise reflection). Importantly, he emphasizes the need for theory and evidence-based approaches, an argument that I strongly support if we are indeed to understand torture from the bottom-up, rather than the more unilateral top-down influence.

It is perhaps Pau Pérez-Sales who expands the developments and expansion of definitions of torture in most depth in his text *Psychological Torture* (2017). As well as addressing CIDT, he maps various cases that relate to the boundary shifts in legal decision-making processes, and which are synopsized for clarity in Table 1.1.

Given the historic dominance of physical violence in narratives and definitions of torture, the Inter-American Convention went some way to addressing psychological violence which Pérez-Sales documents and expands upon (2017; see also Şalcıoğlu and Başoğlu, 2017). As he also highlights, the move away from trying to define severity of suffering to focusing on motivation (that is, purpose and motivation) was broadly welcomed. Indeed, the question of severity is long debated. Tobias Kelly had earlier stated that 'although pain may be a universal and an inherently social experience, it has famously resisted attempts at replicable measurement. Far from creating an easily replicable standard, the emphasis on pain generates the very subjective nature of the experience' (2012: 14). This is an important point – how does one determine another's severity of suffering? As will be explored in Chapters 3 and 4, severity may indeed be subjective, however, there are mechanisms under which this may be measured in relation to forms of violence inflicted (Şalcıoğlu and Başoğlu, 2017). Similar questions have long been asked in feminist scholarship and activism, where the historic legacies

Table 1.1: Developments of definitional boundaries of torture

Year	Body/instigator	Additional or distinctive definition
1969	European Commission of Human Rights, *The Greek Case* (sometimes called *Denmark v Greece*, although other countries were involved)	Distinction between 'torture' and 'ill treatment' as 'aggravated form of cruel, inhuman or degrading treatment or punishment'.
1975	General Assembly of the United Nations	Adopted the above definition in their first Declaration against Torture.
1984	General Assembly of the United Nations, Convention Against Torture	Solidified the Convention Against Torture with no explicit distinction between 'torture' and 'ill treatment' – although articles 4–9 (criminalizing torture, bringing perpetrators to justice); article 3 (non-refoulement); and article 15 (using evidence extracted by torture) apply exclusively to torture, not CIDT, so the *legal* distinction is paramount.
1985	Inter-American Convention to Prevent and Punish Torture	Broader than CAT to specifically include psychological torture as 'the use of methods upon a person intended to obliterate the personality of the victim or to diminish his physical or mental capacities, even if they do not cause physical pain or mental anguish'.
1970–1980s	European Court of Human Rights, *Ireland v UK*	Five techniques used by British army in Northern Irish conflict (wall-standing, hooding, noise, sleep deprivation, deprivation of food and drink) did not amount to torture, but inhuman and degrading treatment.
1999	European Court of Human Rights, *Ahmed Selmouni v France*	Ruled sustained beating and humiliation leaving evidence of physical injury constitutes torture. Also supported qualification of torture based on psychological suffering, namely humiliation, debasement and instilling fear or anguish. Recognized changes for future classification based on critique of the *Ireland v UK* decision.
2001	European Court of Human Rights, *Keenan v United Kingdom*	Court begins to disavow severity of suffering as defining factor, still focusing on deprivation of liberty in its example, but indicating the five techniques may constitute torture (earlier challenged in 1997 in response to Israel's use – see also Danner [2011] on the five techniques from a critical perspective). Motivation, not severity, becomes core criteria.

Table 1.1: Developments of definitional boundaries of torture (continued)

Year	Body/instigator	Additional or distinctive definition
2006	UN Special Rapporteur Manfred Nowak	Proposes principle of proportionality and powerlessness in applying to CIDT and possibly torture.

Source: Adapted from Farrell (2013) and Pérez-Sales (2017: 5–9).

of hierarchies of physical violence and suffering were expanded to recognize a continuum of violence, to consider multifarious forms and impacts (Kelly, 1988) rather than a simplistic hierarchy. Although the value of severity is not always agreed upon, for some at least, severity remains relevant.

Moving towards three epistemological perspectives

The changes in approach to torture are not only evident in law, but at ground-level psychological practice and support for survivors of torture specifically, and trauma more broadly. These various shifts in definition and understanding are often echoed in how practitioners 'see' torture, and how organizations working with survivors define their mandate, which we will explore through the interview excerpts in this chapter. In relation to severity, for example, Klara, a psychologist working with child survivors, argues, "it depends on the frequency and the context and the way it was perceived at the time, the intensity of the violence and who you were with" (interview, 2021). While not using the term *severe*, intensity is considered along with frequency. Unlike UNCAT, however, *context* is not made explicit.

While the ambiguous use of severity or – as Klara puts it, intensity – does not necessarily help in opening out the boundaries of torture in law, the shift to *purpose and motivation* highlighted by Pérez-Sales arguably adds a definitional tripwire for understanding torture in the context of domestic or interpersonal violence, since the motivation does not commonly sit with information extraction, and not necessarily even punishment (see also Ginbar, 2017: 296–299 for debates on this). Given also that the 'fight against torture is usually framed in medicolegal, human rights, developmental or trauma narratives' (Jefferson, 2017 in Dehghan, 2018: 88), this epistemological reality has further opportunities to move towards recognizing or addressing feminist approaches to torture.

As this chapter begins to unpack torture definitions through practitioner perspectives, there appears more obvious limits in adhering to legal definitions in practice for people working in the field of torture support and rehabilitation. For example, Freja, a legal expert who has worked in response to torture across various international regions highlights, "there has been on a global scale, kind of [a shift] away from the more traditional types of torture … much more towards working on violence and really working on that whole idea of where torture comes from" (interview, 2021). In short, while many torture narratives remain dominated by the UNCAT, such deterministic approaches are differentially adhered to. Some are clear on the relevance of CIDT, some less so. Consequently, through thematic analysis and critical discourse analysis of interview, oral histories and torture texts these stances have been separated into three perspectives, namely, *orthodox legalism, legalist hybridity* and *experiential epistemologies.*

1. Orthodox legalism (strictly following legal conventions)

While the boundaries of torture remain in flux and contested, many organizations and legal approaches are fundamentally tied to narrow legalistic definitions of torture. Some are explicit in this requirement – a specification which can determine who can or cannot access or gain support based on whether they meet the threshold of torture in legal terms. Key pioneering organizations such as the Danish Institute Against Torture, Freedom from Torture and the International Rehabilitation Council for Torture Victims explicitly hold the word 'torture' in their title, and as such adhere to legal definitions in their mandates (see mandates online at DIGNITY, nd; Freedom from Torture, nd; IRCT, nd for examples). These echo the overall crux of the literature examined earlier, in that conventions and legal rulings provide a platform from which the rest of their work develops.

While the narratives explored in this section are predominantly linked to the UNCAT, broader uses of torture can also be identified – shifts in emphasis on severity or motivation, for example, may differ. However, unwavering in the *orthodox legalism* stance is that definitions of torture are inherently based on law and legal practice and do not divert from these. As we move through the latter two perspectives, we see that *individuals* may begin to deviate from them, even if the role or organization they are working with does not.

Role of the state

Ida, a project coordinator working on protection of refugee survivors of torture, defines the torturer as:

'[A]lways the police and the secret service, they're the ones who are the perpetrators. So that is not different. The state is the perpetrator. Sometimes it's armed groups, like now with Syria, but that also refers back to the convention, an armed group. It cannot be your father, your brother inducing torture.' (Interview, 2013)

Here we can see that the state is the main perpetrator of torture – it cannot be anything other, including as she says, a brother or father. This is important in highlighting ways in which violence outside of the UNCAT mandate is specifically and deliberately excluded. Similarly, Mila, a psychologist and psychotherapist, reflects that "we also have clients that I would define as having been physically tortured, so that's a government or state agency imprisoning and torturing a person physically or psychologically, so that would be my definition of it" (interview, 2021). In these narratives, the centrality of the state therefore is the backbone of personal perspectives and, subsequently, one's own knowledge-based practice.

Systematic physical and psychological violence

Luna, a clinical psychologist working with survivors of torture, goes further to say, "[t]he term 'torture' is used, in my room at least, when it has been systematic, breaking down both psychological and physical violence from people in power, from the government or the terrorist organization, or when it has been systematically brought upon them" (interview, 2021). Here she positions the state among the systematic nature of violence, maintaining focus on the state but highlighting that the systematic element is of significance.

Christian, a psychologist working with survivors in a clinical capacity considered that, "a survivor of torture is having been exposed to or seeing others be threatened on their life or wellbeing by a state official or other organized groups" (interview, 2021), although later – as we will see, shifts as he reflects on his own experience of treating survivors, rather than in what he is mandated to do. This definition not only draws the state as perpetrator, but considers torture *a threat to life or wellbeing*. This inadvertently induces the psychological dimension of this threat as being torture in and of itself.

Adhering to legal conventions, including changing as they evolve

For a chief executive officer in a torture rehabilitation organization, it is important to:

> '[W]ork and start working with the legal concept. That legal concept is obviously dynamic and evolving all the time. For instance, increasingly neglect from state authorities of preventing some forms of non-state torture or violence is considered, also in classical legal terms, an act of torture. … These things are, of course, contested as to what extent domestic or at least very systematic domestic violence with objects of state or authority neglect constitute torture. As you know, the Special Rapporteur for Torture has suggested that we are getting there … but that's in a grey zone.' (Interview, 2021)

This is particularly interesting in that legal concepts not only guide the direction of the work, but suggests that these also have the power to change this direction. In this case, domestic violence may be under consideration, but *that is in a grey zone*. Subsequently, although laws and conventions are ever-changing in the context of torture, for some working in research or rehabilitation it must still be these norms which determine practice and organizational definitions. They are ultimately bound to law.

2. Legalist hybridity (taking a flexible approach between the application of legal conventions and wider definitions of torture and trauma)

Though legal definitions do influence epistemology, research and practice as documented, this does not mean that such definitions go uncontested, or that individuals working with them don't face their own conflict. For some, definitions only go so far and practice and experience with survivors provides alternative insights that do not always align with wider dominant narratives. For others, definitions may be accepted in relation to mandates, but not in how they practice support or work with survivors of trauma. These positions can be understood as *legal hybridity*, where practitioners – indeed research, scholarship and survivors themselves (see Chapter 4) – may draw from both legal definitions of torture, while applying or accepting torture has been experienced outside of legal norms. Interestingly, as Freya highlights in correlation with my own research, this is a perspective which is increasingly common. She reflects that, "with all the work we've been doing on violence, particularly in Africa and Central America, I think that it's definitely broadened our horizons to look at other aspects of it … also a lot of the donors realize that it's not just conventional torture – there's a lot more to it" (interview, 2021).

The archetypal narrative: multifarious forms of violence can be torture, but torture is separately definable

For Amina, a psychologist working with survivors of torture but with previous experience of working with other forms of violence, "torture is of course mostly for those who have been held captive, been imprisoned. Some would define torture as also when they have been subjected to violence by their partner. Even the fathers – I've had a client who told me how his father tortured him, in Denmark" (interview, 2021). This is an archetypal statement for legal hybridity: although there is one way of looking at torture, the domestic sphere seeps into narratives where a man has been subjected to violence from his father. It is also interesting given Amina specifically refers to a father as a kind of torturer, in contravention to Ida's claim, a point which directly demonstrates that how we 'know' what torture is is not monolithic. Klara, a child psychologist working with families affected by torture specifically, opens this further. She considers war as well as the traumas increasingly induced by flight from conflict and persecution, stating: "I also work with people that are not necessarily exposed to imprisonment and torture, but that have been exposed to other forms of violence during war or the flight from war" (interview, 2021).

This point echoes wider literature on trauma, war and torture, as well as human rights approaches to war-related violence. Some have been much more open to expansion from feminist perspectives than torture narratives and definitions have been, for example the Istanbul Convention (Council of Europe, 2011), Istanbul Protocol (UN High Commissioner for Human Rights, 2004) and UN Security Council Resolutions 1325, 1820 and 1920. These all addressed conflict-related sexualized violence with much more feminist influence than most torture definitions (conversely, and along similar lines to this, it is worth mentioning that although the role of UN High Commissioner for Human Rights has been occupied by several women, currently including former Chilean president Michelle Bachelet Jeria, the role of Special Rapporteur on Torture and Other Cruel, Inhuman or Degrading Treatment or Punishment has only ever been occupied by men[2] – all European except one – since its inception in 1985. See OHCHR, 2021a; 2021b). Given Klara's role, it also allows her scope to support child survivors of trauma who may not themselves have been subjected to torture, but who are affected by its aftermath and/or the traumas associated with crossing borders.

Motivation matters – so does severity and impact

As we saw in the discussion around legal orthodoxy, the purpose and motivation behind torture is becoming increasingly centralized, generally meaning that the perpetrator is more likely to align to state roles or functions such as police or prison guard. Legalist hybridity has the propensity to move away from this, towards the forms, impacts and severity of violence that international approaches have been gradually decentralizing, as Pérez-Sales outlined earlier (2017).

In this context, Mila, who had initially defined torture narrowly, expanded her perspective when asked further if the abuse or incest that she had mentioned a client experiencing could be torture. The dialogue is reflective in terms of her own definition of torture, but also – as Tobias Kelly touched on – becomes uncomfortable when trying to prescribe a hierarchy:

Victoria: Would you consider those to be torture, the kinds of abuse like incest and other violence that your client is inflicting?

Mila: Not in the technical sense, no, they're not, but you could call it that, yeah, of course. It has the same impact, in a way, although it almost has a more challenging impact because it comes from a care-giver, and that of course creates a lot of problems developmentally, so I think it's more. ... I don't know. It's terrible to compare – this is worse or not worse – but I think developmental trauma and abuse and incest is really, really ... has such a profound impact on a person and their life. *You could call it torture, but not technically* [emphasis added].

This is a common conflict for practitioners working with survivors of violence. Comparing violence is not only problematic as Mila suggests, but not really possible in terms of individual experience. What she does emphasize is that it could be called torture, *but not technically*. From the forms of violence and associated impacts, torture may be applied, even though it deviates from dominant legal narratives. As we hear from survivors of violence in Chapter 5, it becomes increasingly difficult to differentiate the two when considering lived reality.

Similar to this broadening spectrum of violence, Klara goes further to specify the experiences of people who are kidnapped, but not held in prison, as a form of conflict-related violence. It is a tactic which also raises concerns for survivors of trafficking, and so-called false imprisonment. She states:

'[I]n terms of forms of violence, there are big similarities between the forms of violence that are used inside the prison and by military groups outside prisons, in people's homes, or it's not unusual that people have been kidnapped during war and that they have experienced torture exposure during kidnapping, even though it didn't happen in a prison.' (Interview, 2021)

So here, not only is the perpetrator somewhat obscured, but the space in which people are subjected to violence is no longer dependent on state-related forms of confinement or interaction.

Survivor narratives do not always encompass the term 'torture', regardless of legal definitions

How survivors of violence – whether subjected to legally recognized forms of torture or not – discuss torture themselves varies. There is no monolithic experience, and no monolithic interpretation (Canning, 2017). This point was raised in the Introduction in relation to kneecapping, and will be raised again in the context of women's oral histories. For now, as the final facet of legalist hybridity, it is worth looking at how violence is defined in secondary narratives.

Christian – who earlier outlined the need to adhere to law, once probed, began to broaden his perspective to consider injustice, but maintaining focus on the role of the state. He contends, 'it's always something about the injustice and an unjust world, and does it really matter then if it's the state or an organized gang or whatever that commits the crime or the violence? For some, it does'. This is an interesting point, and one which solidifies the multifarious nature of violence and who commits it: *for some, it matters*. He later drew from discussions with survivors about the state/citizen nexus that has been broken by a violation, particularly for those who have been actively involved in state building or state defence themselves, only to be tortured later. Assuming this logic, it is worth considering that the perforation of trust in close interpersonal relationships is not any less binding. The difference, then, is *which* relationship we focus on when responding to people who have survived systematic violence: whether they are seen or see themselves as survivors of violence; or whether they are seen and see themselves as survivors of torture.

Like Christian, Luna initially discussed torture in relation to legal orthodoxy. After a longer discussion, she came to reflect that:

> '[M]ost also have experience with torture in *different ways*, and their definition of torture can be *somewhat different*, depending on the country of origin and also depending on the period of them being in the country. So, somebody would describe being stripped naked at a checkpoint as torture, whereas others would not describe that as torture, but rather being exposed to violence in prisons.' (Interview, 2021; emphasis added)

Here, Luna lays out a central facet of this book: the use of the term 'torture'. As with other forms of violence, in particular sexualized violence, applying words that convey violence is incredibly complex, personally as well as linguistically. Aspects of violence which we may apply to fiction, or accept happening to other people, can be much more difficult to name when it comes to the self. As she goes on to say:

> 'So what we do is, we psycho-educate around both the legal definition of torture, which some of the clients minimalize: "What? No, I was just beaten every day. *That wasn't torture*," or, "I saw somebody else get tortured," and defining that violence as torture, but the violence on their own body not as torture.' (Interview, 2021; emphasis added)

As will be explored in more depth, this hybrid approach works in two ways. Firstly, by narrowing torture and depending on legal definitions, practitioners can work towards supporting survivors to understand what torture is in a legal sense, thus – in this case as an example – recognize the gravity of the harm inflicted. Secondly, it is worth considering that this also works in the opposite direction: torture becomes so exceptionalized through discourse – itself intertwined with dominant narratives of legal norms – that people may not recognize the gravity of violence they have experienced because of the narrow definitions of 'torture'. Further, it is worth considering that for some this can be a coping mechanism. By minimizing experiences and avoiding terms such as 'torture', it can be easier to move on from one's own subjections, in the short term at least.

3. Experiential epistemologies (building knowledge on experiences of survivors)

The final of these three perspectives leads us to consider how 'torture' can look when more explicitly defined by experience rather than legal norms. While narratives such as 'experts by experience' – whereby people who have direct experience of an issue or social phenomena (such as migration, prison or probation) – have become more central to practice, advocacy and activism in recent years, the terminology used here is more complex. Rather than situating epistemological knowledge of torture *only* with survivors of torture, this draws perspectives from practitioners, survivors of violence, and survivors of legally defined torture. This section therefore sets the basis for Chapter 5's focus on women's lives, but also explores ways in which supporting survivors of torture can be influenced by the experiences of survivors through a broader social process of long-term engagement with the field, and knowledge of wider structures. This arguably facilitates a dual process of developing experiential epistemologies: knowledge which is developed by and through multifarious actors engaged in or affected by torture, which itself becomes more fluidly characterized.

Defined by experience

The first consideration for developing or addressing experiential epistemologies is to consider how violence is discussed, and through which narrative meaning is produced. In other words, rather than beginning narrowly, such as practitioners commonly did earlier, we begin to work backwards to gauge what is being said and experienced, and consider if and how this would be definable as torture beyond the confines of law. This means defining experiences of torture can themselves be subjective and open to interpretation. Laura, a medical doctor working with pre-assessed[3] survivors of torture, highlights that, "sometimes I may use the word 'torture', but oftentimes I think I refer to it as 'some of the bad things that you've been subjected to', because in that way, I figure then they can also decide what they want to be included in that description" (interview, 2021). Clinical psychologist Luna, who earlier defined torture through its legal norms, reiterates this approach in practice, "I'd rather have the client describe their own experience and then we together can put it into categories of torture or violence or trauma-related violence or whatever suits their own understanding, and building a meaning around their own experiences" (interview, 2021). In both of these narratives, although the boundaries of torture are very much embedded in each person's own work, these are significantly transgressed in reality, where the experiences of survivors become the platform from which knowledge of violence, and in some senses its severity, are situated.

As Amina, the psychologist introduced earlier, expands:

'The clients don't differentiate about violence and torture, meaning that if they have been subjected to severe pain, or even the client that I'm talking about right now, where the father would basically torture the children, used to tie them up or beat them while they were tied up and stuff like that, and even though I know the definition of torture is something else, but it's like the *experience of the patient themselves*; how they experienced the violence or torture.' (Interview, 2021; emphasis added)

A key point here, which is reflected across many later narratives in this book, is that the practitioner is led by the survivor with whom they are working. In this case, Amina's role as a psychologist working with survivors of torture, who are pre-assessed as torture survivors. However, as time has gone on, she has come to uncover other forms of violence which mirror torture, but that are perpetrated by (in this case) a father. Amina went on to reflect on working with other survivors, or 'clients' as termed here, moving from perpetrator (connected to motivation and intention) to forms of violence inflicted:

'[I]t's not the torture forms that are used, like falanga, basically, or even being tied up, continued hanging or something. All that sorts of stuff is not considered in terms of violence, but more like torture, but violence is more like, "Oh, my husband is violent towards me", or, "He's violent to our children." But sometimes, when you dig more into it, then you find out that it's not only violence – *torture methods are also used in some cases*.' (Interview, 2021; emphasis added)

This second paragraph opens up the recognition that some forms of violence, associated primarily with torture under legal definitions, are inflicted within private spheres. The final line allows this transgression – this is not 'only violence', but torture methods. For those reading from orthodox legalist perspectives, this provides an extra conundrum. As is well documented (Rejali, 2007; DIGNITY, 2012), many forms of violence, such as repeated beatings, sexualized abuse and sustained psychological violence, amount to torture in other settings. Why then is it that certain forms of violence may be interpreted by an experienced practitioner as *torture methods*, while others that are common in domestic, familial and interpersonal violence, are not?

Definitions of torture may be organizationally bound to legal norms, but not bound to individual perspectives

As with Amina, Laura and Luna, Christian and Morten work only with clients who have been pre-assessed and identified as having been tortured. The key organizational mandates in these practitioners' cases is to work with survivors of torture, which is normatively defined by legal conventions. However, although this mandate serves as a kind of filter from wider forms of violence, how individuals work with this in practice transcends this. Moreover, as with others, Christian and Morten began their interviews defining torture narrowly, but gradually began to draw their own experiences to different conclusions. Christian reflects, "we don't really think about the definition of torture, but we can get the feel of, is this a trauma that is relevant?", going on to discuss, "dilemmas such as, is the violence committed by Islamic State torture or is that organized violence? But in the clinic, it doesn't really matter because *the outcome is the same for the client*, and *they don't think about the legislative definition*" (interview, 2021; emphasis added).

The first of these brings us to an epistemological crossroad. Although Christian did begin his discussion defining torture in a legal sense, in everyday practice, he explicitly says, he doesn't really think about the legal definition of torture. It does not matter for him in working with a survivor of trauma or torture when it comes to their broader lived experience – when support is put into practice, and experiences of trauma become central to meaning. Moreover, he moves to think more concretely about the outcome (or impact) of the trauma, which he argues here is "the same for the client". Subsequently, and contrary to recent trends within torture scholarship, the severity of violence and its consequences on the person are more pertinent to the space they share than the motivation for the infliction of violence in the first place.

Drawing back to Morten, who had otherwise been clear on the need to maintain a narrow focus on torture in the context of legal norms. In reflecting on who can be supported, he considered that, "The idea of only helping torture victims is almost meaningless, because how to distinguish when victims often don't distinguish? How do we reach, especially outside of this country, torture victims only? It's not really possible. In that sense, we have moved much more from torture to trauma". It is here that experiential epistemologies can be seen to shape practice, knowledge and indeed how torture can clearly be seen to transgress boundaries to more holistically encompass wider violence.

This overall point here was recently – and justifiably – addressed as a concern in a conversation with the director of a non-governmental organization in Sweden. As mentioned in the Introduction, I presented parts of this book to around 100 practitioners over the period of one year as a form of reflexive practice.[4] When holding a workshop at the Swedish Red Cross Center for Persons Affected by War and Trauma[5] in 2022, another risk was outlined that raises further issues with embracing the term 'torturous violence', or even diluting the term torture. Although in agreement with the overall premise of this book's agenda, the director highlighted a recent example where such a definition could be trivially used. During the Christmas period, for example, she had been contacted to comment on the ways in which counter workers were being 'tortured' in high street shops by the repetitive overplaying of Christmas music.

Now, as a union representative, former counter worker, and strong advocate of workers' rights, I do not wish to diminish the dislike of repetitive sound for those working in high street or department stores. I agree though with the director that the trivialization on the points of severity and impact have the potential to be highly problematic, especially for those working in the field of torture support. If such an experience is 'torture', then it would become impossible to distinguish what is *not* torture. However, it is precisely the definition of torturous violence outlined in Chapter 2 which serves to exclude experiences of temporal discomforts which are neither sustained or impactful in the longer term, and still offer the opportunity to more fully recognize violence which is nefariously impactful in its infliction.

Where does 'torture' take place? Gendering torturous spatiality

This question, and its most common answer, provides us with some surface level insight into the limitations of accepting legally dominant narratives of torture. As we saw at the beginning of this chapter, torture is heavily aligned with state-sanctioned confinement. According to the Danish Institute Against Torture, '[t]orture and other ill-treatment most commonly occurs in relation to the arrest, interrogation, and detention of a person … however the international definition of torture does not relate to a specific location' (DIGNITY, 2012: 43).

There is an inherent juxtaposition here: in *not* specifying a location, but focusing on actions undertaken almost exclusively at the hands of state actors and thus in state custody (wherever that physical space may be), we see an inadvertent narrowing of space back to the publicly political. The most common occurrences noted – arrest, interrogation and detention – are bound by state authorities, criminal justice and – in some instances – outsourced, third party (or private and corporate) torturers. It is a space which is reiterated across the literature, but is very well synopsized by Sofia, a lawyer working specifically on cases amounting to torture, who states:

> 'What we see is that torture is undertaken at the initial stages, when people are apprehended, and during interrogation, as this is where incentive lies in terms of extracting confessions and information about other parties that may be implicated in a crime. Or just for punishing people, especially the harsh torture takes place at these initial stages.' (Interview, 2013)

Although accurately reflective of legal definitions, this does not invite us to recognize that *the same or similar forms of violence which may amount to torture in their infliction* are perpetrated much more prominently in the home and other domestic realms, psychiatric hospitals, schools and other 'everyday' settings by everyday people. As such, although there are significant shifts in defining torture in terms of wider narratives, this very statement provides us with a case study example of how torture is typified by when and by whom it is undertaken, rather than the infliction itself.

Given that women remain disproportionately affected by violence from men, and mostly men they know, while men are much more likely to be arrested, interrogated and detained, the public/private dichotomy is reproduced. As Anne, a clinical psychologist reflected:

> '[W]e have been talking about the violence that men are exposed to in war, as soldiers or civilians, and that internationally has been a raised question for a long, long time, but … female experiences of war are still a question of women's rights and not a legal question about violence.' (Interview, 2021)

This issue leads us to a cyclical relationship with definitions: neither violence is less intrusive, abusive, political and sometimes even fatal than the other, yet while definitions move forward, our collective consciousness of what 'torture' really is continues to be confined to dominant legal conventions unless explored fully, as was shown in interviews – whether we intend it to or not.

Torture as a social contract

This draws us back to consider torture as something that is in fact well within the human imagination, and exercised as such through power, powerlessness and control. To do so requires specific agreements between those present – either implied, or overtly stated. Employing again the insights of Rejali, 'torture is not a government policy. It is a *social practice and it lives in society*' (2011: 27; emphasis added). Indeed, for orchestrated, systematic abuses to occur, there must exist some form of spoken or unspoken social contract. In some instances, we know these have been deliberately constructed and indeed literally contracted in collaboration with psychologists, medical practitioners and prison staff (such as in the case of Enhanced Interrogation Techniques discussed later. In others, it is in both the instigation of or agreement to inflicting torture, or indeed in resistance to participation. Green and Ward similarly deduce that, 'It is not an aberrant strategy or punishment employed by individual rogue agents, rather torture needs to be understood as part of a *process of control* through terror' (2004: 132; emphasis added). Note that this broader argument is reminiscent of feminist arguments around domestic and sexualized violence in society more generally – a point we will return to in Chapter 4.

There are three examples from which I will draw for illustrative purposes, although by all accounts this is far from exhaustive. These highlight the extent to which torture – and indeed other forms of violence – is social: group torture, witnessing and surveillance; the employment of and dependence on medical practitioners and psychologists; and multiple perpetrator rape.

Group torture, witnessing and surveillance

Torture – in its narrowest legal sense – is often represented as a one-on-one endeavour, sometimes a lone torturer or a rogue 'bad apple' in the military or police ranks. This arguably makes it easier for us to accept that it is a *deviation from* social norms, rather than a consensus among those present – a different or perhaps exceptional set of norms through which the ends – for those torturing – are presented as justifying the means, even when torture itself fails. Although this is, of course, one example of torture, the 'lone torturer' does not fit the requirements for facilitating endemic or systematic forms of torture as can be seen in various examples of confinement. As Athey highlights in the context of 'Palestinian hanging' positions, 'Indeed the shackling, overhead or otherwise, as well as forced standing and sleep deprivation, not to mention water-boarding or beatings, all require teamwork: to restrain, lift, position, or return the prisoner to consciousness' (2011: 143). In this sense, torture is a somewhat bureaucratic exercise, where various people are required to fulfil roles for the action to be practicably undertaken, and for this to happen, discussion and compliance – if not consensus – is needed.

Perhaps one of the most obvious forms of group torture that has confronted the public imagination, with ample witnesses, was the photographic evidence collected in Abu Ghraib. As has been widely discussed (Greenberg and

Dratel, 2005; Rejali, 2007; Biswas and Zalloua, 2011; Ireland, 2011; Jones, 2014), the release of the images forced us into witnessing a kind of raw brutality that is seldom exposed, at least not where White army officers are responsible for the degradation inflicted. But more than this, we are visually probed into a deeper realization that this is not accidental or individual, but a collective social agreement among those present. For the images to exist, planning was required: to discuss and agree[6] the forthcoming actions; to choose which detainees to degrade; to move them from cells; to collect and leash dogs. It required space to be available; a camera to be collected; and hoods and other tools of torture to be acquired. Like many forms of torture, it simply required social agreement on procedure, and a social contract to do so – one often built around camaraderie and protection of the group, particularly in institutional settings. By returning to the archetypal lone torturer, we undermine the value and relevance of this agreement, and thus avoid confronting the forms of violence that exist not only in individual perpetrators, but in society. This therefore maintains, upholds and facilitates further forms of social silencing (see Canning, 2016; 2017).

The employment of medical practitioners and psychologists

Some disciplines and practices enjoy an elevated status across most societies. Certainly, in many regions, the dominance of law, medicine and psychology are at the fore of these (see Ussher, 2011). Yet, as history has repeatedly taught us, these otherwise admirable practices have also been intrinsic to severe forms of brutality, not least during the Holocaust where medical experimentation was embedded in the methodical tortures of those held in concentration camps, brutal aspects of which were lauded as milestones for biological sciences. Similarly, and as we will focus in more depth on in Chapters 3 and 4, psychiatry and psychology have seriously chequered histories in method and practice, some of which continues to haunt the obsessive pathologizing of women (Thompson, 1998; Ussher, 2011).

It should come as no surprise then that such practices have been intrinsic to some aspects of torture. In her essay on biopower in Guantanamo Bay, Lauren Wilcox highlights, 'the health of prisoners is closely monitored by medical professionals as a means to ensure that death does not come to the tortured, lest its objectives thus be obscured from obtaining information or confession' (2011: 102). This form of biopower works when torturers aim to overcome resistance to – for example – force-feeding, drawing together not only biopolitics in the Foucauldian sense, but sovereignty over the body, and indeed sovereign power over the interrogated (Wilcox, 2011: 108). This requires a level of witnessing, monitoring and indeed training since techniques to torture without killing often require knowledge of the boundaries between keeping a person alive and facilitating their death.

As Wilcox goes on to assess, 'The complicity and assistance of medical personnel are essential to the practice of torture. ... Medical professionals are on hand to ensure that such torture tactics are not taken so far as to permanently damage the bodies of the victims' (2011: 113). Indeed, it is often the *lack* of permanent damage which plays to facilitate further silencing of bodily pains, since it becomes difficult to 'prove' torture on the body and thus impacts of both accountability (of the torturers) or for survivors seeking asylum, the ability to 'prove' torture in claims for refugee status (see Freedom from Torture, 2016).

Of course, it is not only those who are responsible for biological wellbeing who have been complicit. When torture is decided as a strategy, there is an innate requirement to be sure that the subject is psychologically capable, particularly if the objective is on interrogation and information extraction and where testimony is central. Even though we know that torture is not an effective tool to do this, it has been an integral one in the systematic torturing of informants, often by states presenting as democracies (Rejali, 2007). For this, psychologists may be employed to not only evaluate the state of detainees, but to develop strategies which would be most psychologically effective in obtaining information, itself a kind of 'clean' torture. As the Senate Intelligence Committee Report on Torture (Jones, 2014) exposed in relation to the US torture regimes in the Central Intelligence Agency (CIA)'s Detention and Interrogation Program:

> The CIA contracted with two psychologists to develop, operate, and assess its interrogation operations. ... On the CIA's behalf, the contract psychologists developed the list of enhanced interrogation techniques that was approved for use against Abu Zubaydah and subsequent CIA detainees. The psychologists personally conducted interrogations of some of the CIA's most significant detainees using these techniques. (Jones, 2014: 15)

I use this remarkable example, not to suggest these two psychologists are representative of their field, but that the structural decision for employing such individuals to engage to such a level marks the value of psychology to states wishing to advance psychological torture and interrogation. It is not even unique to this case, but endemic to the typified torture regime when self-defined democracies advance their techniques on such a scale (see also Rejali, 2007). Torture becomes a profiteering mission: as the Senate Report went on to note, the CIA outsourced virtually all aspects of the Detention and Interrogation Program so that '[i]n 2006, the value of the CIA's base contract with the company formed with the psychologists with all options exercised was in excess of $180 million; the contractors received $81 million prior to the contract's termination in 2009' (Jones, 2014: 16).

Multiple perpetrator rape

As a final example of the forms of social contract required, multiple perpetrator rape is an incredibly complex form of violence which requires trust, camaraderie, planning and execution. It is perpetrated in many social settings: prisons, during war and conflict, in homes, schools and even the night-time economy (Bastick et al, 2007; Kelly et al, 2011). These range significantly in prevalence rates locally and globally (Gidycz and Koss, 1990; Edinburgh et al, 2014), which can be exacerbated in conflict where organized and militarized violence is extended.

However prevalent, multiple perpetrator rape provides us with a social conundrum: it removes rape from the supposedly private sphere in which it can often reside and places it in a public domain that is clearly influenced and perpetuated by gendered social processes. When an individual man chooses to rape a woman, it can be easy to label him deviant – a loner, pervert, psychopath, all labels which can, if incorrectly applied, ignore that the act itself is embedded in a complex web of socialization processes and institutional power structures. Multiple perpetrator rape, on the other hand, cannot be explained away, since an agreement of values must be reached between more than one man (Canning, 2011a: 44).

Multiple perpetrator rape is a form of brutality which has long-lasting consequences for survivors – as was also documented in the aftermath of the Rwandan Genocide and Bosnian War. However, although often presented as inevitable in reports and academic literature, *it is not an inevitability in conflict*. As Elizabeth Wood has highlighted, sexualized violence was largely absent from the secessionist Liberation Tigers of Tamil Eelam of Sri Lanka (Wood, 2009). This is the central aspect of this section: torture and other forms of group or multiple perpetrator violence is built on social agreements and contracts. As such, these agreements and decisions can be made otherwise – *none of them are inevitable*.

The expanding realms and recognitions of torture

As this book progresses, it focuses more on the notion of torturous violence from an intersectional and feminist-centred perspective. However, as parts of this chapter have highlighted, although much remains anchored in UNCAT and other norms, there is a contemporary shift in what these are in law and – as outlined in depth in this chapter – practice. Three important aspects are worth exploring in respect of this potential for advancement.

Firstly, Michelle Farrell advocates a move to explicitly recognize structural violence, which, she argues in the case of removal of land for reasons of capital accumulation, amount to state crime and the processes of doing so, torture in a cultural sense (2021). As with other forms of structural violence

(Galtung, 1969; Canning, 2017), this increases the prospect of moving away from 'the torturer' as individualized, whereby prosecution is a key objective, to a more holistic understanding of mass forms of state torture. It gives further scope to move away from highly problematic notions of torture in the public imagination, citing the ticking timebomb scenario that Farrell had earlier analysed in depth (2013). This expansion, she positions, also facilitates a shift away from Eurocentric notions of torture to more adequately address state violence which leads to collective and individual trauma.

Secondly, Ergün Cakal recently critically explored the debates separating ill-treatment from torture, highlighting:

> Ill-treatment may generally be described *negatively* in relation to torture, that is state-inflicted harm which does not amount to torture because it lacks one or more of the key elements required by the definition of torture in article 1. In other words, an instance of state violence would constitute ill-treatment rather than torture either if it lacks the required intention, the required purpose (or discrimination) or if the pain or suffering it causes is not considered to be 'severe'. (2021: 153; emphasis in original)

So here we have a critique of the limitations of requiring intention and purpose to call 'ill-treatment' over 'torture'. Cakal goes further to acknowledge the definition of *motive* in relation to sexual gratification in the case of sexualized torture brought forward in the International Criminal Tribunal for Former Yugoslavia (Cakal, 2021: 154). This is a relevant platform on which the focus on torturous violence can build. However, the emphasis here – as with Farrell – remains on the state as an active perpetrator of violence.

Thirdly, the term 'torture' is increasingly used in relation to the state-inflicted pains of border harms. In his book *No Friend but the Mountains*, Iranian journalist and former Manus Prison detainee Behrouz Boochani stated, 'I have always despised waiting. Waiting is a mechanism of torture in the dungeon of time' (2018: 62). Having spent, by that stage, more than five years in the environmentally hostile immigration prison on Manus Island, Boochani became an expert in applying critical structural analysis to the everyday harms of waiting. He reflects:

> I am captive in the clutches of some overbearing power.
>
> *A power that strips me of the right to live life/*
> *A power that tosses me aside and alienates me from the very being that*
> *I was supposed to be/*
> *A power that tortures me/*
> *A power that torments me.* (Boochani, 2018: 62)

Khosravi (2018) refers to this as 'waithood'. With Omid Tofighian, Boochani extended this to look at the 'weaponisation of time' (2021). I termed aspects of border waiting 'temporal harm' (2019b; 2021a) as a means of acknowledging the impacts of a lack of security and certainty on mental, emotional and psychological health. As Cakal goes on to state, 'In the context of migration, intentional infliction of pain or suffering based on migrant status, whether they be border pushbacks, arbitrary detention or poor conditions of detention, have been read as being capable of amounting to torture' (2021: 157).

On revisiting Boochani's work, temporal torture may be a more apt term, not only since states are key to the infliction of these harms through policy, law and practice, but because the impacts of loss of time (which Bhatia and I termed 'stealing time' to centralize the active element of criminally taking sections of people's lives – see Bhatia and Canning, 2021) can be similar to the impacts of torture. Certainly, reflecting on Boochani's poetic reflection on torment and torture, one can place the significance of power and thus *powerlessness*, the very aspect of torture which Manfred Nowak sought to include as a defining factor of torture when considering further inflictions when unable to defend oneself from an aggressor (Nowak and McArthur, 2006). Combining this, then, with Pérez-Sales' definition of psychological torture, *temporal torture* becomes a relevant facet for understanding the endemic infliction of structural harms which seek to reduce humans 'from the very being that I was supposed to be' (Boochani, 2018).

The expansion of the term 'torture' in this sense can be one which moves away from individual state actors to the structural set up of a state-enacted torturous system, even when it outsources to corporate allies. Moreover, it arguably even fits the narrow definition of torture in that it is intentional, built into policy and law as strategies for control (see Canning, 2019b around 'degradation by design'), and with motive, in that although it does not work towards garnering information, it does work towards the removal of the migrant Other from sovereign or bordered spaces (Bosworth and Turnbull, 2015). It does not, however, encompass the objectives of punishment or extraction of information, even if it does this unintentionally. As such, although defined by the authors as torture, they arguably align more coherently with the concept of torturous violence, as we will see in Chapter 3.

Conclusion

At surface level, what constitutes torture is ever evolving, but is inherently and intrinsically tied to restrictive legal norms. As this chapter outlines, this development can especially be seen in research and scholarship around torture that continues to take torture as a given: strongly connected to the

Convention Against Torture even if not explicitly. Even when torture is discussed beyond this, it is still dominated by legal narratives, even though, as we can clearly see throughout, these are ever changing. Debates are in flux, but centre strongly around severity, intention, and mostly in relation to some form of interrogation. They are built on perpetrations of states or their third-party torturers. Furthermore, and as the following excerpts continue to highlight, formal state sanctions and prison are replicated in the social and individual imagination. That is, to whatever degree and however frequently debated, the most common definition of torture remains within the limits of legal frameworks.

However, the narratives of practitioners that are explored throughout the three epistemological perspectives offered in this chapter tell a different story. They highlight that, although torture is normatively bound to legal norms, and discourse cyclically repeats this ontological reality, how torture lives in support practices can differ vastly. Where state, institutional and organizational mandates may require a narrow law-based focus, those working with survivors do not necessarily adhere to this. Indeed, even when they may consciously do so when considering what the *definition* of torture is, their own definitions – and those of survivors – transgress this legalistic fort.

This point forms the crux of my argument and the central facet of this book: that for as long as legal definitions continue to occupy consciousness in ways that sideline experiential epistemologies of what torture is, gendered and intersectional experiences of violence which is torturous – with the same impacts and the same outcomes – remains side-lined in public and institutional discourse, and thus knowledge and understanding.

2

'Wandering Throughout Lives': Outlining Forms and Impacts of Torture

Introduction

This chapter moves to outline forms of torture documented historically, and how torture (in its narrowest definitional sense) is documented. This primarily considers two substantial works: *Torture and Democracy* by Darius Rejali, and *This Side of Silence* by Tobias Kelly. It outlines physical inflictions such as electrotorture, waterboarding, prolonged bath submersion and near-drowning, prodding, beating, induced stress positions and tortures such as noise, light and mock execution. Importantly, Rejali's work has been fundamental in exploring the silencing effects of 'clean' torture – that is, torture which is inflicted in more subtle ways through stealth that become difficult or impossible to physically evidence. As Kelly went on to highlight, this has significant implications for survivors of torture who are seeking asylum, as well as obtaining justice for their subjections, since evidence is diminished and thus so is the burden of proof.

From this, we look at the forms of torture identified by practitioners working with survivors of torture and/or sexualized violence. This chapter broadens the scope of practitioner narratives included to draw correlations between forms of violence documented as torture, and those which are not. The latter part of this chapter shifts focus to look at the consequences and impacts of torture. It is important to highlight the complex specificities of these impacts here, so we can later draw correlations and distinctions in other chapters, as we then shift away from narrow definitions and towards the conceptualization of torturous violence in a broader and more experiential sense.

Prologue: why outline forms of torture?

In his introduction to the text *Torture and its Definitions in International Law*, Metin Başoğlu reflects on being asked to develop the book. His thoughts were that 'what the world needed was not yet another book on the consequences of torture but one that promotes a sound theory – and evidence – based understanding of torture' (2017: xxiv). It is an excellent point, and one which drew me to consider whether there was any real value in what Chapter 2 aims to do: outline forms of violence that are recognized here as torture, and their impacts, or whether this ground is too well trodden already.

My conclusion is that yes, there is merit in expanding on documented forms of torture. There are three reasons that bring me to think so.

The first is that this book is not only aimed at scholars of torture, but also practitioners and students who work in wider fields. In my own work at the University of Bristol, I teach students across social policy, social work, criminology, medicine, dentistry, law and global health. It is an eclectic mix of interesting people doing interesting studies. However, in the same way that I have little (or rather, zero!) knowledge about dentistry, many students from different backgrounds do not have academic or practitioner knowledge of torture in its many forms. They have not necessarily read the 800+ pages of *Torture and Democracy* or the 1,200+ pages of *The Torture Papers*. So, in one sense, this chapter aims to set a platform from which anyone reading at most stages can begin on the same page.

The second reason stems from lecturing also. In teaching about violence and torture, it is often easy to be caught up in theories, debates, and international treaties or conventions. Probably the most common of these rests with the now ample discussions on torture post-9/11, in particular Enhanced Interrogation Techniques. However, this leaves us in the terrain of normative acceptances of the term 'torture'. Yet as we have also seen, even leading practitioners who are at the forefront of working with survivors of torture do not necessarily adhere to narrow definitions of torture. Furthermore, in my modules I am clear to outline exactly the forms of violence we are discussing: to ensure people know the complexity and multitude of what we are discussing; to ensure people recognize the long-term impacts of violence (which is particularly relevant for students who will go into practice); and to ensure students recognize the gravity of what is being said when we visit debates on torture. The last of these is unassumingly important. As the Introduction highlighted, and as many readers will know, the post-9/11 period reinvigorated public and intellectual debates about the legitimacy of torture. Invented scenarios like the ticking time bomb have played to imagination of movie makers and Netflix watchers alike. The option to create a 'best case scenario' where others may be saved if only we torture has unilaterally deflected from the fact that *torture seldom or never works for its purpose* and that even if it did, it breeds further torture (Rejali, 2011). I agree with Žižek on this occasion, when he says, 'The idea that, once we let the genie out of the bottle, torture can be kept at a "reasonable" level is the worst liberal illusion', and that even debating it intellectually is perverse (Žižek, 2002: 104). However, debates on torture exist outside of our influence socially and politically. As a lecturer, then, my aim is to ensure that any such debates among students are informed by what forms of violence are being discussed. To ensure that anyone arguing *for* the use of torture in any capacity (and some do) will be aware that they are arguing *for* the use of grievous, brutal and holistically degrading violence in whatever circumstance they might see as justifiable. This is a first step towards challenging interpretive denial (Cohen, 2001).

Finally, this book is also aimed at practitioners at any level who may be working with violence generally, or people pre-assessed as survivors of torture specifically. While this chapter focuses in places on academic literature and research, it addresses the forms of violence and impacts thereof that practitioners have listened through, worked with or supported. Since practice itself can be somewhat isolating at times, it can be helpful to know that what you are hearing or seeing is not only on you, but that other practitioners and survivors have correlating experiences (as I have heard many times over the past 15 years). Practitioners often see and hear the most brutal forms of violence in individuals' histories, yet – as later chapters will highlight – these go silenced, overlooked or disregarded in many public spheres, in particular for refugees whose histories are undermined in societies where anti-migrant sentiment strongly usurps sympathy or empathy for such experiences, instead demanding integration or assimilation, if not demanding or exercising expulsion (see Canning, 2019b). Perhaps most significantly, some readers of this book will be survivors of violence themselves. Since violence works to silence and break us down, it can be an isolating experience to have. To that, you will see that although experience is personal to you, you are not alone in surviving such violence.

By outlining these I hope to address what Başoğlu highlights as a 'true need': theory and evidence. With these points in mind, I outline forms of violence documented in academic and non-governmental organization literatures and people working with survivors, and the impacts and implications of such violence.

Typologies of torture: situating mechanisms of physical and psychological violence

There are many ways that humans can be broken down, humiliated and degraded. As Hannah Arendt so thoroughly documented in *On Violence*

(1970) and *Eichmann in Jerusalem: A Report on the Banality of Evil* (1963), power and violence are separate, and yet usually appear together. As Nowak later attested, all aspects of torture should be situated in the relative powerlessness between torture and tortured (2006). Subsequently, although not all in power will use violence, and not all violence stems from holding or keeping hold of power, power and powerlessness is required to work effectively for the means and ends of torture, in the context of both state and non-state abuses.

How torture is performed is not monolithic, either spatially or historically. Torture, as Rejali (2007) has documented, comes with many physical and psychological faces and can correlate across global and temporal spheres. In some senses then, torture travels. Eric Fair, a former military contractor in Abu Ghraib, outlined forms of torture he witnessed in Iraq. Of particular relevance was his claim that US contractors were trained in the use of the Palestinian chair – a stress position in which the subject crouches across the chair with the majority of weight on their thighs – by the Israeli military to execute the position effectively to 'essentially break their will' (Fair, 2016). This should not be surprising. In a report on the use of Central Intelligence Agency (CIA) torture (specifically in detention in this case) by the Open Society Justice Initiative, 54 governments across five continents were implicated in facilitating or administering torture (2013).[1] As one psychologist also put it when reflecting on correlations in survivor accounts, "Is there some sort of torture organization that is worldwide, training people in the same methods around the world, because I think, even though there's differences, there is still many, many similarities between different places" (interview, 2021). As such, although torture has differences and no two people experience the same subjections on an individual level, torture – like other aspects of organized harm – is simultaneously corollary *and* highly differential in its mechanisms and objectives.

Torture may therefore be best understood in terms of typologies and techniques. By typologies, I am referring to the broader spectrums of violence which act as an umbrella under which specific abuses may be situated, specifically physical, psychological, sexualized and temporal. This approach draws from zemiology, the study of social harm, which originally established four dimensions of harm, expanding to nine and later more (Hillyard and Tombs, 2004; Pemberton, 2015; Canning, 2018; Copson, 2018; specifically, see Canning and Tombs, 2021: 64–88). Within these, like typologies of torture, one can situate specific techniques – or forms – of torture. However, there is contention around where some forms would situate or fall under – for example, while sensory deprivation may sit fairly solidly as psychological torture, sexualized humiliation may be psychological or, depending on the use of bodily abuse, physical *and* psychological. As such, there is more opportunity to examine the *dimensions of violence* as relational rather than singular in their type, intent or impact.

Forms of infliction: what do we mean when we talk about 'torture'?

How torture is enacted, then, differs over time and space and yet clearly has various links to globalization and indeed democracy. In *Torture and Democracy*, Darius Rejali spans the Ottoman Empire, Soviet methods in Eastern Europe, Chinese Communists, Weimar Germany, the United States, Britain, Cambodia, Iraq, Syria, Mongols in Iran – the list goes on (see Rejali, 2007). From thorough documentary analysis, Rejali outlined uses of violence, which included – and is certainly not limited to – beatings, crushing of nipples, use of stun guns, the driving of pegs into kidneys, the rubbing of bodies with sandpaper followed by alcohol or turpentine, use of cattle prods, electric shocks, pumping with alcohol, excessively spicing or salting meals and forcing ingestion, insertion of irritants to eyes, nostrils, anus and/or vagina, deprivation of sleep, waterboarding, the crapaudine (tying legs and arms behind the head and drawing together on the stomach), blows to fleshy areas, various forms of chairs inducing stress positions, excessive or deprivation of light, sleep deprivation, and holding people in cold rooms or sweatboxes.

I only synopsize here the extensive number of forms Rejali documents as a means to illustrate both the banality of some forms, and the brutally imaginative use of others. Further examples are tabled by Pérez-Sales, who aligns accounts of specific forms of torture with political regimes and countries/states and knowledge sharing, including Algeria, Latin America, France, the USSR, China, Japan and in places such as Guantanamo and Abu Ghraib (2017: 166–168). As we will clearly see, forms of violence – whether defined as torture or torturous violence as we will later explore – are more plentiful than we perhaps like to recognize or be confronted with in everyday social consciousness. As Arendt (among many others, of course) noted in the context of the Holocaust, the range and scope of brutality used when power and violence is unleashed together and without accountability is almost beyond imagination. And yet, as is clearly evidenced, it is not only vast in its reach and dimensions, but in some spaces meticulously devised, developed and shared.

We'll return to the concept of 'clean' torture and the forms thereof later, but these are a reminder of what we are discussing when we discuss torture in the hands of states contemporarily and historically. In the meantime, the objective is to fully recognize the forms of violence we are alluding to, rather than implying without saying and thus leaving gaps for silence or denial.

The glocalization of torture

The final point in the previous paragraph is critical, not only for the reasons outlined in the prologue, but because we will now move to forms of torture that research participants working with refugees have reported in interviews (between 2013 and 2021) which draw together the local and the global. This serves three purposes: firstly, to highlight ways in which torture does not only travel with torture regimes, but through the trajectories of a person's life. While some of these interviews are taken with people working during conflict or in regimes recognized as torturous, and some practitioners have also survived them themselves, many of these accounts relate to the experiences of people living in Northern European countries. As the title of this chapter highlights, impacts of such violence can *wander through lives*. Secondly, if some people are living with such violent histories, why are we not more collectively conscious, and indeed compassionate towards, the experiences of people who could be our neighbours, our practitioners, our teachers, or ourselves? And thirdly, naming sustained and extreme forms of violence as torturous challenges the ways in which such acts are committed in 'other' places by 'other' people. Although Darius Rejali has clearly outlined the complex relationships between torture and democracy (2007; 2011), and even though we are familiar with the proliferation of torture by Western states in the aftermath of 9/11 (as well as before, of course), campaigns against torture often present it as something 'uncivilized' and committed elsewhere. Introducing torturous violence is a reminder that extreme brutality is both global and local to us, and happens in much more banal circumstances than militarized or organized torture.

It is here that I introduce the glocalization of torture. While torture is well recognized as an entity which can be moved across borders, boundaries, time and space, those who are contemporarily subjected to its impacts do not necessarily figure well in this recognition of globalized torture, as the Open Society Justice Initiative terms it (2013). Glocalization refers predominately to business models. It is the means for companies and corporations to distribute business globally, while providing local preferences or cultural demands. However, Roland Robertson, who coined the term, was later clear in stating that it 'facilitates the thorough discussion of various problems that attend a simple distinction between the global and the local' (2012: 191). Taking this invitation for such discussion, we can begin to see that not only is state-facilitated or inflicted torture global, but local in its forms. Moreover, and to get to the crux of the concept as I mean to apply it, torture transgresses the boundaries of its own locale, to perforate people's lives and memories wherever they go, while beginning to occupy the consciousness of those who come to know about them.

This section therefore seeks to uncover, from individual and institutional perspectives, forms of torture survivors work through while living in host countries – often much later after the subjection to violence, as well (in some places) in political states recognized as torturous or torture complicit.

From repetitive beatings to imaginative inquisition

Interviewing practitioners – who are often more used to interviewing other people themselves – is interesting. It allows people to reflect on their breadth and depth of experience, knitting together histories they have heard that for some stretch back to 30 or more years of practice. While individuals' subjections to torture can be focused on exactly that – the individual – practitioners often see patterns in global politics and persecution: the Bosnian War, the first and second Iraq wars, the Sri Lankan Civil War, right up to responding to contemporary survivors of the Syrian War.

Sarah, a psychotraumatologist with experience working in several countries, reflected on working with:

'[P]eople who have been tortured with water boarding, burning cigarettes, noise exposure, people who have witnessed rape of their family members, mothers, fathers, children, wives, you name it. We have people who have been exposed to mock executions, where they hear the click of the gun without being killed. We have people who experienced rape, enforced labour in jails, people who have been forced to drink their own urine. One of the most bizarre tortured that I've heard was a torture performed in a Tunisian jail, where they put you in a sack that they close here, and close at your legs, so your head is out. Then they put a cat that is very hungry in the sack, so the cat just runs all over you biting and scratching. You know, when I think about the creativity of torture, and when I think about how it is used in other ways, it's mind-bugging. We have seen people who have been exposed or attacked with acid. Whatever you read in the papers, it's peanuts compared to what the people who come here have been through.' (Psychotraumatologist who works exclusively with pre-assessed survivors of torture, interview, 2013)

Here we see a combination of particularly common torture techniques, some of which have garnered debate on whether they can be defined as torture (predominately as a means to justify their inclusion in 'interrogations' by the CIA in Iraq, Afghanistan, Guantanamo and other detention black sites, and by the British government in Northern Ireland). They are often repetitive, excruciating, psychologically demeaning and, for some, anxiety inducing in the anticipation of repeated abuses. Sarah includes the witnessing of loved ones being raped as well as rape of the self, most within the context of detention. As she goes on, she begins to consider more performative mechanisms of torture, such as the cat in the sack she refers to here. This kind of imaginative interrogation – or indeed punishment – was echoed by Johanne, a psychologist working in Uganda who spoke with survivors of the Lord's Resistance Army, recalled being told by former child soldiers that they had been asked, "do you want short sleeve or long sleeves, and that would be asking whether they would cut from the top or bottom of their arm" (interview, 2013).

Sarah's emphasis towards the end, like Johanne's example, is on the creativity of brutality: whatever we garner from torture as exceptional, it is inflicted in more elaborate ways than we might like to imagine humans to be capable of. This is arguably somewhat ironic given the increased use of torture in popular culture. From the book and television series *True Blood* to *Game of Thrones*, from *Zero Dark Thirty* to the *Saw* collection, brutal violence (often in some form of confinement) is regularly present in public narratives. It seems then that rather than being unable to confront torture completely, we are less able to confront it collectively as reality – it remains something of fiction, too far from what many of us are willing to accept, despite its continued prevalence globally.

Asta, a physiotherapist working with pre-assessed survivors of torture (see Scarry, 1985), reflects:

'In the Middle Eastern regions, as there is a lot of regional difference, but there it's almost always falanga [beating of the feet]. A lot of beating all over the body where they are hooded or can't protect themselves. Or hanging and suspensions. Isolation, where they are put in dark rooms and not allowed access to anyone else. Also, overcrowded prison cells where they can't lie down, they can't relax. They take turns so half are standing up while the others are sitting or lying, and they just take turns. The most common are beatings on the body, beatings on the feet, suspensions and threats about what will happen to them. Like having a cigarette burning in your eye ... also burnings. Electrical torture. And retractions. Being pulled, that woman was pulled and dragged by her hair, forced to inhale acidic fumes, so she is now asthmatic. There are also some methods you don't see with everybody. And of course a lot of the females, and the males, are also raped.' (Interview, 2013)

Like Sarah's initial outline, Asta's examples of torture are those that are most commonly reported as repeated injuries (Başoğlu et al, 2007), before moving to some which relate more to specific narratives of survivors she has met, including the consequences, in this case, of inhaling acidic fumes. As many others also did, Asta referred to regionality and common techniques, such as the Middle East, although not which specific countries. This kind of glocalization of torture, where the impacts of torture in one region move across borders and into new areas, is something that resonated with survivors – as we will see in Chapter 5.

Laura, a medical doctor who assesses the extent of physical injuries on torture survivors, highlights similar techniques, but moves also to more specifically psychological forms of torture to explore their relationship with bodily pain:

'It's beatings, both with objects, with electrical wires and other things; it's also electrical torture, especially to the genitalia and other sensitive parts of the body. It's a lot of deprivation forms of torture, deprivation of food, deprivation of the possibility to sleep, deprivation of the possibility to go to the bathroom or get medication, personal hygiene and things like that. Mock executions and witnessing other people being subjected to torture, either by seeing it or listening to it or by being forced to perform acts of violence towards other prisoners or other people who are being held captive, and then threats, of course.' (Interview, 2021)

This moves us to a more hybrid recognition of deliberate forms of psychological torture. Although all forms of violence have the potential for negative and severe psychological impacts, some strategies are deliberately and exclusively developed to target and break down the human psyche. Some, such as sleep deprivation or toilet deprivation, have the potential to transgress to actually developing physical symptoms. But others, such as witnessing other people's torture or being subjected to mock execution, are held in the minds and memories of survivors, and can have as or more harmful long-term consequences (Başoğlu et al, 2001; Pérez-Sales, 2017; El-Khoury et al, 2020).

Hannele, a psychologist also working with pre-assessed survivors of torture, identified similar combinations of the physical and psychological:

'To be put inside a wheel and shoved downstairs. Isolation in small, small spaces. Just being isolated. Having to watch other people being tortured is very common. And pointless things. Having to collect all the sand in a yard with your hands in 30 degrees sunshine and pick up the sand. They like to subject people to do stuff that has no meaning. It's very hard for people – as soon as we can find meaning in a task we can motivate ourselves to do it, so they often find pointless things to do. They often try to get them to torture other people. And often succeed with enough pressure. But they make stew out of people, they put them into meat grinders and make people watch them do that. And also beating. Mock executions are very common. Dogs raping people. Tearing nails out, teeth out. All kinds of sick things.' (Interview, 2013)

As with others, witnessing is inherently impactful, despite not always being recognized itself as a form of torture in many legal discourses. Dora even went as far as considering being witness to some forms of brutality as "one of the worst cases – having to face your parents or your close relatives, brothers being killed, shot at, are just harrowing, or being closed up in a prison cell and beaten up thoroughly on a daily basis, and hung up" (interview, 2021). This is taken a step further by Laura, who recalled that, "he [survivor] had to witness his brother's death, the way the brother was tortured and killed, and then he had to prepare his brother's body. … I don't know what kind of ritual was supposed to be performed, but he was supposed to clean up after the act". The psychological impact of witnessing begins to transcend to the physical – not only must this man watch his brother's murder, but he was forced to partake in preparing his body for burial. It is of course customary for family to clean and shroud the body in Islamic burial rites, where possible (if this case is indeed following Islamic rites). However, the deliberate use of a brother as a witness and an agent to clean and bury the tortured, is itself a form of power infliction on the powerless, and one which again requires planning and imagination.

To go back to Hannele's statement, we also see isolation included again. Isolation is one form of deprivation, but as Sharon Shalev has long identified, and Therese Rytter at DIGNITY has long campaigned around, prisons all over the world continue the use of solitary confinement (see Shalev, 2009; Council of Europe, 2018). Conversely, it is worth reading work by colleagues in the Angola 3, Albert Woodfox, Herman Wallace and Robert King, who were held in solidarity confinement, with Albert Woodfox becoming the longest-held person in solitary confinement in American history at the time. Although Wallace died from liver cancer hours after being released in 2013, King and Woodfox went on to campaign for solitary to be recognized as cruel and unusual punishment, which is addressed in both their autobiographies (see King, 2009; Woodfox, 2019). In short, although used as a 'legitimate' tool for punishment globally, isolation and solitary confinement is hugely damaging (particularly after around 30 days), yet not always regarded as torture, depending on the context.

Psychological torture

This brings us specifically to psychological torture. As El-Khoury et al emphasize, psychological torture has long been inadequately defined (2020). Pau Pérez-Sales has gone some way in addressing this in *Psychological Torture* but concludes that, 'The lack of a clear and objective definition within the juridical conception of torture leaves space for uncertainty and discretional interpretations that makes scientists uncomfortable' (2017: 329). To this end, it is clear that defining psychological torture is no easy feat. Yet, as this whole book argues, neither is *torture*.

As such, it is worth looking at how practitioners categorize or define psychological torture here. For Mila, the psychologist and psychotherapist introduced in Chapter 1:

> 'The thing is, you can divide it up into being psychological torture and physical torture, and yeah, they overlap, but I think that some of the most disturbing really often is the psychological element of it, where people come out having had a degrading of their sense of self and having to pretend to be something they aren't.' (Interview, 2021)

Here is the crux of the issue: although some forms of torture are focused only on breaking people down mentally, all forms of torture – physical or otherwise – have potential for serious psychological impacts. As Mila goes on, she gives examples: "[T]hings like being hung up for longer periods of time, starvation, withholding food. The list goes on and on. Just different forms of psychological torture, of promising release and not being released, or withholding toilet; withholding any sort of basic things that you might expect to have" (interview, 2021). In this we begin to see time introduced – in this case, being hung up for longer periods of time as detention goes on. The promise of release and having this removed echoes points made elsewhere (Canning, 2017; 2018; 2019b; 2020a; 2021a) – that temporal harm and, to some degree here, autonomy harm, are unique in their mechanisms for inducing stress and anxiety, and yet temporality is generally completely overlooked as a form of torture.

Finally, Klara, a child psychologist working with children affected by torture, surmises that:

> '[T]he more psychological, demeaning forms of violence, where people imprisoned are being systematically exposed to social practices that are designed to break down integrity and the sense of community and sense of time and sense of having access to basic needs. That can be systematically lining people up in groups, blindfolding them, keeping them from access to hygiene facilities, food, unclear water, but also demeaning names.' (Interview, 2021)

Again, we can see the issue of time being introduced, and the psychological impacts of uncertainty and the threat of what is to come are seen as demeaning. Further, the use of the term 'systematic' is imperative – while debates on the severity of violence are complex and difficult to solidify in reality, as discussed in relation to Tobias Kelly's points in Chapter 1 – *systematic* inflictions of physical or psychological violence can arguably support us to define torture, and the difference between being subjected to a singular violent act or episode and sustained or systematic torture or torturous violence. As I will later argue, it is exactly the systematic nature of torturous violence outside of the remit of state torture which makes it so convincingly torturous – in particular familial, domestic and sustained interpersonal violence.

The move to 'clean' torture

This brings us to focus on the significance of this shift. Where state-sanctioned/inflicted torture has historically focused on breaking the body in obvious and traceable ways, tactics have gradually shifted to embrace stealthy, less evidencable forms of 'clean' torture. In identifying torture, Darius Rejali was clear to document forms of bodily and psychological abuses which did not only work to degrade, humiliate and break people down, but which could do so without being (easily) identified or proven: those which leave few, or no, marks. Many of these we have seen here: falanga, electric prods, sensory deprivation, starvation, enforced labour, mock executions, forced witnessing of other people's murders, torture or death. As noted earlier, the list – unfortunately – goes on.

As the narratives here emphasize, the impacts of psychological and other clean tortures transgress international boundaries to infiltrate survivor histories when living in host countries. It is here, for example, that the burden of proof of having survived torture or persecution becomes even more complicated, since it becomes difficult or impossible to do so. Tobias Kelly outlined the implications of this in meticulous detail in *This Side of Silence* (2012), as standards of proof which relate to credibility and evidence in asylum claims disproportionately weigh towards the physical. This can also be seen in the use of body images in some form of torture assessment, which focus on where pain or abuse has been felt. As Kelly also highlights, although there have been shifts towards recognizing clean and/or psychological torture, evidence collation remains on the side of the pains of the body where asylum claims are considered (Kelly, 2012) although organizations such as Freedom from Torture work to produce expert medical evidence to counteract this where feasible (see Freedom from Torture, 2016, for a full discussion, particularly on the difficulties inherent to this).

The narrative of 'physical harm as paramount' is also one that is engrained in the consciousness of survivors. There have been occasions where survivors of physical abuse and torture have shown me their scars when in fairly regular conversation about their asylum claims: cigarette burns, burns from scalding water, whiplash marks, cheek fractures and other bodily disfigurements. All of these have, of course, not been at my request. Yet, as Amina, a psychologist, also states: "They show me, 'Look what they did to me' – they would lift up their shirts – and sometimes I think, 'Okay, this is not necessary. I totally trust what you're saying.' But somehow they believe that if they can't show what they have been through, then people wouldn't believe them" (interview, 2021). Yet, as we know, not all impacts of violence are visible or produce scars.

All of this is even before we get to fully considering sexualized torture, violence and torturous violence. This type of violence is not set out in its own category by Rejali, and yet arguably is the most successful way of inducing silence, including as a form of torture which 'leaves no [physical] marks' for many survivors.

Deliberate permanency: when histories of torture lack an ending

As a final point before considering impacts, it is worth highlighting that some forms of torture seem deliberately constructed to inflict a kind of permanency which cannot be evaded, no matter where a survivor goes.

Rikke, a clinical psychologist working with pre-assessed survivors of torture, gives one example, "when they torture they put a Coke can at the table because there's Coke all round the world, so no matter where you end up you'll see a Coke bottle and then you'll be traumatized" (interview, 2021). Here we have an almost ironic relationship with glocalization. In one sense, glocalization originates from a business model, as discussed. In this case, a multinational corporation is used as a semiotic marker while inflicting torture. In another sense, and more related to the way in which I have framed the glocalization of torture, survivors' memories are used to ensure that, no matter where one goes, their subjection to torture is always, and uncontrollably, present.

This form of permanency was later echoed in an interview with medical doctor Laura, who recalled, "The types of torture can be really … some of them are just completely beyond your imagination". Laura went on to describe how the survivor had been forced to witness a cellmate being tortured to death before being forced to eat parts of him (interview, 2021 [specific details withdrawn to protect the client]).

Again, here we see reference to the term 'imagination', and the insistence that so much of this is beyond what we can humanly imagine. And yet, it is only humans who have imagined these practices into existence. In this case, after torturing a man to death, the survivor – who was receiving treatment at a European rehabilitation centre at the time of the interview – has been forced to ingest his murdered friend. This tactic was also mentioned in other interviews, including the cooking of people in stews. Even apart from the levels of degradation embedded in this subjection, this moves permanency into a different realm: when we ingest anything, it becomes part of us. Subsequently, in some ways psychologically, if not also physically, this kind of torture takes form as part of the human body, further elevating the significance of biopower and biopolitics.

The impacts and effects of torture

Given the breadth of typologies and forms of torture addressed, it almost goes without saying that the impacts of these forms of brutality are not prescribed, monolithic or deterministic. Individuals respond to abuse, degradation, humiliation and physical and/or psychological subjections to violence differently. Also crucial is that the impacts and outcomes can change at different intersections of people's lives.

As with forms of torture, there is no definitive set of impacts or problems which may develop in the aftermath of torture. Nor are these impacts confined to being outcomes of torture, since some clearly relate to other forms of trauma or loss in a person's life. However, given the (often) systematic nature of torture, it is unsurprising that physical and psychological impacts can be severe, long-lasting and complex to address for individuals and practitioners alike.

The *Field Manual on Rehabilitation* developed by the Danish Institute Against Torture is a useful source to begin with when considering the multifarious impacts of torture (DIGNITY, 2012). Accordingly, problems or outcomes that can develop are separated into two sections: *body functions*; and *activities and participation*.

Reiterating this point, the two lists in Table 2.1 are very obviously relatable to other forms of trauma. Indeed, many feminists have highlighted similar patterns in the aftermath of sexualized or domestic violence. Focusing on the impacts of such violence draws together torture with torturous violence more solidly, beyond the contestable boundaries addressed in the first chapter – in particular, focus on motivation and context over forms of violence and the impacts thereof.

Furthermore, as with addressing the somewhat fluid ways in which physical and psychological tortures may combine in some contexts, the problems outlined in Table 2.1 have similar relational scope. For example, it is not difficult to imagine that bed-wetting has the potential to impact on intimate relations, or that whole-body pain may affect how a person engages in their work or social life. Meanwhile, participation issues such as 'not using transport' has serious consequences for maintaining family or friendship networks, but also the ability to engage in trauma support or rehabilitation itself. I have addressed some of these in different contexts – specifically for people seeking asylum – as relational, temporal and autonomy harms (see

Table 2.1: Problems which may develop in the aftermath of torture, as defined by the United Nations Convention Against Torture or Other Cruel, Inhuman or Degrading Treatment or Punishment

Body functions	Activities and participation
Abdominal pain, anger, anxiety, arm pain, back pain, bleeding from orifice, breathing difficulties, burning sensation, chest pain, cognitive problems, coldness, constipation, coughing, depersonalization, depression, diarrhoea, disfiguration, Disorders of Extreme Stress Not Otherwise Specified [DESNOS], dissociation, dizziness, facial pain, flashback, foot pain, guilt feelings, hand pain, headache, hearing difficulties, heart palpitations, hyper-vigilance, incontinence, indigestion, intrusive memories, leg pain, loss of appetite, loss of energy, loss of interest, menstruation problems, micturition, muscle, joint and bone pain, muscle weakness, nausea, neck pain, numbness, over alertness, pain [acute], pain [chronic], pain [neuropathic], pain [psychogenic], paranoia, paresis, pelvic pain, persistent thoughts, phantom pain, post-traumatic stress disorder [PTSD], posture and balance problems, reproduction difficulties, sense of a limited future, sexual problems, shame, shoulder pain, skin infections, sleeping difficulties, somatization, somatization [children], substance abuse, sweating, swelling, tics, tinnitus, tiredness, ulcer of skin, urge to urinate, urinating difficulties, vision difficulties, vomiting, weight loss, whole body pain.	Aggressive outbursts, alienation, antisocial behaviour, avoidance behaviour, bed wetting, bereavement, community life [participation in], coping and preoccupation with pain, disability, dressing problems, eating problems, exclusion from participation in social and political activities, family life [participation in], friendship breakdown, gainful activities, identity problems, intimate relations, isolation, lifting and carrying objects, maintaining a dwelling, nightmare, night terror, obsessive compulsive activities, performing household work, redress, regressive symptoms, relational problems, risk-taking behaviour, self-efficacy problems, self-harm, self-mutilation, taking care of others, toileting problems, traumatic play, using transport, walking problems, washing problems, worrying about symptoms.

Source: Adapted from DIGNITY (2012).

Canning, 2017; 2019a; Canning and Tombs, 2021), but the key point to make is that they are not necessarily standalone issues, but become the cause and consequence of other problems.

Impacts reported by practitioners working with survivors

This brings us to the final section, where we return to consider some of the issues identified in working with survivors. These are threefold: psychological;

physical and somatic; and social, cultural and relational. Although presented as separate, it is worth considering the possible ways in which each form of impact may be relational to others, for example that sleeplessness can affect how we engage with work or leisure as we become more tired, or how feelings of guilt may affect how we move forward with existing or new relationships. In short, each has the capacity to interact with or develop into other forms.

Psychological

The first thing to note is that many participants working with pre-assessed survivors of torture and survivors of sexualized violence referred to similar impacts. For Annika, a psychologist specializing in torture, war and trauma treatment, these included:

> '[N]ightmares, disrupted sleep, being afraid of sleeping because you can't control or you don't know if anyone is coming to get you … being not able to relax, having intruding memories of trauma, difficult times, flashbacks as if you're in the trauma again though you're here, so you have a difficulty actually accessing that you are here and not in the situation again.' (Interview, 2017)

These are not atypical, and yet as one can imagine, can cause significant distress and disruption for survivors. Solveig, who worked specifically with women survivors of sexualized violence, specifically noted, "typically they have all the classical symptoms regarding PTSD [post-traumatic stress disorder], they can't sleep at night, they have pain all over, they have difficulties being with other people, also their own family, so they're really isolated. All the classical symptoms. Afraid of going out" (interview, 2017). Here we see the combination of the psychological with the spatial, in that people can feel a sense of isolation. This may be literal, given the issues raised earlier about the impacts of using public transport, and here as a fear of going out, but also a key aspect of affecting a person psychologically so that they may feel alienated or alone, an issue which is often compounded by shame and silence where sexualized torture or violence is concerned.

Laura expanded on these to include:

> '[A]lso feelings of guilt, of survivor's guilt, and feelings of shame, shame that they didn't try to resist some of these acts, and also shame that some of them have been begging their torturers to kill them, for example, or to stop, and that is something that quite a few patients have also been describing: this impact of not … of feeling humiliated, having to beg someone that they obviously didn't feel any sort of

sympathy with, but still had to beg them for mercy or for just killing them.' (Interview, 2021)

These forms of guilt can also be relational, particularly if a person survives and other family members or friends do not, an issue which can sometimes also pertain to witnessing torture or even death. Further, humiliation, like degradation, is inextricably linked with the exercising of power over relative powerlessness, the objective within torture being the breaking down of a person. Anne, a clinical psychologist, went on to relate these to "feelings of no worth or severe hopelessness" (interview, 2021), in some sense an indication that the objectives of the torturer or abuser may be fulfilled as time goes by. Anne reiterated the significance of the concept of time, but in this case in relation to the present: "Very often not being present, flashbacks, but with very, very vivid sensory experiences … but mostly just you have this stressor and then you're out for a period of time, or losing contact with your body is very, very common, what I see, so different dissociative symptoms" (interview, 2021).

Temporality and temporal harm therefore seeps into the everyday for some survivors, affecting how time itself is experienced. Although temporality has been side-lined in many torture debates, as Bhatia and I argue in *Stealing Time*, this factor is far from an irrelevance:

> What we do with our time is a form of capital, linked with our own perceptions of success or failure – it is unlike any other capital we possess. We may lose money or friends, and work to claim them back. We might lose a sentimental object that, in essence, cannot seem replaceable, but with which another can replace its function. But no matter how rich we are or what cultural capital we accumulate, we can never, ever re-accumulate time that is lost. (Bhatia and Canning, 2021: xxiv)

Time, and the loss of control over it, is therefore a central, if somewhat under-recognized, impact of torture and other forms of violence.

Physical and somatic

As Elaine Scarry (1985) and later Bessel van der Kolk (2014) have addressed in depth, pain plays out in many ways. This may be long after physical torture or other abuses, such as joint problems in the aftermath of hanging, or headaches after severe beatings to the head. However, they may also be somatic, the physical manifestation of psychological trauma. Importantly, this has been a serious issue for many women I have spoken with who experience stomach pains, itching legs or chronic back pain, but do not wish to disclose histories of violence to their medical doctor. As such, in my experience at least, some doctors – already often pushed for time between one patient and the next – can be exasperated by repeat appointments and tests, only to find nothing wrong.

This is a key point to convey for future doctors who may go on to work with people who may have been subjected to persecution, torture or other violence, disproportionately people seeking asylum or with refugee status, although certainly not confined to this demographic. However, it is a double-edged sword: if people do not disclose histories of violence, probing for disclosure without appropriate time or resources to respond effectively can be problematic, but also overstep a survivor's comfort zone without their consent. Disclosure for many people can take time and requires trust. Dora, a psychotraumatologist working with survivors of sexualized violence and torture, echoes this point, "[w]e have a lot of physical pains that they don't even talk about until after they've said in therapy, 'I have these pains, but I don't know why I get them.' Then you find out later on, through therapy, they've actually been hung up and beaten up" (interview, 2021).

Laura identifies "deficiency impacts", where a physical quality is reduced or lost through physical torture. She states:

'Depending on the specific act of torture, it could be of course also specific deficiencies, like loss of hearing or loss of eyesight, blindness, and negative feelings about themselves, sometimes not being able to look at the part of the body where they have maybe scars. I had one patient, he was beaten several times in the head and he lost his eyesight in one eye. Originally, he had two brown eyes, but then the eye where he lost his eyesight, it became like a faded, whitish-blue, the eye, and he said he hated looking at himself in the mirror because every time he looked in the mirror, he would be confronted with his blue and brown eye and be reminded of what had happened.' (Interview, 2021)

In this narrative, the complex relationship between the impact of torture and the perspective of the survivor, on how they see or view themselves, can itself be a daily reminder of their subjection.

'Wandering throughout lives': social, cultural and relational

As is already evident, torture has the potential for long-term impacts, and although these impacts may look separate on the surface, there are complicated ways in which they may link to, influence or transform others: that physical impacts may have somatic consequences, or psychological impacts may manifest to become physical (such as eating problems or self-harm).

It is unsurprising, then, that the consequences of torture and other forms of violence can nefariously transcend the physical and psychological to impact on the social. This point is important: histories of torture are often silenced, and yet torture remains pervasive globally, thus its impacts have capacity to rupture everyday life and experience of survivors, as well as their families, communities and wider society. Some of these aspects are outlined in this chapter, but it is worth emphasizing that although many cannot be altered, since history is past, living conditions and support for survivors *can be changed in the present*. This is specifically relevant to addressing histories of violence in the aftermath of conflict – which is often arguably perpetual in nature – as well as for survivors who have fled conflict, violence or persecution, with which comes great loss and change.

Mila's outline relates directly to the purposes of torture: the breaking down of an individual, and the implications of this on their relationships with others in terms of trust:

'[A] sort of stripping of sense of self and meaning, and the whole course of one's life has completely changed into a different direction. That's probably the primary impact, I would say, and a loss of trust in other people generally in the world, in a way, in the goodness and potential of the world or being in the world.' (Interview, 2021)

This echoes issues raised earlier about the ways in which people may become isolated, or seek to isolate themselves. As such, one is intertwined with the other: if we lose trust in others, isolation becomes a logical response to protect from further harm, even if this act of self-preservation can prove to be harmful in and of itself.

For some survivors, torture may affect them in the region or area that they were subjected to it. For others, it can be the instigator of significant social change – moving away from one's home, country of origin or region to build a new life away from the threat of persecution. As this book unfolds, this will become more centralized in relation to people seeking asylum. As Laura synopsizes:

'Many patients, they say that they just want to get back to the person they once were before the torture, and that's a big grief that they carry with them. They've lost so many things. They've lost culture, friends, family, work, profession, language, everything, and then they also feel like they've lost themselves. Then also, when they come here, those who have children who are maybe teenagers, they may feel that they're losing their children to society, because the children are learning the new language, faster than the parents are, and they are often times becoming integrated much faster and maybe attracted to parts of the culture that their parents don't necessarily approve of, so that's another impact some steps down the line, but something that can happen eventually.' (Interview, 2021)

As such, loss is compounded – not only may there be a loss of the sense of self, but also of everything one may know, own or love. In the case of people rebuilding lives in a new country, complex forms of integration leave little space for reflection, as we will explore in Chapter 7. Moreover, as generations move on, this loss can be inextricably linked with temporality and change, where a sense of loss over cultures and heritage can diminish personal histories lost to migrating in the first place.

The importance of this is picked up by Mila, who emphasizes the ways in which relationships can change or be affected in the aftermath of torture, and the longer-term trajectories of these relational harms can begin to impact more fully on families, and even people the survivor may love:

> '[I]t affects relationships because I think a lot of these symptoms of PTSD and also just generally meaninglessness really affect relationships in couples or with children. Sometimes we also find in our family projects there can be some dysfunction in families because of that, of one parent's or both parents' experience of torture, sometimes violence in the family as well from the torture survivor.' (Interview, 2021)

These relational implications may be intergenerational, and have ripple effects across families as time moves on, as Mila went on to point out, "it's intergenerational; it has very profound effects that mushroom out into all parts of the family, and it lasts for a long time after. Even one person's experience affects several generations after that". This is reiterated, almost poetically, by Freja, highlighting, "that torture doesn't only affect the person who's been tortured; it affects the entire family and *it wanders throughout the family*, and children of torture survivors, and even if both the wife and husband have been tortured, the kids suffer tremendously from that" (interview, 2021; emphasis added).

This brings us to the stark realization that torture is the violation of an individual, but it also serves as a form of cultural violence which can work to break down heritage, relationships, collective histories, friendships and families. Its harms perforate time and space, where it may *wander throughout* lives.

Conclusion

Forms of torture are diverse, socially and culturally contingent, and as such, are certainly not monolithic. As this chapter shows, there is a breadth to forms of torture which takes us beyond what we may prefer to distance our personal or collective consciousness from. Yet, ironically, torture remains pervasive and, as the next chapter will focus on in more depth, torturous violence is sometimes exercised in the banal everyday life of people who are subjected to it.

The most significant element herein is arguably the focus on the impacts of, and problems which can develop from, torture. Apart from the extent and indeed – whether contested in contemporary debates on torture or not – severity, impacts can be profound, life-altering and relentless. They can change through the life course with different forms affecting the lives of survivors at different times.

The lists outlined by DIGNITY go a long way to outlining the multifarious impacts of, or problems developing from, torture, however it is through practitioner reflections that we can more holistically deduce the ways in which these intertwine with each other, and the complexity of how they undermine the individual's sense of self, as well as wider relations and experiences in the long term. These consequences are personal, interpersonal, psychological, emotional, cultural and social, each of which is significant in its own right. Given that these impacts can be related not only to torture as per legal understandings, but to other forms of sustained or systematic violence, they are arguably the central focus for understanding and responding to violence which goes beyond definitional boundaries. It is with this in mind that we move to conceptualize *torturous violence* more fully.

'I Wouldn't Call it Torture': Conceptualizing Torturous Violence

Introduction: thinking beyond states and state institutions

In the month prior to submitting this book for publication I garnered opinions of approximately 100 practitioners working on trauma, torture, violence and rehabilitation, discussing if or how much the concept of torture is of central relevance to their work. For some, particularly lawyers and legal advisors working on international committees and advising governments accused of torture, it was paramount: without the concept of torture, all aspects of international or criminal justice, accountability or torture rehabilitation would be defunct. Others alluded to the possibility of 'cruel, inhuman and degrading treatment', only themselves to agree that the concept of and terminology around 'torturous' holds a linguistic and discourse advantage in its derivation of 'torture', given torture's common understanding as the most heinous of all violence.

For others, my continued inclusion of legal definitions of torture undoes the objective of transcending definitional boundaries of torture, since some aspects of the book continue to build around it. For some psychologists and psychotraumatologists in particular, the term can be relevant for survivors of torture, but far from relevant to treatment or rehabilitation since extreme violence may have been part of a longer-term trajectory, even from childhood. As a number of people argued, even assessing for evidence of 'torture' can be highly problematic: people receiving support can relay torture as one of many traumatic events or forms of serious physical or psychological violence. Without a torture assessment, they might see many more self-elected survivors of extreme violence who experience the same impacts of trauma. In short, torture assessments may be useful to an extent for responding to state inflicted or sanctioned torture, but they also act as a metaphorical sieve for responding to other forms of extreme violence, even those which may mirror torture in their sustained and impactful nature.

Whether one agrees or not, torture as we have explored it so far remains central to how knowledge around torture is produced, including in scholarly works. Whatever one's stance, torture exists in social, legal and political consciousness and so we cannot move to a space which transcends boundaries if we have not explored what those boundaries are. This chapter therefore aims to probe those boundaries further with the primary focus of conceptualizing and recognizing torturous violence, particularly integrating gendered perspectives.

The legal and epistemological expansion of definitions of violence

To understand torturous violence, especially from a gendered perspective, we must first explore briefly what is meant by 'violence'. Violence was defined by the World Health Organization at the World Health Assembly Resolution as 'the intentional use of physical force or power, threatened or actual, against oneself, another person, or against a group or community, that either results in or has a high likelihood of resulting in injury, death, psychological harm, maldevelopment or deprivation' (World Health Organization, 2002). The World Report on Violence and Health (WRVH) divides violence into three categories according to who has committed the violence: self-directed, interpersonal or collective; and into four further categories according to the nature of violence: physical, sexual, psychological or involving deprivation or neglect (see Rutherford et al, 2007).

It is fair to say, then, that definitions of violence have come a long way since original conceptions as mostly, if not exclusively, a physical act against another person. Indeed, explorations have long encompassed structural violence (Galtung, 1969; Farmer et al, 2006; Vogt, 2013; Canning, 2017); institutional violence (Barak, 2003; Cooper and Whyte, 2017); and other forms of everyday violence (Das, 2006). Definitions also encompass epistemology and disciplinary (and interdisciplinary) perspectives, some of which combine and draw together the nuances of each of these (see, for example, Montesanti and Thurston, 2015).

The gendered nature of violence and its impacts thereof have also extended and solidified. Perhaps the most relevant to international developments is the Istanbul Convention, which defines violence against women specifically as:

- Violence against women: 'a human rights violation and a form of discrimination against women' (Article 3(a)).
- Violence against women: 'all acts of gender-based violence that result in, or are likely to result in, physical, sexual, psychological or economic

harm or suffering to women, including threats of such acts, coercion or arbitrary deprivation of liberty, whether occurring in public or in private life' (Article 3(a)).

- Gender-based violence against women: 'violence that is directed against a woman because she is a woman or that affects women disproportionately' (Article 3(d)).
- The definition of violence against women goes further by including 'economic harm' and explicitly establishing such violence as a human rights violation (Council of Europe, 2011).

Having been built on the foundations of the Convention on the Elimination of All forms of Discrimination against Women (1979 – see Chapter 4), the Istanbul Convention moved further to define multifarious actions as violence against women, namely psychological violence (Article 33); stalking (Article 34); physical violence (Article 35); sexual violence, including rape (Article 36); forced marriage (Article 37); female genital mutilation (Article 38); forced abortion and forced sterilization (Article 39); and sexual harassment (Article 40). UN Women go on to emphasize that most women who are subjected to violence are so by a male partner, former partner or family member, and that '[v]iolence against women and girls is a human rights violation, and the immediate and long-term physical, sexual, and mental consequences for women and girls can be devastating, including death' (UN Women, nd).

Though all of these aspects incorporate complex perspectives on violence, the term 'torture' usually remains peripheral unless based on the legal concept explicitly (such as in the Istanbul Protocol which addresses sexualized violence as torture under the conditions of the United Nations Convention Against Torture or Other Cruel, Inhuman or Degrading Treatment or Punishment [UNCAT]), if included at all. This is an interesting omission for some of the forms of violence discussed, particularly the Istanbul Convention which mentions torture only once (see Chapter 4 on torture and non-refoulement). Yet we would likely agree that forms of physical violence (Article 35), sexual violence including rape (Article 36), or female genital mutilation (Article 38) would be physically torturous, or that being forced into an unwanted and potentially lifelong marriage (Article 37), particularly given the often sustained nature of this (Article 34), is psychologically torturous.

In short, even though such forms of violence could be prosecuted as 'torture' or even cruel, inhuman or degrading treatment or punishment, or as other forms of human rights violations, such acts are not inherently framed as torturous in Conventions, even if being subjected to them is experienced as so. The torturous nature of such violence is reduced by its side-lining of dominant torture discourses.

What is torturous violence?

For the purposes of this book, torturous violence is the infliction of emotional, psychological, sexualized and/or physical violence which mirrors acts normally inflicted as torture (defined in Chapters 1 and 2), but which fall outside of the dominant legislative requirements to be recognized as such.

Torturous violence is sustained, psychologically impactful and harms to the same or similar extent as violence which is definably torture. It can be enabled by coercive control, marital rights, relative powerlessness between perpetrator(s) and victim/survivor(s), and on structurally violent familial or cultural norms. These norms include patriarchal norms, and so transcend usual representations of cultural violence as 'Other', or somehow disconnected from society in the Global North. It may be in familial and/or interpersonal relationships. Torturous violence may be the continuous subjection to sustained violence over a period of months or years or one sustained violation by an individual or group which has deep and long-lasting psychological or psychosocial impacts on the survivor. Individuals may be subject to torturous violence at different intersections of their lives, in different places or spaces, and with different forms of infliction by different people or social actors. This element is particularly relevant to those living in abusive familial settings, in conflict, during flight from conflict or persecution, or when seeking asylum or safety from domestic violence.

With this definitional lens, we can see that torturous violence opens many spheres in which it is previously invisibilized in its extremity and impact. It also begins to include survivors who are otherwise under-recognized in the study of torture, including children, women, and trans victims/survivors – as we will more concretely see as this chapter and indeed the book moves on. For those concerned with the extreme violation of animals, torturous violence may be a tool in identifying, naming and addressing physically and psychologically torturous abuses of non-human species in a way that a narrow lens of torture will be unlikely to allow. Considering the concerns outlined earlier about the possibility of trivialization, this definition should also go some way to telling us what is *not* torturous.

Moving from who perpetrates violence and why, to the infliction and impact of violence

Torturous violence becomes an issue we can more readily see in the everyday lives of those who are subjected to sustained and impactful violence, something which breaks down the false public/private divide about where extreme violence takes place (Das, 2006). Marina, an immigration lawyer, emphasized the role of non-state actors as perpetrators of violence against women, "the majority of women that I come into contact with have been subjected to violence, it's been by private actors, so family members, I think, almost exclusively" (interview, 2017). This sets out a gendered differential on who is subject to such violence and where, in particular for women, by private actors. Izabella went on to make a similar point, elaborating on the ways in which trust and relationship building can develop into violence through coercion and control (see also Walby and Towers, 2018):

'There are obvious differences between torture and domestic violence within a detention setting but you might feel more unfree in a home because you have relationships with that person, it might have been a nice relationship in the beginning even, and then that one that is supposed to love you becomes the abuser. In the prison you know clearly that they hate you because of your opinions, political or your sexual orientation or whatever it might be, and you don't have an attachment to them from the beginning.' (Interview, 2018)

This is a particularly interesting juxtaposition, which refers to the home not as a space of confinement, but as 'unfree'. Here we see the public/private discourse intertwine – the home is not formally prison, and is not formally regulated as such. Like the term 'false imprisonment', there is a recognition that limits are in place for gaining freedom from an abuser, but the extent to which these are recognized do not quite mirror the state-sanctioned trajectory of imprisonment or prison industries. Moreover, and as we'll unpack later in this chapter, the relationship between torturer and subject can be much more complex, where power is similarly embedded in coercive interactions, if for different means or ends (that is, extracting information rather than increasing interpersonal power or control). Indeed, Elizabeth Stanley highlights the humane relationships some torturers develop with their victims – supplying luxury items, introducing victims to their children, taking them out for dinner between torture sessions (see 2004: 15) – for this very purpose.

'It's non-stop. The violence continues': domestic and interpersonal violence as torturous

In their research which disentangled the impacts of stressors associated with torture and those defined as 'Other Cruel, Inhuman, and Degrading Treatment [CIDT]', Başoğlu et al concluded that, 'Ill treatment during captivity, such as psychological manipulations, humiliating treatment, and forced stress positions, does not seem to be substantially different from physical torture in terms of the severity of mental suffering they cause, the underlying mechanism of traumatic stress, and their long-term psychological outcome' (2007: 277). The findings presented in their work, and outlined by others in the previous two chapters, contributed greatly to subsequent debates on severity and the long-term impacts and psychological implications of CIDT (see also Edwards, 2006 on disucssions on the 'feminization' of torture).

Ten years later, Şalcıoğlu and Başoğlu would go on to publish their theoretical and empirical comparison between torture and domestic violence (2017). While there is not scope to outline the full context of the chapter here, it is an important contribution for various reasons. Firstly, as the authors identify, 'although gender-based violations, including rape and domestic violence, are already recognized as coming under the definition of torture in international law [although they do not outline where specifically], there is still widespread disbelief that domestic violence can be a form of torture' (2017: 109). I would go further than this, and say that for many, legal routes in many places are so marred by safely accessing facilities to report, poor reporting procedures, and the harms of the criminal justice system, that exercising laws which would do so can be wholly or at least partially irrelevant in the everyday. That does not mean they are irrelevant in their existence, but that lived experience does not register this violence as such.

Secondly, the chapter is particularly interesting in that it reinvigorates discussions on the effects of domestic violence, before looking at the severity of trauma, severity of mental health outcomes and mechanisms of traumatic stress. Most interestingly, these were based on identifying forms of stressors, and comparing these between women survivors of torture (n=109), and women survivors of domestic violence (n=228). It is worth reiterating findings on the nature and severity of trauma, in excerpt:

> The two groups were remarkably similar in the rates of exposure to physical stressors, ill-treatments of sexual nature, fear-inducing or humiliating treatments, and deprivation of basic needs. Domestic violence survivors were exposed to a mean of 21 stressors over a period of 11.3 years, whereas torture survivors experienced a mean of 20 stressor events during a mean of 20 days detention. ... The most common form of domestic violence was beating with hands or with an object, which was reported by all survivors. ... Furthermore, 70% of the women reported an experience of asphyxiation through attempted strangulation, compared with 19% of torture survivors. Thus, although domestic violence did not involve some of the extreme forms of physical torture reported by torture survivors, it was nevertheless of comparative severity. (Şalcıoğlu and Başoğlu, 2017: 117. For fuller methodological information and findings, see Şalcıoğlu and Başoğlu, 2017: 107–137)

There are many ways in which correlations can be made between torture and domestic violence that might bring us to concretely recognizing intricacies of power and control as facilitators of torturous violence in sustained cases of abuse. These include introducing focus on the *goal* of abusers.[1] Some may not be so deliberate in nature, yet by default of extreme violence may have the same multifarious impacts. For Elaine Scarry, 'the goal of the torturer is to make ... the body, emphatically and crushingly *present* by destroying it, and to make ... the voice *absent* by destroying it' (1985: 49, emphasis added; also in Stanley, 2004: 12). Inherent to this is a form of both inducing presence through pain, while silencing the person suffering. Stover and Nightingale argue that 'the purpose of torture is to break the will of the victim and ultimately destroy his or her humanity' (1985: 5, in Green and Ward, 2004: 125). One's humanity then, a sense of self, is under attack from externalized forces which break one's own will to theirs. Inherent then is the removal of autonomy, and forced compliance with another. Finally, as Elizabeth Stanley mentions, 'The words spoken by torturers as part of the violence – "if you tell anyone, we will be back" – live on with isolated survivors' (Stanley, 2004: 13). In this instance, the harms inflicted through torture are done so not only through the power/powerless nexus on the relationship between the tortured person and the perpetrator, but manifest through threat of repeat violations. In essence, the spectre of torture hangs over one's own future, sense of safety, temporal stability and, indeed, one's own life trajectory.

Luban goes further to focus on this dynamic between torturer and victim, in that:

> Torture aims, in other words, to strip away from its victims all the qualities of human dignity that liberalism prizes. It does this by the deliberate actions of a torturer, who inflicts pain one-on-one, up close and personal, in order to break the spirit of the victim – in other words to tyrannise and dominate the victim. The relationship between them becomes a perverse parody of friendship and intimacy: intimacy transformed into its inverse image, where the torturer focuses on the victim's body with *the intensity of a lover*, except that every bit of the that focus is bent to causing pain and tyrannising the victim's spirit. At bottom all torture is rape, and all rape is tyranny. (Luban, 2006, in Athey, 2011: 140; emphasis added)

These statements are all written explicitly about torture, by scholars exploring the fields of torture and state violence, and yet any of these could be related to domestic and interpersonal violence. Indeed, Luban even goes so far as to reference *the intensity of a lover* without recognizing that a lover's intensity can also work to tyrannize the victim's spirit. In Stanley's point, the threat that 'we will be back' is arguably the very threat which limits survivors of relationship violence unable to safely exit an abusive or even torturous relationship. Ultimately, the goals – whether explicit or predetermined – are similar in outcome and impact, and power and powerlessness in these senses are along parallel trajectories. Coming back to some points highlighted by practitioners, Izabella's points here synopsize the overarching premise of employing the concept of torturous violence more fully in discourse, and indeed responses to survivors:

Victoria: Do you think that the impacts of long-term experience of domestic violence are similar to torture?

Izabella: Yes, it's also torture I would say, even though the definition of torture being someone in power, which is often the case in domestic violence, having the power to detain you, to abuse you, to make you afraid of doing different things, limiting your freedom of movement and limiting your freedom of speech or whatever. So yes, I think so. (Interview, 2018)

Similarly, Anne argues that "the severity, the methods, the impact, the consequences, they are equal to those of torture" (interview, 2021) while Dora reflects that "it's non-stop. The violence continues" (interview, 2021).

Childhood and families: recognizing trajectories of torturous violence

Over the past two decades in particular, there has been a marked proliferation of investigations into institutional abuses in care homes, schools and psychiatric institutions. One key example is the landmark Admissibility Decision before the UN Committee Against Torture in the case of *Elizabeth Coppin v Ireland*, which investigates the abuse of women and girls in Magdalene Laundries. These asylum-like establishments were set up from the early 1900s (cited as active from 1922 to 1996 in Coppin's complaint – see Hogan Lovells, 2020) to house women and their children, specifically women who were deemed sexually deviant, including unmarried pregnant women and mothers, prostituted and sex-working women, women who were accused or convicted of criminal offences, and women with psychiatric disorders. Institutions were prevalent in Ireland[2] but spanned also Canada, England, New Zealand and Australia. Abuses included, but were not limited to, sensory deprivation, starvation, beatings, solitary confinement, psychological abuse and routine humiliation.

According to the Committee Against Torture's report in 2013, 'evidence of direct State involvement[3] in the committal of women to the Magdalen laundries was found of 26 per cent of the cases it examined. State responsibility for funding and regulating the laundries was also established, as was the role of the police in returning escaped women to the laundries' (cited at Point 2.10, UN High Commissioner for Human Rights, 2020). Furthermore, Coppin was noted as 'not asking the Committee to consider *what happened to her* in the Magdalen laundries, but to examine the *present effects of the abuse that she underwent* in the light of the State party's current obligations under the Convention' (Point 5.3, UN High Commissioner for Human Rights, 2020; emphasis added).

I include this example not only for its position as a landmark case, but because it has state involvement and admissibility. The complainant – Elizabeth Coppin – both centralizes violence against children, but also moved from intent to effect for her motivation in bringing the case to the Committee against Torture. This is clear in the emphasized sections of the previous quotes, where the case focuses not only on the violence she was subjected to, but the effects of the abuse. While this case may relate to torture due to state admissibility, the example shows that a focus on effects might more concretely lead us to broaden subjections as *torturous* beyond these realms if and when similar abuses are enacted against children and young people outside of custody.

Although this book does not aim to address or explore children's experiences in depth, there was a clear increase in consciousness around childhood trauma and its relationship to violence against children, war and conflict, as well as border-related harms in later projects (from 2016 onward). As Marcus, a rehabilitation director at a torture support organization, stated, this was an institutional process where "we've become very aware of the effects on children, the direct effects of trauma that they may have been exposed to but also very much the indirect effects of living with a parent who is traumatized" (interview, 2017).

The issue of continuums and trajectories of violence throughout the life course was similarly mentioned by some practitioners working with young people and unaccompanied minors. Christian offers one example: "A younger patient of mine, who started treatment with sort of having experienced war, attacks by the state, but now the treatment has sort of shifted towards him being violated as a child by, I think, his uncle or a relative, and that's the main thing for him" (interview, 2021). As with domestic and interpersonal violence, torture may not be the only form of violence but one of various severe traumata. Again, as with other survivors of multiple abuses, if this young person had not met the threshold of 'torture' in assessment, the other violations he had endured may, alongside their subsequent psychological impacts, have gone unsupported.

"I wouldn't call it torture, though": conflict within discourses

It is therefore in addressing the intricacies of serious violence that the term 'torturous' becomes more relevant, and should be more fully employed. Quite often, practitioners stated what they would or would not call sustained or extreme violence, as we saw in Chapter 1. However, this is not always static, and asking further questions opens more complex dialogue. Dora, who worked with pre-assessed torture survivors, offers an example of this complexity. She states, "I deal with families as well. I wouldn't call it torture, though", before going into depth on an ongoing case of father incest, where the father survived torture and now routinely sexually abuses his children. On probing whether this specific violence is torture, Dora responds, "No, I think *they* would not call it torture. Maybe I wouldn't call it torture as well, but I look at it as torture, because when is it torture?" (interview, 2021; emphasis in original).

Of course, this question is the basis of the whole book and – depending on how the reader interprets this case example – may be named torturous violence (as I consider it to be) or indeed torture (as others – including Dora – may consider it to be).

This juxtaposition between naming and not naming sustained violence as torturous also creeps into discourses of trafficking, where Mila argues, "You can make these overlaps of torture and trafficking, because there's also a denigration of personality, denigration of the person's sense of self and stripping of all rights and stripping of freedoms. That's primarily what characterizes also trafficking" (interview, 2021). She goes on later to specifically encapsulate the psychological element of torturous violence which is not always recognized in reporting of violence beyond sustained physical abuses, arguing, "it's [trafficking] a psychological removal of freedom, really, because a lot of trafficked people aren't necessarily stuck in a house, they're not always locked in, but through indoctrination and threats and so on, freedom is removed and they're exploited for various reasons".

Take another example outlined by Amina, who works with both survivors and perpetrators. She reflects on some case examples that include:

'Burning them with cigarettes or even cutting off their fingers, putting boiling water over them – all sort of stuff. Then there have also been stories about taking this person to the woods and subjecting them to torture, but we don't hear that much about it because, again, it's classified as violence.' (Interview, 2021)

Two of the first examples are directly reflected in oral histories with women in Chapter 5, correlating exactly with ways in which torturous violence can go unnamed as such. The latter case Amina refers to, however, is one of few which drew controversy in Denmark as being named 'torture'. It is the case of Phillip Mbuji Johansen, a 28-year-old man of Danish and Tanzanian heritage, who was murdered by White Danish brothers Magnus and Mads Moeller in June 2020 on the Danish island of Bornholm (BBC News, 2020). Although the prosecution controversially did not include a hate crime motive, the brothers' links to far-right groups drew significant critique of the handling of the case and invigorated Black Lives Matter protests and interventions.

While this is important in and of itself, so too is the way in which some media relayed the murder. Thirty-nine separate wounds were identified:

> Johansen's legs were broken and he suffered burns, stab wounds and brain damage in a sustained bout of violence that lasted at least 15 to 20 minutes, the court ruled. The brothers had beaten him with a wooden pole and a bottle, stabbed him with a knife and pressed a knee against his neck. (BBC, 2020)

So severe were his injuries that the *New York Times* led with the headline 'A Black man was tortured and killed in Denmark: The police insist it wasn't about race' (Erdbrink, 2020). AP News stated Johansen was tortured for 20 minutes, a statement they say was given in the Medical Examiner Reports (AP News, 2021).

There are obvious concerns here pertaining to far-right violence, racism and xenophobia, with a clear mirroring of the case of George Floyd who was murdered by White police officer Derek Chauvin in Minneapolis only one month earlier – both victims were subject to having their neck kneeled on by the perpetrators, an image of violence which perforated public consciousness in the aftermath of Floyd's murder, and still continues to do so today. However, also important is the application of the term 'torture' in the violence used against Phillip Mbuji Johansen, since his murderers do not fit the limitations of the UNCAT, yet very clearly the abuses against him and the sustained nature of the fatal violence are absolutely torturous.

Expanding the realms of infliction: witnessing, borders and sociospatial shifts

Witnessing violence, abuse or death was commonly referred to in interviews with psychologists and psychotraumatologists as one of the key forms of trauma affecting survivors, and which was integral to their therapy or support journeys. As Klara stated, "it can also be witnessing other people's torture, so even though you were not exposed yourself, bearing witness to close relationships being close to torture, can also be a very traumatic memory that people would bring up" (interview, 2021).

Forced witnessing has been a strategy of collective and community violence (Al-Nuaimi et al, 2015), engraining degradation and humiliation in many wars and conflicts, including – but certainly not limited to – the Rwandan Genocide, the Bosnian War, torture in prisons in Iraq, Iran and Syria, in the Democratic Republic of Congo and during the conflict in Northern Ireland.

The use of violence against family members by state perpetrators or paramilitaries works to induce the shame of defeat, in particular the sexualized abuse of a friend or family member when the person witnessing cannot intervene. As Amina described, "guilt is there also if they have witnessed some people being sexually assaulted as well, and not being able to help or intervene, and it could be family members, it could also be other inmates" (interview, 2021). Similarly, for survivors whose sexualized violence is witnessed, it can be "humiliating to not only be forced to have something penetrated within you, but also that happening with witnesses, other prisoners, for example, other guards, family members in the worst cases, and the shame that follows that kind of torture" (Luna, interview, 2021). Indeed, humiliation can be compounded by being witnessed by others, and forcing people to engage in humiliating acts or nudity has itself been documented as torture (Einolf, 2018a).

However, witnessing violence also transcends the (sometimes inaccurate) dichotomies of war/peace or public/private. Many studies have documented the harms on children who witness domestic violence, some of which can be torturous (Sternberg et al, 2006; Moylan et al, 2010). While there may not be consensus on whether being subject to violence is more or less impactful than being subject to direct violence, the potential for negative psychological impacts of witnessing over the life course is certainly open to exploration as being torturous. Klara emphasizes this in the context of working with children, in that:

'A lot of children have experienced war-related violence. That can mean those who've been exposed themselves to physical violence, but often they have also witnessed killings ... and that can be different forms of violence, both the psychological terror from being under threat, or threatened in concrete situations during war and invasion of their homes. But it can also be witnessing a beating or extreme violence against their caregivers or more distant others, and we sometimes experience that the children have been witnessing sexual torture towards their caregivers.' (Interview, 2021)

Similarly, the impact of rape being witnessed by family members is one which can perforate familial relationships and induce shame over long periods of time and, as we will see in the following chapters, inflicts a kind of collective trauma that can go completely silenced, a kind of secret that everyone knows but does not speak. Luna considered that, "some of the women I've worked with, being raped either in prison or on the way up to Europe, it happened in front of their children, and that is the most shameful experience, more so than the rape itself" (interview, 2021). While it is not necessarily helpful to create immeasurable hierarchies in women's experiences of shame, this does provide a lens by which we can begin to realize the impacts of such violations as being torturous not only in their physical infliction, but in the psychologically torturous consequences of collective memory and humiliation.

Spatial continuums of torturous violence through bordering

In their Annual Torture Report 2020, the Border Violence Monitoring Network (BVMN)[4] documented in-depth accounts of violations enacted against migrants crossing the Western Balkans, as well as Greece, Turkey and a 'growing focus on chain-pushbacks from central European states such as Italy and Slovenia' (2020: 3). Adhering to Article 3 of the European Convention on Human Rights, the report considers whether some cases may constitute torture or inhuman and degrading treatment. The report collates evidence which includes the use of excessive and disproportionate force; forced undressing; threats of violence with a fire arm; inhuman treatment inside a police vehicle; and inhuman treatment inside a detention facility. It is a litany of abuses, some of which are enacted by state actors, some by outsourced corporate actors, some in custody or detention, and some beyond either of these facets pertaining to UNCAT explored in earlier chapters.

Whether or not each action can or will be determined as torture or CIDT, all accounts included arguably fall into the broader definition of torturous violence. Moreover – and importantly – the report is one of many expansive forms of documentation of torturous violence against people crossing borders not only in Europe, but globally (Ghosn et al, 2019; Gineste and Savun, 2019; Amnesty International, 2021; Al-Dayel et al, 2021; Bhatia and Canning, 2021; Iliadou, 2021).

If torturous violence can be part of a trajectory of violences in a person's life, then certainly the proliferation of militarized bordering has contributed greatly to the proliferation of opportunities to inflict it. This is not only in the physical and psychological inflictions outlined here, but by creating more dangerous routes in closing safe passage, temporal and spatial opportunities for torturous violence to be inflicted through extended time spent in secure spaces, time on the move, and in creating further dependence on partners or families for those subjected to interpersonal or domestic abuses that are torturous (see Canning, 2017).

These trajectories were very much a part of the lives of survivors I have met and spoken with, including the oral histories we will explore in Chapter 5. They were also increasingly fundamental to the consciousness of many practitioners, who were clear on connecting the roles of bordering to the experiences of trauma that the people they were working with had been subjected to. For example, Izabella, a psychologist working with survivors of torture and war-related trauma, states:

'A lot of people experience being wounded in war, being forced to witness relatives or close family being killed by bombs or by shootings or different kinds, and then during the flight can be different kinds of traumas from the boats across the Mediterranean and witnessing people die and being very, very terrified yourself on the boats, and being maltreated in the recipient countries. People can talk about the detention in Turkey or Greece as they've been very badly beaten and badly treated in the detention centres there. So that can also be part of the trauma.' (Interview, 2021)

This was reiterated by Luna:

'I hear more and more stories about traumas on the way from the country of origin up to Denmark, and it comes in waves and also it takes a longer time, and what's heart-breaking is that, when they finally come here, they are met with hope and help and money and a safe place to be. But also in the camps where they live in Denmark when they've just arrived, there's also a lot of violence and shit going on there as well, because of all the trauma placed in one place. It's presenting itself as a bigger issue now.' (Interview, 2021)

Similar references to violence in camps were made by Karim, a social worker focusing on lesbian, gay, bisexual, transgender and queer (LGBTQ) support for people seeking asylum:

'[I]t's this waiting time that kills people and also living in a camp that is like a closed place and there is a lot of aggression. I see a lot of violence and it's actually very much affecting. There are periods where almost every day you see police coming and taking people and people going crazy and violence and blood and all that. People are frustrated. Frustrated, angry and sad and powerless I think.' (Interview, 2017)

Although Karim is herein implying the prevalence of physical violence, this also encapsulates forms of structural violence built into the conditions under which people seeking asylum are made to live (in these two cases, in asylum centres – or camps – in Denmark – see also Canning, 2017; 2021a; 2021b). Moreover, the reference to a 'waiting time that kills people' brings us back to the points made by Boochani (2018) and Boochani and Tofighian (2021) in Chapter 2 on the weaponization of time as torture.

Finally, this takes us to the issue of borders and torturous violence in the lives of children. Klara found that, "[o]ften the children have been witnessing death during their flight overseas. A classic example is the *Gummiboots* [inflatable boat], crossing the sea where there are often a lot of accidents, and often we hear reports of fights along the way" (interview, 2017). She went on to outline some serious concerns for addressing tortuous violence and exposure, even when violence was indirect:

'The children I work with in my everyday life are usually double exposed, in the sense that they can carry their own traumatic events with them, but they also live in a family environment where their parents are naturally affected by the traumatic events they have been exposed to, and then they have often a shared history of other exile-related stressors during flight, but also after arriving in their new country.' (Interview, 2017)

In this reflection, we can see histories of trauma collide with the effects of torture and trauma which 'wander through lives', as we explored in the last chapter. For people in camps, camps for internally displaced persons, asylum centres or indeed survivors of violence who have refugee status, further issues are inflicted through and embedded in bordering practices, whether bureaucratic borders (Abdelhady et al, 2020) or physical borders.

A note on discourse: the outcome of being gender neutral is not neutrality

As a penultimate point in this chapter, is it worth reflecting on ways that the neutralization of gendered language influences law, policy and practices surrounding torture and thus further emphasizes the value of conceptualizing tortuous violence. With the exception of the terms 'his, him and he' in reciting torture conventions and declarations, much of the torture literature uses gender-neutral language and, unless otherwise specifically stated, it is assumed that the victim or survivor is male (sometimes explicitly so, for example when names are used). This serves only to perpetuate two things: firstly, that those targeted for torture are only male unless otherwise specifically disclosed; and, secondly, the denial of gendered social and political roles in many societies more broadly. If survivors in a study or report, prison or regime are men, then say so. Likewise, if torturers are predominantly or exclusively men, state so. The consequences of this are not only that women's experiences become side-lined, but that the gendered nature of violence against men is under-recognized in torture discourses, narratives and texts (see Einolf, 2018a; 2018b for interesting discussion on this).

Spatially and politically, men *can* be – and often are – disproportionately imprisoned or targeted for torture on the basis of interrogation, precisely because they hold or are seen to hold political or economic power. By addressing this we can address gendered power relations more broadly in repressive regimes, conflict and gendered violations in terms of the endemic imprisonment of men in many countries. To reiterate the words of Sarah, "often if you talk torture they are mainly focusing, and believing, I think, that torture is something that happens against a man" (interview, 2013). This is not to overlook that many women are political agents, and have historically and contemporarily been active – indeed tortured – in military, paramilitary and oppositional forces, but that they often continue to be viewed as less powerful or politically insignificant.

The implications are that on the whole, fewer women accessed the organizations I researched that were providing torture-specific support and which disclosed clientele ratios. These varied between 20/80 women to men clientele ratio; 30/70 women to men clientele ratio; and 40/60 women to men clientele ratio. The last of these had, since the 2015 Refugee Reception Crisis, been working to broaden the remit of the organization to address this issue, since they were finding in their own research that very few women were accessing their services, but those who were (that is, who met the threshold of torture) had been disproportionately subjected to multiple forms of interpersonal violence beyond this. Therefore, as outlined from the outset of this book, there are implications on how we implement narrow legal definitions of torture, since it can mean that survivors of torturous violence fall through the support net. As Chapter 4 goes on to demonstrate, this is not only a barrier for women with regards to accessing torture support, but possibly also for men accessing support relating to sexualized torture/torturous violence.

Conclusion

While there is no universally agreed definition of violence, the term has developed exponentially to address multifarious ways in which violence can be physical, psychological, structural, institutional and gendered. These perspectives have provided a platform from which this chapter has established a solid definition of *torturous violence*. This has moved away from narrow legal definitions, even if the book itself does not altogether abandon relevant laws, conventions and indeed the UNCAT.

This chapter charts ways in which this critical lens can support researchers, scholars, practitioners and survivors to recognize extreme and sustained forms of violence as torturous. It draws together complex social, global and interpersonal issues to expose impacts on people over life courses. Importantly, it does so by highlighting the limitations of focusing on who perpetrates extreme violence and why, to centralizing what is inflicted, and what the impacts of these inflictions are.

Chapter 3 has more fully implemented a gendered recognition of torturous violence, which sets the foundations for the following chapter in which we will now move to examine sexualized forms of torture and violence, and the consequences of these from an intersectional perspective.

Sexualized Torture and Sexually Torturous Violence

Introduction

Whether rape and sexualized violence is inherently perceived as torture is the subject of debate. For feminists such as Copelon (2004) and MacKinnon (2006), rape is in and of itself torture, while for others, such as Green and Ward (2004) and Rodley (2015 cited in Davis, 2017 and Rodley, 2002), defining rape as torture lies in state participation or culpability. For practitioners interviewed across my research projects who counselled survivors of rape in any capacity, sexualized violence has been variously defined: some as torture because of the levels of pain and humiliation inflicted on survivors, as well as any resultant traumata; some adamant that state involvement is a crucial aspect. This is the case in relation to publicly political realms, such as prisons, but also domestic and interpersonal spheres, and outside of typical conflict or persecutory violence, especially violence by partners or other family members (see also Herman, 1992; Peel, 2004).

To a degree, this chapter addresses the implications of endemic levels of sexualized violence in conflict which is seldom discussed as 'torture' but as tactical rape (Peel, 2004; Fitzpatrick, 2016). Relevant UN Security Council Resolutions are critically explored, and more recent steps taken to define and understand such violence as torture is evaluated (for example, the recent special editions of the *Torture* journal which focus on sexualized, gender-based and gendered torture [2018]). However, the primary objective of this chapter is to determine what separates these categories of violence, and if or how these are contingent with case study examples of violence when we focus on forms and impacts, rather than motivations and context.

Why set this chapter as a standalone form of torture and torturous violence?

One of the key objectives in writing this book has been to challenge the ways in which discussions around sexualized violence are too often shied away from, or even directly resisted, in relation to torture narratives, conventions and even rehabilitation. This is something that happens at various levels. Many of the texts outlined in Chapter 1 go into significant depth on many forms of brutal tortures, but either skim over sexualized abuses, or discuss them as one of various but equal components of torture. Even in undertaking research for this book, I experienced a multitude of questions: why was I always talking about sexualized abuse when other abuses are 'just as bad'? I was informed at one point early on that I had 'ruffled feathers' by discussing sexualized torture, which made people suspicious of my objectives. In one postdoctoral interview, knowing the scope of my research, one participant stated:

'[T]his idea about women and children as the most vulnerable people in conflict is bollocks. ... All the rules that you could interrogate women and children were much more lenient than the rules under which you could interrogate men. So that basically stems from a right to perpetrate violence on men and women and children and being differentiated so that women and children were exposed to less violence and interrogation than men.' (Interview, 2013)

Again, the implications of adhering to narrow definitions of torture – here, as a means to interrogate – undermine the broader experiences of sexualized or torturous violence outside of this. In the narrow sense the interviewee is correct – men are more likely to be tortured since it is men who are disproportionately politically targeted as well as detained in state facilities.[1] However, it is not true that 'women and children' – very different demographics who are often grouped together – are exposed to less violence. It simply depends on how one defines, understands or recognizes violence.

Even though feminist discourses, international laws and conventions have evolved so significantly, particularly since the 1990s, research experience – and delivering scores of seminars, workshops, conference talks and keynotes to many almost exclusively or exclusively women audiences – suggests to me that sexualized violence is still not consciously or unconsciously recognized by all in terms of its harm and consequence. Indeed, a number of prominent people working in international roles around torture have declined to take part in interviews for these projects. Obviously, I can make no claim as to why, since they did not take part, but one might at least suspect that either such issues are secondary 'women's issues' and not – as the interviewee insinuates – what we are assumedly talking about when we talk about torture. Another may be the discomfort that mentioning sexualized violence can induce. This is relatable for some people, particularly survivors who may not wish to engage in discussing something they themselves have lived through.

For others, my thoughts are that this is seen more as a 'women's issue' than an endemic form of torture or torturous violence.

This echoes points made by the renowned, pioneering feminist lawyer and campaigner Rhonda Copelon when she noted resistance from an all-male commission, until they were made to consider why, for example, electric shocks to the penis constituted torture, but rape by penetration did not (in Davis, 2017: 330). I mention these points here because – as we will now see – there have been historical recognitions of sexualized violence and abuse in relation to torture. However, there remains in academic, political and some practitioner narratives a chasm, arguably due to the continued dependence on the United Nations Convention Against Torture or Other Cruel, Inhuman or Degrading Treatment or Punishment (UNCAT). It seems less difficult to reconcile sexualized violence as torture when in detention and increasingly in conflict settings, but this can be more ambiguous for other scenarios, however brutal they may be.

Sexualized violence, sexualized torture and sexually torturous violence

How sexualized violence or other forms of interpersonal harms are discussed can be contentious. Historically, the pathologizing of women in particular influenced terms around hysteria early on, and Battered Wives Syndrome later, both insinuating illnesses or disorders when women were responding quite reasonably to unreasonable violent circumstances (Ussher, 2011). Terms have continued to be challenged in relation to violence, something which comes up regularly in seminars, and when I previously trained volunteers at a rape support clinic. Interpersonal violence can be quite broad; violence against women is discussed as exclusionary of men, even if emphasizing disproportionality and prevalence; domestic violence inherently suggests that violence is confined to the domestic sphere or the home; and partner violence excludes wider familial abuses. It is a complex area. For me, all of these terms, and more, have their place since all can relate to each specificity in different cases and contexts.

This chapter, however, focuses on three forms of violence: sexualized violence, sexualized torture, and sexually torturous violence. One of the key reasons I opted to use *sexualized* rather than *sexual* has been because the term 'sexual' also opens up other kinds of discussions. It relates to lifestyle, pleasure and sexual orientation – all things which can and should be free from violence. As we will see as this chapter goes on, the infliction of sexualized violence is not only interpersonal, and undermining of one's own autonomy over the sexual self, but it can be difficult for survivors to recognize acts of abuses as violence, rather than sexual acts. For example, practitioners report people experiencing confusion if they have reacted to abuse by developing an erection or orgasm (conversely, also a form of harm experienced by women in institutions historically, who were treated for 'hysteria' through enforced vaginal massages – see Thompson, 1998) as well as questioning one's own sexuality or orientation (see also Shin and Salter, 2022).

Instead, by separating sexual from sexualized, we can open further questions which work towards dissolving the turmoil for individuals about, 'Is this my sexuality? Is this my sexual pleasure? Why has this happened and did I invite it?'. All of these are normal for survivors to experience, particularly given that sexualized violence is so intrinsically linked with shame and, for some, highly problematic ideologies of honour. It is therefore a means to recognize that it is actually a process of violence and torture: the sexualized infliction of violence.

As such, terms included here are as follows:

- Sexualized violence in its broadest social sense is a continuum of sexualized violations which can include penetrative rape, oral rape, sexual assault and unwanted sexual advances or intimidation (see Kelly, 1988). I also take Claire McGlynn's point on the importance of retaining the label 'rape' where accurate, given its 'gendered meaning and powerful associations' (McGlynn, 2008: 71).
- Sexualized torture refers to the archetypal forms of torture addressed in earlier chapters: those which are inflicted in conditions which meet those typified in UNCAT. Former UN Special Rapporteur on Torture, Nigel Rodley, argued, 'What makes torture *different* [from Cruel, Inhuman or Degrading Treatment] is that it is inflicted by or with the tolerance of the state for certain purposes, the *state's* purposes. If, in this context, the pain inflicted is by means of rape, then it is torture. Outside this context, it is, in the absence of due diligence by the state to prevent it, CIDT' (email correspondence between Lisa Davis and Nigel Rodley, 2015, in Davis, 2017: 353).
- Sexually torturous violence refers to forms of violence which inflict physical and emotional harm in ways similar to sustained torture, but to include abuses undertaken by a range of social actors, including domestic abusers. It is the first and last of these which stem most obviously from the experiences of women I have worked with, while men who are subjected to sexualized violence as torture are more likely (although not exclusively) to do so within the parameters of confinement by an interrogator as per the second definition.

Saying and seeing sexualized violence: linguistic barriers to recognition

Related to this, putting words to experiences is a fundamentally complex issue in discussing, disclosing or addressing the *violence* element of *sexualized violence*. As Anne, a clinical psychologist, put it, "I don't think that they define it as sexual violence, but being forced to engage in intercourse or sexual activities with their husbands, but also physical violence, beatings, stuff like that, and also more controlling them, not allowing them any economic or influence in the family" (interview, 2021). Klara, a child psychologist, reiterated this point in saying, "often we experience that it's easier for survivors to name and describe the more physical and psychological forms of exposure" (interview, 2021).

This has long been inherent to my own experiences of working with survivors of sexualized violence within activism, advocacy or research. Terms such as 'he did sex with me', 'he hurt me', 'he touched me' are common in place of specific references to violence such as 'rape', 'sexually abused' or 'assaulted'. While this may be picked up by some practitioners experienced in supporting survivors, it is easily overlooked in its non-consensual or abusive nature by more generalized practitioners and, in seeking asylum, people interviewing asylum applicants – an issue which can affect the likelihood of gaining refugee status if not recognized as persecution or violence. On the other hand, and as Chapter 6 will elucidate in more depth, it can also be inappropriate for practitioners or advocates to make assumptions, or press for specificities of experience if trust has not been built to facilitate fully consensual disclosure of experience.

Lastly, it is worth noting that even the terms may be contestable. As mentioned, for some feminists, all forms of rape understandably equate to torture. The interpersonal manifestation of violence, as well as the potential for significant and long-term impacts, make this a reasonable statement. However, a survivor may not wish to reflect on their experience as being torture, torturous or even recognize it as violence. As a survivor of multiple forms of sexualized violence myself, even I would struggle to consider my own subjections as torture, and did not even recognize one form of violence by a man in a Northern Irish paramilitary organization (at 14 years of age) as rape until much later on. I recognized the harm, and felt the threat and fear (at the time and after). Yet society around us has created a myth that unless one fights or screams, violence is not present – even if we are screaming inside.

It is exactly these mythologies, assumptions and perspectives which reiterate the need for sexualized violence to be explored in all its complexities.

International developments on the recognition of sexualized violence as war crimes, crimes against humanity and torture

As Lisa Davis documents in depth, there has been a sustained effort to have rape recognized as a form of torture. Simultaneously, there has been resistance to this recognition (Davis, 2017). In 1986, rape appeared in a list of official forms of torture, where Pieter Kooijmans – then the UN Special Rapporteur on Torture and Other Cruel, Inhuman and Degrading Treatment – included it in a report to the UN Commission of Human Rights. He would later state, 'it was very clear that rape or other forms of sexual assault against women in detention were particularly ignominious violation of the inherent dignity and the right to physical integrity of the human being, they accordingly constituted an act of torture' (Kooijmans, 1992, in Davis, 2017: 327). This was followed by his successor Nigel Rodley's report in 1994, which included an exclusive section on the sexualized abuse of women.

From here, how rape, sexualized violence and other abuses have been documented in legislation and conventions has been expansive. While these early reports were fundamental, they remained strongly centred on abuses in detention. More relevant and specific policies have been developed since the endemic rapes of women in Rwanda and the former Yugoslavia in the early–mid 1990s, specifically the Čelebići torture camp case (International Criminal Tribunal for the former Yugoslavia [ICTY], 1998), and the case against Anto Furundžija, the first in the ICTY to deal entirely with charges of sexualized violence (although not without its controversies – see Davis, 2017: 347). The ad hoc International Criminal Tribunal for Rwanda acknowledged rape as a crime against humanity, and the establishment of the International Criminal Court in 1998 was a marked milestone for human rights. Since then, the United Nations Security Council's Resolution 1325 (2000) addressed the gender specific impact of war and conflict on women, Resolution 1820 (2008) finally identified rape and sexualized violence during war and conflict as a threat to international peace and security and a war crime, and Resolution 1960 (2010) began to directly address the issue of impunity.

As these were developing, and even before, significant advances were being made through various platforms and conventions for recognizing the rights of women and girls. This included the introduction of the Convention on the Elimination of All Forms of Discrimination against Women (signed 1979) which came to force in September 1981, the landmark Beijing Declaration in 1995 (see UN, nd) and the Council of Europe Convention on Preventing and Combating Violence Against Women and Domestic Violence in 2011, better known as the Istanbul Convention (see Council of Europe, 2011).

These are fundamental landmark changes for addressing gendered inequalities, discrimination and violence against women. Conversely, as discussed in the last chapter, the term *torture* is largely absent – featuring only once in the Istanbul Convention, in relation to non-refoulement in Article 61.2. This is not a minor omission, and leads us to question gendered recognitions of torture.

Moreover, the concept of non-refoulement is, like other aspects of gendering torture, related to the wider social and cultural rights of women survivors of sexualized torture or sexually torturous violence. Rather than recognizing the harm and pain caused and inflicted in the very abuses, the seriousness is not always situated in the impacts, but in the potential consequences. Freja, a legal expert on torture, for example, states:

> 'One of the examples that we always use for whether or not it was inhumane, degrading treatment was that if you had been raped and you were gonna be sent back to a society where you would be ousted by your entire society because having been raped would make you dirty and not accepted, then that would be an added aspect and it could actually mean that what you had experienced was torture because of what the effects of it were, making it torture. So, if I was raped and I could go back and things would be normal for me, the burden wouldn't be as big, so in that sense, yes, then it would be different, if that makes any sense.' (Interview, 2021)

What we can see here is a narrative that sexualized violence is recognized as *accompanied by* further threats of ostracism, rather than surviving the abuses alone. The idea that sexualized violence is not inherently torturous is inadvertently reiterated by Brenda Fitzpatrick, who highlights in the case of the Rwandan Genocide that, 'The rapes were often accompanied by severe torture and mutilation, particularly of sexual organs, which emphasised degradation and violation' (for which she gives examples, see Fitzpatrick, 2016: 68). Rape is not presented as torture in and of itself, but is *accompanied by* torture. Yet as practitioners regularly state, rape, sexualized violence and sexualized torture are all deeply inherently rooted in degradation and humiliation.

Sexualized violence as torture when perpetrated by state actors in state facilities

As outlined earlier in relation to Rodley's points (2015, in Davis, 2017), the state-sanctioned or inflicted nature of torture is central to the UN Conventions' definition (Stanley, 2008). Sexualized violence may be legally definable as torture if a public official is directly or indirectly involved; if it inflicts a severe level of pain (which is difficult to determine); and is inflicted with the intent to gain information or a confession, coerce, intimidate, discriminate or punish. Thus, according to most participants, where *legally* recognized sexualized torture had occurred, perpetrators were usually police officers or state agents who held women in custody or their own homes while making political arrests, and prison guards when women or men were held in detention or visiting someone in prison. Some of these heavily reflected forms of sexualized torture identified by Rejali (2007) and later

Einolf (2018a and b). For example, Mila recalled "a lot of sexual violence. I don't know why that's the definition of it, but let's call it physical violence that is of genitals – that seems to be a really significant one, especially Iranian clients" (interview, 2021).

Luna outlined the impacts of humiliation and witnessing, reflecting that it can be "humiliating to not only be forced to have something penetrated within you, but also that happening with witnesses, other prisoners, for example, other guards, family members in the worst cases, and the shame that follows that kind of torture" (interview, 2021). As with discussions in Chapter 3, witnessing and forcing people to witness violence is inherently torturous. Here, however, is the forced breaking of taboos, particularly where any form of sexualized violence, or even sexual activity more broadly, may be withheld from discussion, particularly for family members or children.

Medical doctor Laura highlights similar strategies, but which draw in the use of a parent to inflict humiliation on both detainee and visitor. She recalls:

'[J]ust plain humiliation. Women who've been ... forced nudity, being forced to ... one woman, she was forced to serve ... she came to visit her husband in prison and then they forced the husband to undress, and they forced the wife to undress and then she had to serve tea for him while all these people were watching, so it's also very unusual and very degrading.' (Interview, 2021)

While this may not be 'usual', it does reflect some wider strategies of sexualized torture in detention, where women's bodies are used as a tactic to shame detainees. In this case, shame is embedded in the woman's degradation and humiliation, in which her partner cannot intervene. In others, as documented by Kelly Oliver (2007), women officers or torturers are used to inflict cultural sexualized violence on men, as in the case of Abu Ghraib. This was noted also by Mark Danner, who highlighted that sensory deprivation there was often enacted alongside sexualized violation in detention, specifically:

Shame – the use of shame. You see this in Abu Ghraib and at Guantánamo: this focus on sensory deprivation together with shaming the prisoner. Female interrogators were often used to magnify this affect, for they were thought to be more effective in shaming Muslim men, who now found themselves naked and vulnerable and impotent before the women. (Danner, 2011: 55)

Likewise, former US intelligence soldier Erik Saar revealed the use of 'fake menstrual blood and other sexualised assaults on detainees' but did not consider them to be 'torture' at the time (Athey, 2011: 129; see also Saar and Novak, 2005).

A key gendered disparity can be the timing of sexualized abuse. For men, interviewees generally reported that sexualized torture was perpetrated early in the process, such as during arrest or the first few days of detention, when interrogation and dehumanization is integral (Sexual Violence Research Initiative Resources, nd; Sivakumaran, 2005). For women, however, this took place in prisons, camps, the home, and in slavery imprisonment, where state or paramilitary actors committed the abuse but not necessarily with the intention of interrogation for information. Participants reported working with survivors of forced bestiality, rape in prisons, multiple perpetrator rape, rape with an audience, forcing to watch a family member being raped, rape with objects, including rape with bottle tops, groping, and threats of rape (reported in this study predominantly for male rape, especially in prisons – see also Peel et al, 2000). As Oscar – a psychologist and researcher – points out: "There does seem to be a lot happening when it comes to conflict and war, but when it comes to daily policing and standard operation procedures in terms of torturing people, taking advantage, forcing confessions, forcing advantages, all these things in the daily life are not really focused on" (interview, 2013).

Although not explicitly identifying the gendered nature of the argument I aim to make, many points mirror feminist arguments in terms of developing the recognition of everyday violence as part of a continuum (Kelly, 1988). Drawing back to critical scholarship and activism, it is worth reflecting on Elisabeth Stanley's point that, 'Criminologists must become minded of the ways in which victims suffer a continuum of violations, across time, at the hands of diverse actors who support, organise and inflict them' (Stanley, 2008: 190).

For some participants, the requirement to adhere to the UNCAT specifically meant that sexualized violence such as that inflicted by partners, husbands or fathers *could not* be considered torture. For example, Sofia centralized the UNCAT specifically, stating:

> 'Well it depends on who commits it. I mean the UN Convention on Torture; it would be a state official that conducts this … [for example] domestic violence is going on all over the place and the state are not held responsible, so it has to be within the custody of the state.' (Interview, 2013)

However, as wider narratives have highlighted, there are instances when actions come under debate even in prisons or detention, such as the use of cavity searches. Although strip searches and cavity searches are commonplace in many prisons, there remains ambiguity around whether they can be considered torture, despite the degradation, pain and powerlessness inherent to the act. As one example, Athey outlines, the *New York Times* described the sexualized assault of Ehab Elmaghraby with a flashlight – a Muslim New Yorker who was detained in the Metropolitan Detention Centre following 9/11 – as an 'unnecessary cavity search' (Athey, 2011: 130). This neutralization of language is a common mechanism for reducing the severity of sexualized assault which – even under the parameters of the UNCAT – can be classed as torture in its narrowest sense.

The view that sexualized torture could only be perpetrated by state actors, or due to negligence in a state facility, was reiterated across various discussions, although as we saw in Chapter 1, some participants began to waver when probed on how they defined torture themselves. This again tells us that some narratives of torture continue to depend on legal definitions, even though legal definitions have long been contested. Moreover, the marker of what *is* considered as torture in these two quotes is directly relational to what *is not* considered as torture.

In some ways, this also relates to more recent arguments regarding the banality of torture in people's lives. Tobias Kelly and Steffen Jensen have argued, in relation to Nepal, Kenya and Bangladesh, that the most common forms of torturous violence that people face are not in torture dungeons or in prisons, but as part of a means to control and terrorize populations in everyday life (Jensen and Kelly, 2016).

Sexualized violence as torture when perpetrated by non-state actors, outside of state institutions

The view that legal definitions were required to fall within the rubric of sexualized torture was challenged by some participants and outright rejected by others, including people working only with pre-assessed survivors of torture. The perspective that the personal is political ran through some narratives, which itself breaks down walls between how violence is seen, in particular familial violence and sexualized violence in non-state settings, including the home. For Sarah, a psychotraumatologist working with torture survivors, sexualized violence "is a political torture. The definition of torture is the infliction of pain and humiliation to another person by a human being. Then it is within the definition of torture. I would go further and say that paedophilia and incest in the family is torture" (interview, 2013).

Similarly, Lisbet – a psychologist who worked with survivors of sexualized violence during and after the Bosnian War – argued that "rapes are not casual. They are *always* tied to the political" (interview, 2013). Also considering regional experience, this time from her work with Afghans, Liv addressed the domesticity of sexualized torture in a way that resonates with feminist arguments, such as Judith Herman's interpretation of gendered terror (1992): "Women from Afghanistan, most had been sexually tortured, but that was from their husbands … it can look like a personal problem, but it is also a structural problem" (interview, 2013). Thus, rape is seen as politicized, bound with the intricacies of gendered inequalities – in that most is perpetrated by men against women – and that violence is facilitated by power and, importantly as Nowak argued in terms of torture (2006), powerlessness.

Some forms of sexually torturous violence were combined with further forms of violence against women. Dora drew from one example where:

'[T]wo ladies were just raped and then beaten up, and then one of them said she was run over by a car, and the other one was shot and thrown out with the dead bodies, so she said she literally crawled out from between these dead bodies. They thought she was dead.' (Interview, 2021)

This was similarly experienced in the context of trafficking by non-state actors, an issue which I have come across repeatedly when working with women seeking asylum (see also McGregor, 2014). Mila, who had previously worked with survivors of trafficking before moving to work with survivors of torture, outlines a clear example of sexualized violence being perpetrated in conjunction with other violences which would very clearly be considered torture if in state custody, many of which feature in the examples of torture given in Chapter 2. She states:

'[In trafficking] sexual violence obviously is a primary one, both if people are in forced prostitution but also domestic servitude, then there's a lot of violence and sexual violence, physical hitting, slapping, teeth being pulled out, some horrible stories, like teeth being pulled out and them being given fake teeth, or finding ways to really scare someone so much that they do what they're told.' (Interview, 2021)

This is an interesting example: sexualized trafficking is predominately experienced by women (European Parliament, 2016), as is the exploitation which follows. Forced prostitution is itself a removal of bodily autonomy, which is replaced by a degree of powerlessness in the given situation. Similarly, Narzanin, a barrister specializing in human trafficking cases, reflects on commonalities across her client cases, where there is:

'[O]ften a diplomat or rich individuals who can afford to bring a member of staff over, and they live in the employer's household and their role is normally described as a nanny or housekeeper. And then their conditions of work are appalling, and they're exploited, sometimes

sexually exploited by the employer or the employer's wider circle.'
(Interview, 2018)

Again, we can clearly see entanglements between power and powerlessness
which, in the case of trafficking, is also intricately tied to citizenship,
nationality and statehood (Lee, 2010; O'Connell Davidson, 2015). However,
we seldom (if ever, in my experience at least) hear it referred to as torture. Yet
it is a subjection which mirrors and inflicts torturous violence, often carried
out in literal or existential forms of confinement, but usually (although not
always) perpetrated by non-state actors. Nonetheless, the levels of violence
inflicted would quite simply be considered torture if inflicted by states.[2]

This brings us to two final thoughts. Firstly, how sexualized violence is
defined is changing in relation to torture. Some interviewees refer to shifts
in how they or their organizations recognize or respond to this, and indeed
I have seen similar changes when revisiting some organizations over a period
of years. Pauline, a member of the Queen's Counsel, reflects on shifts in
client cases over her more than 20 years as a barrister:

'When I started, I would have a lot more cases of sexual torture by
the state. I think now the sort of more classic case is sexual torture
or sexual abuse, however you want to define it, by private members;
it might be your trafficker, it might be your family, it might be a
sort of community assault. Where you have state persecution, like
Syria, we don't get so many of those cases because they are accepted
and they're not going on appeal. The cases that we get are the
ones from broken states in a way or where you've got civil conflict
that's an absent state rather than a proactive abusive state, and in
those sort of cases then you've got your non-state agent problems.'
(Interview, 2018)

As discussed earlier, the upsurge in academic and legal recognitions of
the prevalence of rape and sexualized violence in conflict becomes more
pronounced here. Although the case of Syria is referred to, there is growing
realization that conflict-related sexualized violence occurs beyond state
perpetration. In the case of new wars (Kaldor, 2013), these are not always
formalized conflicts, have increased use of paramilitary violence (rather
than typified state violence), and are much longer in duration with higher
civilian mortality and morbidity rates. It serves to reason, then, that the
forms of violence recognized as torturous also transcend the definition of
the UNCAT to encompass shifts in patterns of conflict-related violence.

Secondly, is that patriarchal violence and abuse within relationships is
increasingly being recognized as torturous. This narrative is present in many

of the quotes, and many further discussions and interviews with practitioners in my own research and activism. One example to illustrate this comes through Anne, who considers the conflation between conflict and non-conflict situations in relation to her women clients:

'[I]t's just a part of being a woman or a wife, and that's awful. So, I think we have two groups of women being subjected to sexual torture and violence. First, it is within the marriage or the immediate family, and then in prison or detention or whatever. I also think about my female patients from the former Yugoslavia. They were not in prison, but as we know, sexual violence was a part of the war methods. Also, up until now, before patients from Syria, female patients from the former Yugoslavia were the most traumatized patients that I ever met, and I connect that to their sexual experiences, experiences of sexual torture and violence.' (Interview, 2021)

Similarly, Marina, a lawyer working with survivors of torture emphasized:

'[A] lot of women come here, they've been subjected to different kinds of sexual violence, it can be sexual violence in their home countries, so maybe at the hands of a partner, in a family situation, and it can be the reason why they decided to leave in the first place or it can be violence that they encountered on the way here.' (Interview, 2017)

These statements bring two key issues to the surface. The first is that, however it is termed, violence in women's lives can be part of a trajectory – in childhood or by family, as well as in conflict or detention. It is pervasive through patriarchy, not only as a tactic of war or conflict or a means to torture or punish. Secondly, as we will explore in relation to impacts of sexualized violence in the penultimate section of this chapter, the effects of sexualized violence can be long-lasting. In the example given by Anne, one of the key client groups is women from the former Yugoslavia. This is a demographic which came up repeatedly with practitioners working with survivors of torture and/or sexually torturous violence. Given that the war and subsequent conflicts and genocide discussed here were in the 1990s, this serves as a reminder that the impacts can be lifelong, manifesting much later after the events occurred.

An analogy I have always appreciated on this came from Liz Kelly, who likened the legacy of sexualized violence to carrying a backpack. Some days, the pack is empty and does not weigh the carrier down. But on other days, the backpack is full, and the contents become burdensome. But empty or full, the backpack is always there on the survivor's shoulders (Kelly, 2014).

Sexualized violence against men and boys

Although sexualized violence can be experienced as part of a continuum of patriarchal violence for women, subjections to sexualized violence for men and boys, as well as trans people, has recently become more recognized in social and academic consciousness. While disproportionality is an essential consideration – in that women are disproportionately subjected to sexualized violence globally (UN Women, 2021) as well as being killed by male partners or acquaintances – sexualized violence against men is arguably part of this continuum. Often when we consider issues from a gendered or intersectional lens, this is interpreted as a 'women's issue'. However, since most men who experience sexualized violence do so from other men or boys,[3] centralizing such abuses as a form of men's violence is a useful way to draw further accountability towards structural sexualized patriarchal abuses. This is also a point which can be somewhat frustrating when working on gendered violence and violence against women: sexualized violence is inherently gendered, including if and when women are perpetrators or complicit in abuse. A gendered lens requires complex analysis and critique of the nuances of power, and in particular their impacts. As such, relegating gendered harm or violence as a 'women's issue' is not only undermining of its severity, but fails endemically to recognize that sexualized violence is harmful for everyone in society, as we will see later.

Although men may experience sexualized and sexually torturous violence outside of detention, the same problematic political and ideological differentiation between the public (or state) and private (non-state) which underpins the non-recognition of some violence as sexually torturous is ironically that which also makes sexualized abuse against men in detention more easily recognizable as torture. Since more men are detained in state facilities and for political reasons, particularly during conflict or by failing states but also in prisons more generally, the scope for sexualized abuse at the hands of the state increases. This is of course not to say women are not detained or sexually tortured by state actors – and far from it. Rather, once the stone is unturned in relation to prison abuses, sexualized violence against men – and its multiplicities of complexity – becomes simultaneously more visible, and yet still significantly silenced.

As we have seen so far, there are some regions where sexualized torture against detainees is endemic. Indeed, during interviews, some participants would refer directly to prisons where clients had been held, most notably Evin prison in Iran. Abu Ghraib in Iraq and Bagram air base in Afghanistan have similarly infiltrated public and academic consciousness, including in the systematic use of sexualized torture. For others, generalizations were made, such as: "In the Middle East, they use sexual violence towards men [which is] much more widespread" (Martin, researcher, interview, 2013).

Research into the extent and prevalence of sexualized torture or sexually torturous violence is complex and continues to experience barriers in some areas, and voids in others. This is similarly the case for sexualized torture against men. However, focus on this area has been increasing, particularly in the aftermath of the occupation of Iraq and invasion of Afghanistan, but also in central African contexts including the Democratic Republic of Congo, and the ongoing war in Syria. Perhaps one of the most well recognized contributions to this area has been from Sivakumaran, who contributed greatly to discussions on sexualized violence against men in conflict specifically, documenting examples from Ancient Persia to the Great African War in the Democratic Republic of Congo (see Sivakumaran, 2007, for example). Valerie Oosterveld later elaborated on this, again in the context of armed conflict as well as mass atrocity (2014), highlighting ways in which endemic sexualized violence has been increasingly prevalent in detention in Libya and Syria (see also Chenowyth, 2017, in her report on sexualized violence against men and boys in Syria). Interestingly, she identified an issue with the labelling of sexualized violence against men as more 'categorised more generically as torture, inhumane acts or cruel treatment' (Oosterveld, 2014: 109). This angle is effectively the other side of the coin which we have been looking at: since torture is more easily recognized as such from within detention settings, the same kinds of sexualized violence are often overlooked in their torturous nature beyond state institutions. Simultaneously, and picking back up on my earlier point, without recognizing the gendered nuances of violence, sexualized violence against men can be inherently stripped of the sexualized element, in the same way that sexualized violence can be stripped of its torturous element in, for example, domestic violence situations. The implications of this also come into effect later, when the impacts of sexualized violence – and silence around it – intersect, as we will see in what follows.

Christopher Einolf has subsequently created secondary documentary analysis of sexualized torture in Iraq, specifically among Shia Muslim men and women imprisoned during Saddam Hussein's rule (Einolf, 2018a; 2018b). He found that out of 47 cases of torture, sexualized abuses were frequent including rape (n=36); groping (n=9); beating to sexual organs (n=13); nudity (n=24); lewd comments (n=8); and sexual insults (n=12) (2018a: 68–69). Conversely, while there were fairly equalized representations of rape in terms of proportion to detainee gender, there was an over-representation of men in relation to electric shock to sexual organs. In terms of verbalized abuse, all cases of lewd comments or sexual insults documented were done so against women, and no men. This is therefore a very useful way to disaggregate the complexity of sexualized torture, and consider the nuances in how power, powerlessness and violence are inflected from a gendered lens.

Forms of violence against men

For practitioners working with survivors of sexualized torture and sexually torturous violence, similar forms of abuses were evident in narratives, as have been outlined by Einolf as well as Rejali (2007). Annika reflects on her work as a psychologist, indicating:

> '[T]he clinical experience that I have, for example from Syria and Iran, being quite sexually aggressive towards men, like electrodes on the testicles and the penises and also penetration of the anus and it's a lot of shame around it also so it's difficult for them to deal with and to talk about afterwards.' (Interview, 2017)

This was reflected by Dora, who argues: "In Iran, they used the sexual torture as just a method of torturing the men, the same as in Syria, the early days of their war there. I've just seen how it damages. It just completely breaks down the individual" (interview, 2021). We can see here especially the references to torture in early parts of the war – an aspect that relates to points raised in Chapter 1 when we asked where and when torture takes place. What Dora is inadvertently noting here reflects the specific period around people being detained and thus interrogated for information on a systematic basis, as was widely reported (Oosterveld, 2014; Chenowyth, 2017). These forms of torture correlate with the UNCAT, thus more adequately reflect typified forms of torture that are responded to as such. Indeed, by 'completely' breaking down the individual, sexualized torture has obtained its objectives.

Amina similarly refers to specific regional spaces, which is also reflective of conflict patterns in wider global spheres, "in Kurds it's mostly men, and sometimes we have women as well, but the torture survivors are mostly men, I think. I've had many women through as well, but right now, if you should look at our patient list right now, then it's mostly men" (interview, 2021). Shortly after the refugee reception crisis of 2015/2016, which saw more people move through Europe fleeing conflict and persecution than at any other time since the Second World War, the rise in Syrian nationals seeking asylum also changed the demographic of people who were being referred to torture rehabilitation. Rikke considers, "Syrians coming in, they have experienced a lot of sexual torture ... who have been raped by prison guards systematically, I won't go into detail but ... I mean the psychological consequences of this is devastating" (interview, 2017). This was an important liminal phase for Syrian refugees. Whereas my earlier research found most people seeking post-torture support already had refugee status and had already been living in Denmark (in that case study example) for an average of 14 years (Canning, 2016), there was a marked reduction in this waiting period for Syrian survivors in the second and third studies, likely due to refugee resettlement schemes which have much more holistic approaches to support than arduous periods in asylum systems. Nonetheless, as Rikke highlights, the psychological consequences have been devastating.

As we have seen, sexualized torture against men can manifest in physical sexualized abuse by a person in power, such as, "a person, a guard-type person, who would rape him regularly, and for him, it was sexual abuse, really, and that also then led him to question his own sexuality now, with his partner" (Mila, interview, 2021). However, similar to wider reports of sexualized violence including during the Rwandan Genocide, Bosnian War, the war in Democratic Republic of Congo, among others, the use of forced witnessing of sexualized abuse of women and/or children was highlighted by Luna. She states:

'I don't want to call it sexual because I think it's violence, the same as any other kind of torture, but what I hear more and more from the male patients, especially if the torture that even forces them to be witness to sexual violence towards a family member or experiencing penetration of different objects within themselves, sexual humiliation, and I think what is the most difficult for these, especially men to talk about, is being witness to sexual torture of women and children. That is something that really breaks their spirit.' (Interview, 2021)

There are a number of significant aspects of this particular quote. Firstly, Luna is the only practitioner to challenge the use of the term 'sexual' in relation to sexualized torture, since she argues it to be violence. Secondly, although not explicit here, one can only imagine the personal consequences of this form of witnessing as torture for men who are forced to watch such abuses. Indeed, the positionality of a man being powerless to intervene is a clear and deliberate strategy for emasculation of power in conflict or detention contexts. However, violence on women's – and in this example, children's – bodies become recognizably problematic for people beyond the survivor.

Masculinity, sexuality and violence

Practitioners working with male survivors of sexualized torture or sexually torturous violence highlighted complex relationships between masculinity, sexuality and patriarchy. Some relayed somewhat problematic assumptions about homosexuality, at times conflating this with sexualized abuse which, as noted so far including in the context of torture, centres around power and powerlessness. The idea that manliness or masculinity was eroded was a common point of discussion. Laura reflects that, "some of the men say when they say, 'I'm not a man anymore,' for example. With the men, you sometimes have to guess a little. You have a good idea, but they may not say things directly" (interview, 2021), adding that, "I think they feel that if they've been raped, then they've been put in a position where they're not a real man, what they describe as a real man, which would be a homosexual man" (interview, 2021). This had been an earlier theme where similar discussions had developed. In 2013, Ida noted:

'Especially for torture in the Middle East there is a whole respect thing with men. If you want to really hit somebody in the face, raping a man is one of your best options. He would be scarred for life – he would not want to talk about it to his family or his wife. He is totally emasculated.' (Interview, 2013)

Concepts of masculinity have long been documented in relation to sexualized violence against men, indeed Sivakumaran (2007) has explored this in depth. However, there are a number of themes which come through the discourses in these interviews that benefit from further consideration. Firstly, there is an assumption of what a 'real man' is, which relates to false dichotomies still prevalent globally that there is a typified set of roles between women and men which cannot be transgressed. This also subsequently breaks down roles between heterosexual men and gay men, which reiterates a hierarchy of masculinities, where gay or indeed bisexual men continue to be perceived as deviant or subordinate (Sivakumaran, 2005). Katarina alludes to this more clearly:

'[I]f you have a man who has been raped by another man and obviously when rape is something completely different than a sexual orientation, it's an act of violence, but in some societies if you have been raped you will be labelled as gay, maybe, or in that spectrum, maybe you're not labelled as gay but you're labelled as someone who's gonna do something sinful and therefore you're cast out.' (Interview, 2017)

Other participants similarly outlined ways in which such abuses lead some men to question their sexuality, or even instil feelings of homophobia, including that one young survivor of sexualized torture felt "every time that we talk about the past or talk about homosexuals or relating to his experiences, then his whole body starts shaking and his mind becomes unfocused, and I think that's very typical" (Christian, interview, 2021), indicating a clear issue in understanding sexualized violence as *violence* rather than *sexuality*. This brings us to the second point: it is worth disaggregating uses of language in relation to 'sexual' and 'violence' more broadly. Luna talks us through how these are differentiated in her practice:

'I had one man who came to me having been subjected to sexual torture as a child, and what was the most difficult thing for him to accept was the fact that once he was gang-raped by a group of soldiers and what bothered him the most was … he actually got an erection, and he couldn't comprehend why. What did that mean, what did that say about him as a boy, and was he gay, was he not, didn't he like it? And the whole talk about, well, it's a bodily response, just as when you get hit, you bleed, or when you get beaten, you bruise, or if you get hit enough on your toe, your nail is gonna fall off. It's just a bodily reaction. It doesn't say anything about who you are as a person or who you should be as a man. It's just a bodily reaction. That was quite helpful for him to just know that fact.' (Interview, 2021)

She emphasizes: "It was violence in the same way that everything else was violence, and it had a purpose, which was breaking him down, which often brings us to the whole sexuality talk: what is sexuality? What is intimacy? What is pleasure within the body?" (interview, 2021). The inherent issue of homophobia or even a fear of being gay is not fully addressed. However, this fear opens up discussions on the complex differences between sex, sexuality and violence that are often otherwise presented as interconnected, including by conflation through language.

Finally, it is worth stating that discourses across various interviews from 2013 and 2021 – projects which focused on sexualized violence – routinely exceptionalized sexualized violence against men in its impacts, referring to men being silent, and some stating it was easier for women to disclose sexualized abuses. Given what we know about silencing and sexualized violence, this is not a helpful tool of analysis, since it is seldom easy for anyone to disclose. Moreover, that men are 'emasculated' leads me to question: what are women? Unfeminized? Refeminized? This exposes the problems inherent to this discourse when we flip the angle towards women. As such, it may be worth recognizing that simplistic notions of silencing as part of a hierarchy are not useful, but instead unpack *gender-specific* barriers to discussing or disclosing sexualized violence so that we might more holistically move towards addressing them.

Sexualized violence and sexually torturous violence in broader social narratives

We have thus far focused predominately on forms of sexualized violence related to conflict or UNCAT adherent forms of sexual torture. This in part is due to the demographic included in research and participation, and because sexualized torture is easier to align with societies or situations which are already facing endemic levels of (physical, but also structural) violence.

However, once we begin to consider ways in which we can comprehend violence as *torturous*, it becomes possible to recognize sexually torturous violence more consciously beyond the limitations of UNCAT, within societies around us and presented as exceptional in the everyday. News media, women's magazines and television documentaries regularly, repeatedly cover examples of abuses which are not dissimilar to those which we have unpacked here. Even in newsagent shops, a quick glance across the women's magazine section opens up a world of torturous abuses: sustained sexualized violence against children, the long-term effects of sexualized childhood exploitation on adult survivors, systematic beatings, threats, burning and psychological violence from partners and, not uncommon, the stories of families whose daughters, sisters and mothers have not survived. These narratives are commonly represented as exceptional – heinous crimes by evil or demonic men. However, as the United Nations Office on Drugs and Crime suggest:

> A total of 87,000 women were intentionally killed in 2017. More than half of them (58 per cent) – 50,000 – were killed by intimate partners or family members, meaning that 137 women across the world are killed by a member of their own family every day. More than a third (30,000) of the women intentionally killed in 2017 were killed by their current or former intimate partner – someone they would normally expect to trust. Based on revised data, the estimated number of women killed by intimate partners or family members in 2012 was 48,000 (47 per cent of all female homicide victims). *The annual number of female deaths worldwide resulting from intimate partner/family-related homicide therefore seems be on the increase.* (2018: 7; emphasis added)

It serves to reason, then, that although torturous and even deadly violence is omnipresent (and *on the increase*, as the United Nations Office on Drugs and Crime argues), the severity and frequency of it too often goes silenced. This is also the case with narratives around 'sex games gone wrong', a form of defence which has gained traction in femicide cases in Great Britain which present the killing of women as accidental outcomes of consensual sadomasochistic sexual activity, however violent the preceding subjection before death has been, including in the case of Natalie Connolly, who was 26 years old when she was killed by her partner John Broadhurst in 2016. The case was described as a 'sex game gone wrong' – one of more than 40 such cases (Yardley, 2020). Even though Natalie was more than five times the drink driving limit, case narratives still assumed consent on Broadhurst's accounts. The Crown Court proceedings document that:

> On your [Broadhurst's] account, after beating her, Natalie's requests became more extreme. She asked you to insert a bottle of spray carpet

cleaner into her vagina, as a sexual stimulant. This was a large object with a trigger. It became lodged in her vagina and you could not get it out. You went to get a bottle of lubricant to try and remove it. The pathological evidence was that the bottle caused lacerations to her vagina resulting in arterial and venous haemorrhage. When you pulled the bottle out of her vagina, you said that 'I had to put my hand inside her and twist and pull it out and some blood came out at the same time. ... She discharged some blood. ... There was a reasonable amount I mean reasonable amount of blood' (Interview 1, p7). You said she said she was fine but 'she slurred cos she was very drunk so it was a bit gobbledy gooky'. (Judiciary UK, 2018: 7)

The forms of violence speak for themselves, and yet despite the alcohol content, sexual consent overshadows the clearly torturous nature of Natalie Connolly's death by a man who went on to leave her to bleed to death while he went back to sleep. As with many sentencing remark reports in similar cases, the terms *torture* or *torturous violence* did not feature, nor in subsequent research (see for example Yardley, 2020).

However difficult *severity* may be to define (Kelly, 2012; Pérez-Sales, 2017), there seems a significant disjuncture between severity in the case of state violence, and that which is inflicted by private actors or violent partners. It is simultaneously there for all to see, while going unrepresented as torturous when states are not direct inflictors of systematic torture as per reflected in narratives based on the Convention Against Torture. Moreover, and although such cases may be situated as related to increased normalization of kink cultures and sadomasochism, it is worth noting that deaths are not routinely documented as 'sex games gone wrong' in kink clubs, swinging clubs or bondage, discipline, domination and submission (BDSM) specific communities, which also often push boundaries with consensual pain infliction. Although I'm not suggesting violence – as in non-consensual sexualized abuse – is never present, this narrative seems to deflect from what *is* most commonly documented in 'sex games gone wrong': the killing of women by men with whom most victims had some form of relationship (see also Monckton Smith, 2021).

Cavity searches as state-sanctioned sexualized torture

A somewhat different but controversial example of state-sanctioned sexualized torture is the continued, routine use of cavity searches in prison and detention. If we consider the purpose of torture, according to UNCAT, as extraction of information, cavity searches are legally authorized bodily inflictions which would – in any other circumstances – be considered sexualized torture. They can include searching the anus, mouth and vagina, all of which can be severely humiliating and painful, as well as compounding earlier subjection to sexualized abuse for survivors who are subjected to it. Rivera (2020) describes cavity searches as 'not comfortable experiences, and *should only be performed by law enforcement personnel* with the proper training and only under the proper legal circumstances' (2020; emphasis added). I italicize part of this sentence to draw attention to the exceptional nature of what is central to cavity searches – that it is a case in which the state is actively sanctioned to interrogate a detainee in a way which would specifically be considered sexual torture in any other scenario. Indeed, Corey Devon, imprisoned in Fishkill Correctional Facility, contrasts this with his own experience of strip-frisking and cavity searches, arguing it strips people of humanity. He recalls:

> I was so scared, I couldn't comprehend how to strip naked in front of two men or why I had to do this. Motionlessness was my response. That provoked more shouting from the officers. The situation escalated into them shoving me and pressing my face against the wall. After I lowered my boxers, they made me face them and lift my penis and testicles. Then they ordered me to turn around, bend over, spread my buttocks and expose my anus for their inspection. (Quoted in Arthur, 2021)

It becomes difficult to disaggregate this narrative to that of survivors of sexualized torture in state facilities and detention. This brings me back to an earlier point: that torture is a form of social contract, one which depends on state-based priorities to be recognized as such, including the non-recognition of sexually torturous violence in multifarious settings.

As a final point here, I am not suggesting that the term *torture* is never used in these discourses or narratives. Cases where people have been subjected to perceptively exceptional and 'newsworthy' cases – predominately at the hands of strangers or serial abusers – torture is sometimes alluded to. This has been the case for men who have inflicted severe torturous abuses, including for example Jeffrey Dahmer, John Wayne Gacy and Dean Corll, whose forms of torturous violence cumulatively included drilling holes in bones or skull, repeated rapes accompanied by other violence, and the use of boiling water and hydrochloric acid, and the use of torture boards or other forms of hanging and suspension. As narratives become ever more immortalized in docudramas and popular streaming series, they become more visible and yet arguably more exceptionalized: the actions of individual, deviant or psychopathic men. It is presented as separate to society, a transgression of norms, even when sexualized and torturous violence is similar in its forms and systematic nature, specifically in the case of abusive partners or familial child abusers inflicting it.

Conclusion: moving from *intent* to *effect*?

'Women sexually abused during incarceration ... it can be [for] humiliation, degradation, pregnancy – but not all these come under definition of torture. Yet the *impacts are profound.*' (Oscar, interview, 2013; emphasis added)

Although not all forms of sexualized violence or sexually torturous violence fall under the official rubric of torture as according to UNCAT, the impacts of torturous violence and sexualized torture can span whole trajectories of individuals' lives (Herman, 1992; Kastrup and Arcel, 2004) with scope for affecting relationships within families or partnerships over time. This is a significant point when considering that one of the organizations involved in this study had a high number of refugees who had long been settled in its base country. Clients seeking trauma counselling and psychotherapy included survivors of the second Iraq War, Iraq–Iran War, war in the Democratic Republic of Congo, as well as more recently settled refugees, particularly from Syria. Practitioners who worked only with refugees (rather than people seeking asylum) were experiencing increases in the uptake of psychological support and counselling from women who had been subjected to rape and sexual abuse during the Bosnian War, which was officially declared to be at an end more than two decades prior to this research.

As Green and Ward similarly elucidate, torture does not necessarily end with the end of being tortured:

The extent of port-torture suffering is extensive and involves somatic sequelae (gastrointestinal disorders, rectal lesions and sphincter abnormalities, dermatological disorders, organic brain damage, cardiovascular disorders, difficulties in walking etc.); psychological sequelae (anxiety, depression, psychosis, lethargy, insomnia, nightmares, memory and concentration impairment, hallucinations, sexual problems, alcohol intolerance etc.) and social consequences of the somatic and psychological sequelae (inability to work, impairment of social personality, negative self-image, inability to relax, inability to relate positively with family members etc.). (Green and Ward, 2004: 139)

Thus in shifting from action and intent to psychological, physical and social impacts, we are perhaps better placed to recognize subjections to sexualized torture and sexually torturous violence. Women and men who are subjected to sexual violence in any capacity can be affected in a multitude of ways – there is no narrowly prescribed reaction. Some individuals may consider themselves as survivors or victims, and some may feel they can 'cope',[4] while others struggle for long periods of time to recover, if they ever fully do (Herman, 1992). This can be the case for survivors of one instance of abuse or many and, therefore, from a feminist perspective at least, it is not necessarily helpful to create hierarchies of seriousness, but rather see such violence as a continuum (Kelly, 1988).

In her research for the UN report on violence against men and boys in Syria, Chenowyth noted:

> Sexual violence, particularly sustained sexual torture, had profoundly debilitating and destabilising psychological consequences. Physically, rectal trauma, often due to sexual torture with the use of objects, in the form of anal fistulae and fissures was reported, resulting in ongoing pain and faecal leakage. Socially, male survivors were shunned and shamed, and some were threatened with death. Economically, adult male survivors faced numerous impediments to employment—under already highly competitive, often exploitative conditions—due to poor mental health, community marginalisation, or compromised physical health. Some boy survivors left school, jeopardising their education. Entire families were impacted: community ostracization, the onset of domestic violence, and poverty due to loss of livelihood were reported as direct results from the sexual victimisation of a husband, father, or son. (Chenowyth, 2017: 7)

Although this focuses on men and boys, similar impacts are evident in the lives of women survivors, who may also bear the burden of pregnancy, birth or abortion in the aftermath of vaginal rape. This can be compounded in societies where women do not have equal access to labour markets of economies, and where 'honour' is intricately associated with virginity or monogamy – again a conflation between 'sexual' and the 'violent', as well as a challenge to women's sexual autonomy even in her own consensual relationships.

In looking to support survivors of conflict-related sexualized violence and torture, practitioners and organizations may adopt strategies based on levels of torture-related trauma. In describing her theory of 'complex Post-Traumatic Stress Disorder', Judith Herman highlights that 'prolonged, repeated trauma' can have multiple impacts that are 'best understood as a spectrum of conditions' (1992: 119). Arcel argues that 'war-based trauma is one of the most complex traumas if not *the* most complex because of the many potential traumatizing events experienced by the individual before', with specific focus on sexualized violence (2003: 20; emphasis in original). Looking at this from a gendered perspective, Kastrup and Arcel highlight that polytraumatization may be more common among women refugees since 'many women have been subjected to numerous human rights abuses and traumatic experiences' (2004: 554) as well as the possibility of trajectories of abuse in domestic spheres and as part of structural gendered violence.

In alluding to 'human rights abuses' the definitional grey area of torture per se is avoided, instead emphasizing that women may be subjected to forms of violence prior to, or indeed after, sexual violence or torture as defined in the UNCAT. In reference to sexualized violence specifically, Sarah, for example, similarly stated that "therapeutically I would say that men and women who have been raped are the most difficult to help in treatment" (interview, 2013). This was corroborated by various participants, including psychological impacts, and the long-term impacts of pain:

'The patients that I know that have been subjected to sexual torture, they are very often very severely traumatized, so the psychological impact of sexual torture is enormous and very, very debilitating.' (Anne, interview, 2021)

'Sexual torture, is one of the worst ... probably one of the most difficult ones to treat.' (Dora, interview, 2021)

'She will continue to have pain, she will continue to be troubled, but she's never been healed or talked to anybody about her rapes. So there can be a lot of physical signs of trauma. And we see that both with men and women.' (Hannele, interview, 2013)

As many survivors have told me over the past 15 years, shame, stigma and humiliation are exacerbated by the sexualized nature of these forms of torture and torturous violence (see Canning, 2014; 2017), which was consistently reiterated by practitioners:

'There's a lot of the shame element with sexualized forms of torture – let's call it that – and self-recrimination, questioning, the kind of things you would find with rape generally or with sexual violence generally, co-exists among other feelings in the torture dynamic as well, I think, and then questioning of sexuality later and questioning of, yeah, sexual life.' (Mila, interview, 2021)

'The way it damages the individual, the way it damages the. ... There's the guilt, then there's the silence around it, what do you call it, the stigmatization around it.' (Dora, interview, 2021)

Importantly, prolonged and repeated trauma is not confined to conflict, state-inflicted torture environments or sexualized torture itself. It is endemic in violent relationships, patriarchal environments and across some people's whole life trajectories. And yet, as Dora clearly highlights:

'[T]he thought that being sexually abused happens within the family, in a safe environment. Well, torture seems to be. ... I still think it's just as violent as the other one, but maybe for a person out of the family, it's easier to say, "Oh, this is just what happens in this family".' (Interview, 2021)

This is compounded by wider forms of violence, some of which has been earlier constructed as structural torture or temporal torture, and which requires significantly more attention in the framing of sexualized torture and sexually torturous violence if we are to understand, speak about and respond to such abuses more coherently.

Experiential Epistemologies: Embedding the Lived Experience of Women Survivors

Introduction

As this book has charted so far, there are various ways in which violence can be interpreted and recognized. For the most part, academic and legalistic frameworks often depend heavily on fairly narrow legislative definitions, specifically the Convention Against Torture and its protocols, which I defined as *orthodox legalism* in Chapter 1. Those working at grassroot or practitioner level more often combine lived experience with legal understandings, defined as *legalist hybridity*, or indeed a more free-flowing focus on experience as the most significant factor in approaching survivors of torturous violence, defined as *experiential epistemologies*.

This chapter moves to focus almost exclusively the latter of these three categories. It is here that I draw in the oral histories of women who have survived violence at various stages of their lives, all of whom, at the time of undertaking oral histories and ethnographic research (2016–2018) were seeking asylum or had recently obtained refugee status.[1]

Women's words in a chamber of echoes

The first point of note is that the accounts outlined in this chapter do not adhere to the legal specificities addressed in earlier chapters – and deliberately so. As you will see, unlike accounts from organizations documenting torture, such as Freedom from Torture or the Danish Institute Against Torture, the narratives here are not confined to the legal definition of torture – indeed, few include the infliction of violence from state officials, and even fewer where the perpetrator was working in an official capacity at the time of violence.

This is the key pattern that ultimately brought this book about. Speaking with women, as well as psychologists, psychotraumatologists and other key practitioners, the use of sustained and often extreme violence may not always amount to torture in this sense. Over the years, I have spoken with survivors of rape, multiple perpetrator rape, forced pornography, sexual and domestic trafficking, rape by border guards, sexual harassment in asylum accommodation and camps, burning, scalding, beating, threats, intimidation, imprisonment, so-called 'false imprisonment', and forced abortion. The most common perpetrator was a partner or husband, outside of state capacities, and there have even been occasions when abuse was ongoing without whole communities or support groups realizing for some years. So far, few (if any) of the women I spoke with ever used the word 'torture'. Indeed, of the few times the term has been used, it was when discussing the process of seeking asylum, a point that will be picked up on at the end of this chapter.

However, like many of the hundreds of refugee women I have spoken with over the past 15 years, the physical and psychological violence each is subjected to has been intentional, often sustained over long periods of time, and sometimes within some form of unofficial confinement, including the home or in refugee camps or asylum housing. Sexualized violence, where women are subjected to such abuses, is often sustained, physically and emotionally destructive, and deliberately degrading. Other forms of threats or coercions limit women's freedom, autonomy and sense of self. Some are arguably forms of existential confinement. They reduce women's safety through fear. Yet as Antonia, Asma, Faiza, Jazmine, Mahira and Nour powerfully demonstrate, this objective has ultimately failed. Each survived, and went on to survive exhausting and unnecessarily, deliberately harmful asylum systems (see Canning, 2019a; 2019b).

These six accounts are somewhat short in comparison to each woman's oral history. One key point to emphasize is that some were tens of thousands of words in length, others shorter, but, where possible, contact was maintained for some years and indeed, in some cases, contact remains. This form of research draws from participant observation, intersectional feminism and activist academic methods (see Canning et al, 2023, for information on International Activist Criminology). What we can glean from this is that *women do speak and speak out*. As this chapter will detail, sexualized violence – and sexualized torturous violence more specifically – are heavily silenced across most facets of society. Despite the plethora of arguments made that it is women and survivors who are silent, given time, space and trust, this is exposed as a problematic and sweeping assumption. Women may choose *not* to speak about certain aspects of their lives, for which I never press, and certainly – understandably – choose not to relay histories when they do not feel safe to do so to people they do not want to speak with. This reflects more on the failure of conditions under which society expects survivors to discuss deeply personal experiences that often draw out sadness, upset, shame, stigma and even self-loathing. The grinding, gnawing attempt to erode women's self-worth is not only inflicted through the violence itself, but through silencing voices at one end of the social spectrum, and forcing disclosures at the other (such as through repeated, lengthy asylum applications and interviews, often with strangers, often in wholly unsuitable settings).

These are social and societal failures. As the following chapter addresses in depth, experiences of torture and torturous violence are routinely invisibilized through various facets of silencing. Some are structurally deliberate, some are individual methods of self-preservation, some are well intended and wholly appropriate efforts to avoid further harm. However, once we begin to lift the curtain on women's experiences of extreme or systematic and sustained subjections to physical and psychological violence, we can begin to more fully recognize that torture – as it is defined in most laws – may be vital for addressing state crimes and violence, but falls short of recognizing and addressing that which causes as much or more emotional and psychological harm: *torturous and sexually torturous violence.*

Intersectional continuums of experiential knowledge: insights from survivors

Antonia

Antonia spent three months in North African desert and forest after she left her home in a West African country. For the part of her journey accessible by road, she was driven by smugglers, recalling "They take us together like, I don't know how to call it, like chickens". She mimics how she sat in the truck packed with people and dogs, by hunkering down with her arms firmly wrapped. When the terrain became inaccessible, she says, "By your feet. Get so where the car can take you. The car cannot take you more than that". Antonia remembers, "it's not easy. Because we saw people, dead bodies, when there is no water. So people can give you their urine to drink. You know? So, it was like that. It was really difficult".

Antonia's departure point for Europe was Morocco. As with many boats trying to evade border police, hers left North Africa at night. She recalled, "You know when you are looking at the lights from Morocco to Spanish [coastline], you would think they are closer. It's not closer. … You know the water, when the water gets into your mouth. It makes you to throw up all the time. So, it was not very easy". It took Antonia and the other people on the boat almost 24 hours to reach safety. They were rescued on shore by Spanish police and taken to hospital before spending one month in a camp, where women and men lived separately.

From here, friends of one of Antonia's original smugglers drove her further into Europe, arriving in Italy. Having now been trafficked through EU borders, she spent seven years living in prostitution to make enough money to pay her original fees, little of which she received herself. She silences this period when she speaks, feeling that "I cannot be proud of things when I tell someone I worked in prostitution. I can't say that. You understand? So, I have to keep that one to myself. I don't have to say to anyone". As for many survivors of sexualized trafficking, the actions of others are internalized as shame. Antonia reflects, "I don't want to, if I talk about my life, I will be sad when I get home today".

Even though she was recognized as a survivor of trafficking, Antonia's case was not reviewed as part of a 'Particular Social Group' under the Refugee Convention, "They say when you are trafficked, they say they don't give paper to traffick[ers]. Because they said you are a slave to somebody, you are working for somebody. They don't give paper for that". But Antonia cannot return 'home'. Like many people who are trafficked, she is still labelled as in debt to her original smuggler and subsequent traffickers, and one in particular who,

'is still waiting for me to pay her. Which as I don't pay her, I can't go home, if not they will kill me. Or they will kill my child. It's like that. If I'm going to my home country, I am making sure I finish paying her. … Or they will kill me'.

Antonia did not have the money have do so.

Having survived crossing the sea, trafficking, forced prostitution and regular beatings over the seven-year period, Antonia felt that life in asylum was now her greatest challenge. She reflected that, "I want to go away from the centre, but when I'm there, I have a lot of stress in my head. It's not what the teacher is teaching me in the school. I don't know anything". As many survivors of abuse experience, she was unable to concentrate in any classes, and could seldom afford to leave the centre due to childcare responsibilities. Instead, she felt, "You have to make yourself happy. If not, you would one day just stand up, you would go hang yourself, you will just die. It's not easy to live in the camp, my sister. It's not easy, camp life is not easy to live".

Accessing free psychological support is very difficult in Denmark when seeking asylum, and the asylum centre was no exception. When we discussed any counselling or psychological support, Antonia stated that, "I don't know if there is anyone like that in Denmark here. I've not seen, since I've been in Denmark. Since I been in the asylum system. I've not seen [anyone]". As a survivor of torturous violence and forced prostitution, she had never been offered sustained emotional or psychological support.

Faiza

When we first met, Faiza had already been living in asylum centres in Denmark for two years. Her case has been complex – based originally on an application for asylum, she subsequently applied for family reunification so that her former husband – who was physically and emotionally abusive and has Danish citizenship – could have access to their children. At the time of research, she was living in her eighth centre with her two children, one of whom had lived in asylum centres for almost all of his life.

Unlike many of the women I met in asylum centres, Faiza comes from a relatively wealthy background – she had gone through secondary level education and had little experience of poverty before moving to Denmark. Her first application to live in Denmark was to move with her former husband and was based on religious reasons – as a Shia Muslim both of their families were critical of their partnership as he is a Sunni Muslim. She also experienced gendered persecution that she did not include in her claim for asylum: having worked on women's rights, she experienced intimidation which once included her life being threatened with a gun. She recalled:

'[W]hen I was with my baby I am working with women's rights, and I have like meetings with the women. Yeah, but in one meeting – it's a Shia meeting – when I come back to home like, some guys come in a car, they stop our car and say, "Come out!" Yeah. And he says "Be careful! Be careful if you want to see life, be careful!".'

Although Faiza recalls having problems in her marriage from the beginning, it was on moving to Denmark that she first experienced physical abuse. As she stated:

'Once he's put shoe [stood] on me, while I'm pregnant, with my second baby. On my head. And second time he takes violence with the mobile phone. He threw me his mobile phone. And he hit my shoulder. But that time I said, no, he had no right to hit me'.

Prior to this he had been coercively controlling, including taking her money and threatening with violence. Her fear of him affected her claim for asylum in the first instance:

'He is outside [the initial arrival accommodation centre in Denmark] and that time, my husband warned me that, "Don't tell anything about my father and mother and sister." I said OK. I get pressurized and I said OK, because he said, "The interview you get, you know, I can read now. I can read it. They give you copy, and I can read it." Then I get scared, and I said OK.'

For this reason, Faiza did not tell the authorities that she was experiencing physical and coercive violence, some arguably psychologically torturous.

After this, Faiza's sister-in-law moved in with them. She reflected that,

'[F]rom the start of my married life I had problems from my husband, from the first day, but I can manage it, I can tackle it, I can manage it, I bear it, but when his sister come, then I don't know ... they make, they want to make me their servant, they want to make me used as their slave, and that case I can't be, because I'm a human being. I have my own life. I have right to live my own life.'

Faiza refused and applied for asylum separately, now also based on fear of retaliation from her now ex-husband's family. Throughout the duration visiting Faiza, she communicated an intent to end her life twice, and attempted to do so once. These led at one point to her isolation in a secure unit of a psychiatric hospital, which none of the support staff at the asylum centre visited.

Jazmine

Having left her country of origin with a visa, Jazmine applied for asylum as soon as she entered Denmark. As a trans woman from a country where being openly transgender was (at the time) illegal, she sought safety from state and family persecution under the Refugee Convention.

Jazmine has experienced persecution almost all of her life. She remembers family 'suspicions' (as Jazmine termed) developing as a child, and the impact of being found to have undergone surgery when, "My grandfather said, 'Throw a stone on her, throw a stone,' because I did haram and I did my operation they want to throw a stone on me, so it's very difficult for me." Following an illegalized castration at 20 years old, she was seen by a family member who told her mother and father. Following threats of violence, Jazmine fled her home and moved to a city some hours away, where she lived in prostitution for five years.

During this time, Jazmine was financially controlled by pimps, or gurus, some of whom were physically violent: "I'm very, very experienced with my gurus because they want to take money from me, and I don't want to give them. They beat me a lot, they hit me, and I was in very difficult situation." She recalled she had "a very difficult life, I say, six hours, seven hours, I stand on the road. Sometimes police beat me, car want to hit me". In all, her time in prostitution was a decision made based on poverty, and a lack of other legal opportunities for trans people due to social and economic exclusion in many areas. She spoke strongly of her dislike for the role, remembering she had, "very bad clients, very dirty, they smell, smelly, and I don't want to do sex with them but force, due to money. If I do not earn money, what do I eat?" and that, "I do not like it, by force people do with me sex, they want to rape me but what I save money is very important for living a life, without money you cannot survive". Even through her dislike, she feigned happiness, remembering "one customer come, I do fuck or do everything, then he goes, I go and shower. Then again, he come, then again someone come, fuck, then again, I take shower. Four times a day I take shower" and that, "after two customers you get tired. Because one time you do sex you get tired, after the second customer come and you're not happy, you must smile on your face."

As well as experiencing beatings and rapes from multiple clients who refused to pay, Jazmine was sometimes paid to dance at illegalized underground parties. It was at one of these that men came into the function room and fired shots, before killing one her friends, "my one friend got killed, dead, due to function people. ... She gets eight bullets on her body in front of me". At another, men fired two shots. She recalled:

'[T]hen I say, "Why you are doing like this?" and I'm getting more distressed. I did not want to get stressed, then we go from function. They say, "OK, you want to go? Sit here!" Two people come and sit on me here, I sit, and they burn my hand with cigarettes. ... Then he wants to do with me rape, then what I say, I say, "OK, do sex with me." He did sex, his friends, do sex with me, then I go from function.'

In an attempt to save her own life, Jazmine complied with the men who raped her, while one burned her hands and arms. When she lifts her sleeves, the deep pockmarks still act as reminders of her abuse.

Having been subjected to violence in her country of origin, Jazmine had hoped that she would be free from persecution when she reached Denmark. She recalled that:

'[W]hen I was coming, I thought Europe was so nice, so good, very nice country and people are so nice. But here I got same problem, I'm facing [the] same problem, nothing different from my country to here, only I'm safe due to my own family, my family is not here.'

Even though she was no longer at risk from abuse from her family, Jazmine still faced transphobia in the four asylum centres she lived at. In the second centre, she recalled that "a woman wanted to kill me with a knife, with bottles, she wanted to kill me, I have very bad experience in asylum centres". This led to her third move within only a few months.

In the asylum centre, Jazmine was popular among her fellow residents, feeling that, "People come and knock my door. Because in my woman centre every woman loved me." Even through the resentment, she was a key part of the collegial set-up that women had established, sharing cooking and holding celebrations for birthdays and any successful granting of refugee status. However, she still faced transphobia from some of the men who lived at the other side of the centre, and regularly felt propositioned (some of which I witnessed). She felt that, "Every time boys come and knock my door, I was so much scared at nighttime that they want to rape me." On the day before one of our meetings, she recalled an incident with a man living in a nearby block:

'He want to talk with me. I say, "What for you?" "Come in my room, we just talk, and we do something." Then I was alone on bicycle, I was riding on bicycle, he was following me. He was following me in this camp, in this Denmark, he wanted to do bad with me sex'.

Even with prostitution and familial abuse behind her, other aspects of harassment still seeped into her everyday life.

Mahira

Mahira first came to Europe in the late 2000s. Living with her former husband, she was routinely abused. Her arms and feet are testimony of torturous violence – her husband regularly poured scalding water on them so that even today, many years later, the scars run deep on her skin. Living for two years in another European country, Mahira had a child. While walking through a city centre, her husband began to beat her, and witnesses intervened. Criminalization ensued: Mahira's husband was arrested and charged for assault, subsequently to be deported to his country of origin. She recalled, "He slapped on my face and police and some people saw him. They called the police in." Mahira went home with him on release, only to face further abuse: "I came back with him, but he promised me we have to go back to our country now, and we went. Then he snatched my baby from me, and my passport, her passport ... and they locked me in the room for six months." Mahira did not want to discuss the six months she was falsely imprisoned. However, when she escaped, her sister applied for a visitor visa in Denmark. Intending to apply for asylum in Sweden and gain family reunification with her child, Mahira left home and flew to Denmark. Until the time of writing, she has never been able to trace her child's whereabouts.

Although a family member was able to support her visa application, Mahira's intention was to apply for asylum in Sweden, which – at the time – had the potential for supported family reunification. Having travelled over the Oresund Bridge, Mahira applied for refugee status in Malmö and was moved to an asylum centre slightly further north of the Skåne region. Having waited six months, Mahira was deported back to Denmark – under the Dublin Regulations her case for asylum would be processed in the first safe country that she had arrived in, and where she had been granted a 14-day visitor visa.

On arrival, her experience of asylum took a turn for the worse when she was moved to Center Sandholm, the first point of all application processes in Denmark. In all the discussions we had, Sandholm featured as a particularly negative experience for Mahira, who recalled that:

'I have been in Sandholm three months, which was very bad experience … people living in the same centre, which is terrible. And they are standing in the kitchen or café, all waiting for the food, and plate in their hands and waiting and there is a lot of people, maybe 200,[2] 300, 400 people and they just open the café for the one hour. You have to come in one hour for the morning, the breakfast, lunch and dinner. It's three times and otherwise everything is locked, closed. So, you have to come for the one hour a day and it is a long queue, about 500–600 people. And they don't think that people can be sick cause they don't want to wait for one hour, just for one lady. So, I haven't eaten anything, I just got something in the breakfast and just I have to eat for the rest of my day, because I don't want to go to the café and wait for one or two hours between 500–600 people.'

As with many other women I spoke to or spent time with in asylum centres, Mahira avoided interaction with others as much as she could as she found it to be stressful.

Her assessment of the centre is damning: "Sandholm is very terrible. Just like a hell or just like a jail, you are in the jail … you cannot decide because you don't have money and you cannot go out if you don't have money so how do you pay for the bus, for the train?" Alongside feeling like she was in a prison, Mahira struggled with the darkness, cold and isolation of Center Sandholm. She recalled that:

'October is snow weather. Snow fall. And Sandholm is also very big area. You had to walk, it's very cold and you don't have enough clothes, enough jacket, shoes, and you have to come down from your room and go to the café, it is far from … the room without a jacket, without warm clothes.'

When I asked Mahira if she thought asylum centres were acceptable places for people to live, she answered "No. Not in Denmark and not in Sweden.

I think it is better they say stop refugees. It is better." On my probing on the justification for such a strong response, Mahira stated:

'[W]hich kind of life they give to the refugees? It is not acceptable. So, I think it was better to say stop refugees. They can say in a very respectable way, stop refugees instead of they treat the refugees like animals, like wild animals, not pets. You can love pets, but not wild animals.'

Mahira was offered the opportunity to change her identity as a safety measure to avoid being tracked by her ex-husband. Since she wanted to restart her education and thus needed her earlier certificates, she chose not to but reflected that "if you're an asylum seeker you cannot start your life again". Her reasoning for this conclusion is that she can't undertake studies now in any case: "I tried to start my education 10, 15, 20, 25, 30 times, maybe more than 30 times, but something stopped me. My past always disturbing me." Like many other people I spoke to, and as can be common for survivors of torture, Mahira's concentration was affected by her past, and the uncertainty of her future and the whereabouts of her daughter. She argued that, "You cannot forget. I would say if you're an asylum seeker so your life will be stopped here where you get your asylum."

Although Mahira still suffered from the impacts of her subjection to violence from her ex-husband – specifically that she worried constantly about the whereabouts of her daughter – her life as a refugee in Denmark caused quite significant stress. As with many other European countries, Denmark has seen a gradual shift to the right with regard to its treatment of migrants.

At the time of writing, I still keep in contact with Mahira, receiving updates on her efforts to reunify with her child. While she is feeling positive about a 'new start', she still feels unsure of her future in Denmark and asks if she should try and gain a visa for another country. On reflection of her life there, she said:

'[W]hen I think I was in my country, it was just happened once I would die, but here I am dying for the last ten years. Every day, everything, every minute I'm dying here in Denmark. I think in the past ten years I died many times. Yes. So, it was easy to die once in my own country. And I feel why I am here in Denmark now? Why I am not dead?'

Asma

Asma had been married to an abusive husband for three years before she entered the UK with him on a short-term visa. While growing up, she experienced various forms of domestic violence, threats and intimidation. A key point she remembers is of gendered control, "by brothers and my father, they were very strict. They don't allow girls to go easily like outside with friends or even friends' homes" and that "they don't allow to women to go out and they don't want you to go to like university. Now the girls are going, but before, long time, 30 years ago now!" This violence extended to her married life, with an emotionally and physically abusive husband, "basically he was beating me a lot, he broke ... he was punch me, he ... this, my bone is broken". She points to the part of her cheekbone which remains partly broken due to one particularly horrific attack. She still experiences headaches and depends on medication.

Asma also experienced intimidation from her husband's family members. She recalled, "he was beating me like that, you know the 7-Up Coke bottles, he throws them too much, beat me too much. Even he broke my phone as well, my computer, and even my clocks, he was ... they were very bad people, you know, even his mum, very bad" and that, "they beat me. Other girls they married, and they brought home and they beat them, too much, another sister-in-law, another brother's wife, they're beating them". In our discussions, she even described one of her sister-in-law's deaths as an outcome of familial violence, as she progressively got sicker without support or intervention.

To get to the UK, Asma's original idea had been to stay with her sister and claim asylum to escape further violence. On hearing the plans, her husband joined her. She recalled:

'I don't want to go with him, but it was ... he wasn't allowing me to go alone. So, it was trick to come here! I was playing it. So, I say, "OK, go with me." I thought when I go there, I will not call, I will call the police'.

When she arrived in London, Asma was advised against applying for asylum by her sister and falsified documents instead. The falsification would prove a significant mistake. She was immediately transferred to the UK's immigration detention facility for women.

Asma recalled being driven in handcuffs to immigration detention in Yarl's Wood, a closed detention centre for women which has been plagued by histories of sexualized abuse, suicide attempts and racism, stating:

'[M]e and another woman as well, both handcuffs. They put handcuffs, like we did any crime, in the UK or like we are prisoners, or we are. I say, "What they do? With women like that! And where are they taking us?" We don't have any idea, because anybody ... we don't know how far they're taking us'.

When I asked if she had ever been held by police in handcuffs before – since arrest itself can be a degrading experience even prior to incarceration – she argued no, but it was "Very bad. Even I was very crying, too much crying. I was new that time, you know."

She went on to reflect on the feeling of incarceration as:

'[T]here is nothing, life, you know, inside it's just lock lock lock lock and there is nothing. You have to eat on time, they can count you in the room, even you can't see your face in mirror, you are not allowed to watch TV or nothing. Like a prison, you are in a prison. So, you can imagine the life of prison?'

Once at Yarl's Wood, Asma describes how:

'[F]our days I was there, and my interview was there and everything happened and my case worker said, "I will give you a decision in two days." So, and she said before two days, and she said, "OK, if you want to go from here, I want to give you a chance of the bail. And if you know somebody, they can take you and give bail," and I talked with my husband and I said, "They said if you can do the bail I can go from here" and the one man came, he was a friend of my husband, and he give the bail for me and he took me to London detention and then I came out and she didn't give me my decision two days, it took three years for decision!'

Nour

Nour moved to Sweden with her partner in the mid-2000s. Travelling with a one-year visa, she had decided to flee violence from her ex-husband, who had already taken her son from her. At the time, she recalled that:

'[H]e was threatening me, and the main reason was that I was not allowed to see [her son] and if I would try to see my son then he said he would really hurt me. The worst time was when he took the leg of a table and hit me with it.'

After falsely imprisoning her in her home, spending the night threatening her with further violence, Nour decided to leave her home country. She never felt that she could report his violence, since:

'I am Christian, and my ex-husband is Muslim. He is a powerful man within Hezbollah. I couldn't go to the police and report him because he was a very powerful man, and the police couldn't enter the area where he lived in. The police there take a lot of bribes and so they will not help.'

When her visa expired, Nour applied for asylum on three occasions. After the second application, she recalled being so nervous waiting for a reply that, "I was very nervous, and I didn't eat for 20 days". Her claim was considered under Particular Social Group of the Refugee Convention but rejected on all three occasions as Lebanon is considered a safe country for return. She recounts that, "they [Migrationsverket – the Swedish migration authority] listened but they didn't believe me, and I don't understand who gave them the information that I was safe in my home country because I really wasn't".

When we met, Nour was being held in an immigration detention centre in Sweden. Having been refused asylum, she had spent many years struggling to access healthcare, feeling that "when you're here in Sweden without legitimate papers they do not care, and they do not help you". Her biggest barrier was administrative, as her lack of documentation meant she could not access a doctor legally. Recalling one incident, she remembered, "the woman on the phone told asked me why do you have your four last digits in your personal number and LMA card [Lagen om mottagande av asylsökande – asylum identification card]? I hung up the phone and then never called back". Instead, she relied on friends to get her medication for high blood pressure.

Like many people I spoke with who were living or working in the asylum system in Sweden, Nour did not even know what immigration detention centres were. From her home, "the police forced me to stay there [at a police station] all night in a small room that was really, really, really disgusting smelling, and I was cold all night, freezing almost to death. ... It was the very first time I had experienced something like that". The impacts of her incarceration spread also to her friends. Nour stated that:

'[A] friend came with some of my belongings to the police station and we have been friends for over ten years, and she wanted to go inside to see me, but the police wouldn't let her, and so my friend stayed outside crying the entire night, outside of the police station, with some of my belongings.'

When she arrived at the centre, Nour said that:

'[T]hey left me in that really small, awful room and I doesn't like to sit for very long, so I was walking around, pacing, in that small, disgusting room and then all of a sudden a man just opened the door telling me to go sit in the corner and not to walk around so much.'

As someone living with by Obsessive-Compulsive Disorder, her confinement made her feel suffocated, recalling that, "when I was showering and the water was falling down, I could see bugs all over the place even though they were not real" and that, "the first four days I didn't eat at all. But now I'm starting to adapt to the environment".

As with many people in detention or prison, Nour struggled to adapt to the feeling of social control. She felt that, "there was always someone constantly watching me, and I don't understand why because I'm a nice person". On one occasion, she was faced with an emergency response from two male guards when her lawyer accidentally hit a response button instead of a call button after a meeting. She recalled that, "all of a sudden two huge men came in thinking that I was trying to hurt my lawyer, because that is assault alarm. And that made me really, really sad because I told them I am not dangerous! I was not trying to hurt someone". Indeed, Nour often reflected on her time in detention as being made to feel "like a criminal".

Nour felt that staff did try to help her, for example, "staff lent me several DVDs and I was watching these in the TV room, and also they gave me an extra blanket for my room because it's really cold and the staff here, they are really nice to me", but that freedom was her main concern, since "I will do what Immigration tells me to do but I want to be free". Unlike the other women I met, Nour and I were only able to meet on two occasions. She was moved to another detention centre, and subsequently deported.

Recognizing torturous violence and its impacts

First impressions of the experiences of Antonia, Asma, Faiza, Jazmine, Mahira and Nour do not necessarily correspond with classical narratives of torture. Not all forms of violence were systematic, in the stories presented none correlate with state actors as perpetrators (at least not working in 'official capacity'). None are for the purposes of confession or extracting information. Although all women experienced some form of state confinement, only one experienced prison: five of the women were subject to incarceration in immigration detention facilities and although evidently harmful, none relayed any experiences of torture or cruel or inhuman treatment while being held there. Indeed, many aspects may not register as torturous, even if they are harmful.

Drawing back to the points raised in the first three chapters, while torture is not evident in its legalist sense in these specific oral histories, they demonstrate the significance of understanding, recognizing and confronting forms of torturous violence. When we take time to listen to trajectories of violence in the lives of survivors, the impacts and implications of them becomes more apparent.

It is useful, then, to consider what *can* be identified and recognized in the lives of the women in this chapter.

Asma outlined long-term subjection to threats, intimidation, psychological violence and physical violence. Indeed, so impactful were these that she lived in the British asylum system for more than ten years rather than face internal relocation to her country of origin. The physical impacts were almost debilitating: she suffered from constant headaches due to the breaking of her cheekbone, and had been dependent on anti-depressants for some years.

In Antonia's story, we can see a history of actions which may be seen as torture if the environment in which she was subject to them were to align with the Convention's definition. She received regular beatings from her male and female pimps in Italy and – due to a form of border confinement which will be discussed in more depth later – was unable to move away from her traffickers, people who might otherwise be recognized as captors. Witnessing violence and dead bodies – which Antonia experienced – can have serious emotional and psychological impacts. Although strongly debated and contested in some torture literatures, since seeing violence does not have the same actual threat of sustained bodily harm as being subjected to it, there can at least be consensus that such experiences are harmful unless in some way the witness is desensitized. Moreover, and like any people's testimonies highlight in crossing by sea (McMahon and Sigona, 2018; Yahya, 2021), Antonia spent a long night in an overcrowded boat at sea, unsure if she was facing death. This in and of itself is a monumental event in a person's life, although the significance and impacts of it are often reduced in discourse when it is refugees who face the threat of it.

Faiza is the only woman in this chapter who was not subjected to sustained physical violence, but whose claim for asylum did relate more clearly to what is more likely to be recognized as 'political': her involvement in women's rights and the implications of this in relation to her religion which included her life being threatened at gun point. Although she did not determine whether the assailants were state-affiliated, it is almost ironic that Faiza did not base her claim to asylum on this threat of persecution under the Refugee Convention's 'Particular Social Group' or even 'Religion' categories, but on the fear she had from her coercively controlling and psychologically abusive husband. The latter was not deemed politically motivated or indeed anything related to torture, and yet it was this that led to her decision to stay living in soul-destroying conditions to avoid refoulement. Her experience of the grinding, banal life in asylum was a key contributor to her attempt to take her own life. As discussed in the previous chapter and later in this chapter, the prospect that time is torturous is incredibly far from the United Nations Convention Against Torture or Other Cruel, Inhuman or Degrading Treatment or Punishment (UNCAT) definition, and yet the impacts are, as Monish Bhatia and I have outlined in depth in *Stealing Time* (Bhatia and Canning, 2021), severely negatively impactful on people's mental health, as they had been for Faiza.

Jazmine was the only oral history participant who was granted refugee status within a year of application. Although based on threat of persecution as a trans woman, her experience also reflects forms of torturous violence and yet – again – under an orthodox legalist perspective, does not correspond with the four requirements to be defined as torture. Jazmine was subject to multiple perpetrator rape, burning with cigarettes and forced prostitution. Her life was threatened, and she witnessed the murder of her friend and fellow sex worker, again where such witnessing may not be equated with torture. Even in asylum, she was subjected to harassment and indeed, as I outlined in field notes, some incredibly dubious propositions from her male doctor – texts that I saw myself and a phone call I was present for. Harassment – transphobic as well as sexualized – was endemic for her. She attempted suicide while in the asylum system and, like Asma, was dependent on anti-depressants.

Like Faiza and Asma, Mahira was subjected to sustained beatings, threats and psychological violence. This culminated in the abduction of her child, which has had intense and life-altering impacts on her mental health and sense of future, which is a continuous effort to locate her child, and which she is prevented from doing by the very existence of borders and her own refugee status: if Mahira leaves Denmark to find her child, she can face detention and deportation on return. Mahira was subjected to repeated scalding and six months of a form of false imprisonment, the only period that she will not discuss, and which I asked no further about. In any case, had any of these subjections been inflicted by a state actor rather than her husband, in a state facility rather than her home, the extremities of violence used would be – without hesitation – categorized as torture.

Like Mahira, Nour's story is one of psychological violence at the hands of her husband who, unlike any of the other women, *was* politically connected and affiliated with the state but who *was not* working in official capacity when inflicting violence. Nour experienced threats and false imprisonment, although for a shorter period. Importantly, Nour's own assessment of immigration detention stands out here in relation to the psychological impacts on people. Her depiction is one of helpful staff and access to leisure activities. And yet it is, ironically, Nour's experience which so clearly situates the need to recognize the impacts and implications of confinement for people with mental health problems, since this was not considered in relation to her Obsessive-Compulsive Disorder or previous subjection to false imprisonment which, according to Nour, led to other forms of mental and emotional harm during her incarceration including nightmares and illusions.

Making the personal political in practice

The objective of this chapter is not to attempt to shoehorn women's experiences into the legal definition of torture in relation to UNCAT and its protocols. Rather the opposite: the centralization of survivor experience shows us that many aspects of abuse, violence and harm go unrecognized in their severity, systematic and often sustained nature, and indeed in the impacts of their affliction because they are not recognizable as 'torture'. Instead, this chapter seeks to emphasize why the distinctions made in the previous chapters are demonstrably important in terms of simultaneously focusing on state crimes (that is, official narratives of torture) while exploring and accepting these abuses as torturous violence.

One of the key issues evident in many women's experiences of violence, not only in this context but globally and specifically in relation to extreme and even lethal violence, is that it is predominantly perpetrated by male partners or former partners. Although statistics on sexual or domestic violence and intimate partner or family homicide are notoriously difficult to establish, as stated in Chapter 4, the United Nations Office on Drugs and Crime suggest that 'a total of 87,000 women were intentionally killed in 2017' alone (United Nations Office on Drugs and Crime, 2018: 7; emphasis added). Like conflict-related violence, like systematic torture in prisons, violence against women is pervasive, endemic and, as we can see, lethal.

However, unlike the deliberate infliction of torture by state actors in state institutions for the means of confession or information, men's violence against women remains to be seen as separate from political violence. That 'the personal is political' is not proportionately reflected in law or conventions, including the Refugee Convention (see Canning, 2017). However, as a psychologist specializing in torture and trauma responses in Sweden highlighted in an interview in 2018:

'Creating a bond or an attachment and then using that to hurt as much as possible can occur in domestic violence as well as in a torture environment, in a detention or a prison. But in a sense the domestic violence might be more difficult to get away from because it's so ingrained in your family system also, and harder to flee from or put in brackets.' (Interview, 2018)

Here we can see the implications of a form of existential confinement, created and maintained through coercive control, threats and the embedding of fear. It is corrosive (Canning, 2020b) and – like torture itself – works to degrade, reduce, humiliate, abuse trust and break spirits. Similarly, the grinding impacts of temporal harm through borders and waithood (Khosravi, 2018 Boochani, 2018; Bhatia and Canning, 2021) have clear impacts on people's mental health, which for survivors can compound trauma, and for all subjected to extended periods of temporal uncertainty, can induce it.

For all intents and purposes, then, torturous violence is as harmful as torture, and as the research undertaken for this book indicates, should be recognized as such.

Conclusion

This chapter has drawn together the points made in the previous four chapters in a way which empirically and epistemologically moves us closer to understanding torturous violence from the perspectives and experiences of survivors. The key and central focus here extends the point made in Chapter 2: that by doing so, we can find ways to address the silence around systematic abuses while taking more seriously the impacts as similar to that of torture (see also Başoğlu et al, 2007).

As the following chapters will outline in more depth, this omission in consciousness has the potential to silence the complex multitude or continuums of violence in women's lives where the impacts can reflect or amount to the impacts of torture. This is not superficial, and nor is it a solely academic issue: the failure to recognize torturous violence as political can affect women's access to torture support and facilities. As will be discussed in the concluding chapter, participants from leading torture rehabilitation facilities register significantly higher numbers of men accessing services, and this in part at least results from the dependence on narrow legal definitions of torture.

By replicating narrow screening processes to identify survivors of torture (see, for example, Pérez-Sales, 2017: appendices four and five as examples; and the Istanbul Protocol in relation to definitions), we continue to risk undermining the realities of extreme forms of violence, distorting how torturous violence is recognized or, more importantly not recognized, reproducing false dichotomies of what is and is not forms of state inflicted or sanctioned violence when their intentions and impacts reflect those of torture.

6

Unsilencing

If we are to avoid past mistakes, then we must learn to speak
intelligently about cruelty.

(Rejali, 2011: 28)

Introduction: unpacking the shroud of silence

Green and Ward argue that, although often undertaken as a way to press for
information, torture serves to silence through humiliation and degradation
(2004; see also Scarry, 19885; Rejali, 2007; Kelly, 2012). Interestingly,
although this is recognized in torture literatures, as we can see thus far
little emphasis is placed on sexualized torture and silence. This is despite
the prolific evidence presented by feminists that demonstrates sexualized
violence to be a tool to silence, and that is in and of itself socially silenced
(Kelly, 1988; Ahrens, 2006; Canning, 2011a; Jordan, 2012). Even in my
own experience, throughout the duration of this fieldwork I was regularly
informed by participants and other members working in the centres
I visited that this area was under-researched, and that sexualized violence
was not always (or for some, often) specifically addressed, even though
survivors of sexualized torture had been supported by staff. As mentioned
in Chapter 4, I have even been informed that I had created an 'air of
suspicion' for asking questions related to sexualized violence generally,
and sexual torture specifically – a further indication of its sociopolitical
sensitivity, even among those who challenge some of the most silenced
forms of violence.

As one interviewee put it, sexualized violence may be "one of many
traumas". This perspective is perhaps understandable given multifarious
forms of torture that some practitioners support people to work through.
Yet the context of such violence, which is shrouded in stigma and silence
(Ahrens, 2006; Canning, 2011b; 2014; Jordan, 2012), can lead to outright
exclusion for some survivors. That is not to say that other forms of torture
do not induce humiliation, but that this is not often as taboo or stigmatized

as sexual violence generally or sexual torture specifically, including for male survivors of sexualized torture.

This chapter therefore draws from practitioner perspectives, survivor perspectives, and my own experience in working with survivors. Some of these insights develop from conversations with people working in criminal justice which have forced me to reflect on how torture is construed, but also how sexualized violence is discussed in some professional spheres. In some sense, this relates to language and sensitivity, for example a disagreement on the appropriateness of terms with a Detective Inspector who told me he was a "Rape Champion, but don't worry – I'm not a ripper". Apart from the utterly tasteless joke reference to Jack the Ripper by an officer investigating rape, 'Rape Champion' was at the time (the early 2010s) a title used to describe the officer with most prosecutions for rape. In another reflection, a meeting between Merseyside Women's Movement (a group I helped establish with a group of five other women in the North of England) and the local Police and Crime Commissioner (PCC) got off to a difficult start when we met to discuss the financing of rape support organizations in the area. The PCC repeatedly referred to "domestic violence services" as we repeatedly requested this be rephrased to the topic under discussion – rape and other forms of sexualized violence. Our efforts were unsuccessful and domestic violence terms prevailed.[1]

In short, this chapter centralizes mechanisms of silencing which can sometimes pervade how we see or respond to violence. In some areas it focuses on sexualized violence, and in others on torture and torturous violence more broadly. In all, ten mechanisms of silencing are identified and drawn out: epistemological silence; social silence; survivor self-silence; institutional silence; practitioner self-silence; spatial silencing; temporal silencing; protective silencing; preservation silencing; and capacity silencing. Some are fairly self-explanatory, others less so, but all will be expanded on to demonstrate the specificities of each form.

Architectures of silence

Before we move to address the specific forms and processes of silencing, it is worth setting a more generalized landscape of how silencing works, and the ways in which it is facilitated. Firstly, not all silence is deliberate and understandably (given the sensitivity of the subjects at hand) can work as means to avoid inflicting emotional harm on others, or avoiding placing the self in a position where one might feel uncomfortable. Annika, a psychologist, for example, emphasized that:

'[T]o meet trauma and to actually understand it means that you need to go into someone's story and someone's head, but that is very scary because that means that you will be affected by it emotionally, so that's also a kind of a distancing and in a way avoidance from the general public.' (Interview, 2017).

Similarly, Lisbet – who has a long career in supporting survivors of conflict-related sexualized violence, surmised that, "Many people who treat refugees are very reluctant to take the issue of sexual violence up and discuss it" (interview, 2013). The point inherent in this statement is that even those who are most exposed to discussing violence and trauma may still have a tendency to avoid sexualized violence specifically: an issue Lisbet had also been working to resolve. It is a reasonable approach for anyone to take, especially for people who are not regularly exposed to discussions on torture or other forms of violence. This is also something I have had to take into consideration in teaching and lecturing. Having spent my adult life working on sexualized violence, torture and conflict-related abuses, there have been times when I have not proceeded with as much recognition that violence in any sense is not something that forms everyone's knowledge base. This has been the case with students and where teaching violence has been a process of sensitization, negotiation and simplification, but also recently in a keynote session to older women in a national feminist association. At the end of the session the audience relayed a mixture of shock and exasperation, some commenting that certain findings (some in this book) were too awful or 'depressing' to believe could be true. In this instance, silence around violence has facilitated the maintenance of distance between traumatic realities and how we go about functioning in our everyday lives – all of which have been learning curves in understanding how silence can sometimes have its own benefits for individuals, yet does require challenging when appropriate or necessary, as we will go on to see.

Secondly, silence is multifarious in its reasons for being pervasive, particularly for survivors. In relation to her research on torture under Pinochet's regime in Chile (1973–1990), Elizabeth Stanley argued that, 'Silence for survivors has reflected concerns regarding protection, coping resistance, control, the inadequacy of language, the lack of listeners and the management of identities or recognition' (2004: 6). She goes on to point out, 'the reasons for this silence are varied, encompassing: the difficulties in communicating pain; desires to protect the self and others; attempts to manage identities; and confusion in the recognition of their perpetrator's humanity' (Stanley, 2004: 11). As such, silence should not be considered monolithic in form, but highly complex, often difficult to identify and pervasive, particularly in relation to torture, and sexualized violence specifically. To unpack and address this, we will now move to examine ten mechanisms that facilitate, reproduce and embed silence around torture, torturous violence and sexualized violence. These relate to ten forms of silencing, as presented in Figure 6.1.

Figure 6.1: Forms of silencing

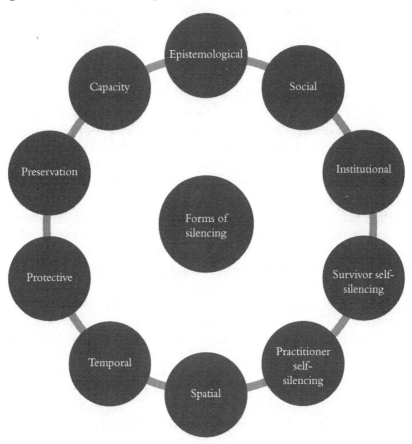

1. Epistemological silencing: Endemic forms of torturous and sexualized violence situated beyond the legal remit of torture are under-represented in torture literature. This silence is iterative

As we saw in Chapter 1, literature and discourse on torture seldom deviate from narrow legalistic definitions of torture. In one sense, that is understandable: it is up to researchers and practitioners to determine how they work with the subject area. However, one shortcoming is that torture in the wider consciousness is often determined by this definition itself, rather than in considering forms of violence which may be torturous in infliction or impact. This was identified in the discourses of practitioners, some of whom began their points based on law, but whose own experience of working with survivors drew them away from this as the discussions developed. Moreover, as the discourse analysis of pivotal texts and reports concluded, scholars and researchers seldom set out any contestation of the legal bases of torture. This means that even though legal definitions are often changing or expanding, the scope for recognizing or addressing violence beyond that inflicted by states, usually in confinement and for the purpose of information extraction, leaves significant voids in organically exploring violence that is torturous, which as we have established by now, is highly gendered in determining who is subjected to it.

A particularly useful approach to exploring epistemological silence, as I term it here, is Lois Presser's work on narrative criminology, and specifically her efforts to determine 'what goes unsaid in dominant narratives' (2019: 409–424). Her interest in this particular chapter is to consider what absences are inherent to a specific text or narrative. She considers three strategies: subtext, or evaluating figuration and multiple meanings; understatement, or assessing patterns of elaboration and explanation; and silencing, or asking what and whose knowledge is missing. She draws from Terry Eagleton who addresses power, stating:

> A dominant power may legitimate itself by promoting beliefs and values congenial to it; *naturalising* and *universalising* such belief so as to render them self-evident and apparently inevitable; *denigrating* ideas which might challenge it; *excluding* rival forms of thought, perhaps by some unspoken but systematic logic; and *obscuring* social reality in ways convenient to itself. (Eagleton, 1991, in Presser, 2019: 410; emphasis in original)

This is central to this book, and to the definition of epistemological silence – where the construction of knowledge is dominated by replications of powerful discourses and disciplines. Drawing from this, in her essay 'The torture device', Stephanie Athey argues that, 'While seeming to make torture visible, the archetype works to suppress historical memory of torture's trauma and enable its perpetuation in the present' (2011: 137). As such, the archetype is both useful in its narrowness, but limits other histories of trauma.

In some senses then, and even though many have worked to challenge it (see Nowak, 2006; Cakal, 2021), the narrowness of the definition of torture continues to facilitate a form of exceptionalism that reiterates the very hierarchy of cruelty that has been sought to be dissolved. This arguably influences the reduction of violences which *would* amount to state inflicted or facilitated torture, such as was seen with the use of Enhanced Interrogation Techniques. In his controversial book *Inside the Wire*, Erik Saar – a military linguist who worked interpreting at Guantanamo Prison – claimed 'I didn't personally see anything that I would label torture as most people understand the word' (Saar and Novak, 2005: 247). This is even despite the clear evidence of endemic levels of torture that had filtered through files and later biographical revelations from former detainees (Slahi, 2015), and as evidenced in the Senate Intelligence Committee Report on Torture (Jones, 2014). However, it is a curious statement because it tells us that even when one is face to face with torture in its legal sense, we can find other things to name it. When it becomes routine and the dominant social images of torture – the spiked chairs and over-stretched bodies which adorn many torture book covers – are extended to 'clean' and more mundane forms, then torture is longer exceptional. Instead, as Stanley Cohen so intricately detailed, we create forms of literal and interpretive denial to call what we witness or engage in something other than what it is (Cohen, 2001).

These forms of epistemological silence transcend expressly to sexualized torture and other forms of sexualized violence, which if not addressed in their specificity, risk being either written out of text – subsequently silenced – or subsumed with all other forms of violence even though it is specific in its inherent attachment to shame and stigmatization. Two examples come to mind: one is in Rejali's text *Torture and Democracy* (2007). A fundamental text for studying torture and a remarkable example of rigorous scholarship, it contains 24 chapters, many of which are dedicated to specific forms of torture. However, none address sexualized torture as a specific form of violence, with specific social implications and impacts attached, but rather refer to these as part of wider mechanisms of torture, such as electric shocks to the genitals. The second is a point raised by Christian, the psychologist we met earlier. When I asked whether there were any particular strategies or requirements for working with survivors of sexualized violence, he noted:

'I tried researching is there any protocols for specifically sexual violence. I couldn't really find any, but every trauma protocol, psychological protocol, would have a section about sexual trauma. I think it's very interesting, because apparently it's something that's always there but it's not specifically focused on. I think maybe that says a lot.' (Interview, 2021)

Herein lies the practical implications of epistemological silencing with the example of sexualized violence: if it is subsumed with other violence, or silenced altogether, an already difficult topic for practitioners is made even more difficult in the absence of supporting materials or protocols. This thus has the potential to cyclically silence survivors – if the tools are not there to support the practitioner or the subject is subsequently avoided, there is less opportunity for confidently supporting survivors of this specific, stigmatized form of violence.

To summarize, by adhering to dominant torture narratives, we continue to silence torturous violence and sexualized violence. This, however, is the simplest form of silencing to overcome: what it requires is for those researching, writing and practising in fields of trauma, violence and torture to more readily work towards centralizing it.

2. Social silencing: Sexualized violence provokes forms of social stigmatization that other forms of violence do not

Leading on from this and keeping to the issues of shame and stigma, torture and torturous violence attach complex senses of social silence – as Freja summarized:

> 'When you get to torture and you start to talk about it and you get to the second or third sentence of something that people have experienced, and people start to shut down, because it's so horrible that they can't deal with it, really. That's what makes it so hard.' (Interview, 2021)

This also resonates with the oral histories in Chapter 5, where although torturous violence and sexualized torturous violence are alluded to, little depth is developed and specificities are often avoided altogether. Indeed, torture and torturous violence are often around us in media and news representations, yet something we tend to avoid when confronted with realities head on.

In relation to social silence, sexualized violence has a particular potential to induce stigma and shame. Its intimate nature – often engulfed in socially constructed gendered ideologies of honour, masculinity and femininity – and conflation with sex and sexuality, means sexualized violence degrades and humiliates in ways specific to its infliction, as well as in its impact. As Amina outlines, even for survivors of torture in rehabilitation, it is a difficult violence to broach and disclosure often comes after a long build-up of trust, "it's not like it's the first torture form they tell me about. It always comes late in the treatment, if it even comes up, it's associated with shame and guilt, so people don't like talking about that part of it" (interview, 2021). Similarly, Laura states that, "sexual torture or violence is something that is not often first talked about when we get into the treatment. I can't even remember any patient who's offered that information in the beginning of a treatment period" (interview, 2021).

These issues will likely resonate with anyone working on sexualized violence. Certainly, they have been recurring themes across various projects for this book (see also Canning, 2017). For example, in 2013 Elias, a psychologist, reflected that "sexual problems are never mentioned", while Martin, who was working internationally on documenting torture, stated: "The kind of violence that women are exposed to is clearly sexual violence, but they do prefer not to talk about it" (interview, 2013). These two claims are understandable, since sexualized violence does silence. However, it is not accurate to state that it is never mentioned or that women prefer not to talk about it, but rather that there are social structures in place that prevent or restrict environments which are conducive to discussing sexualized violence. In these two examples, one may be the gender of the interviewees – both men – which can have implications for disclosure. This requires some level of self-reflection for practitioners, such as Christian who was deeply concerned with how clients might perceive him if they had been subjected to male violence, also concluding that, "I think it's also very good for them to have a male psychologist because they're sort of exposed to the idea that not all men have to be perpetrators" (interview, 2021). In some way then Christian is working to change assumptions of masculinity, while recognizing that this is a complex feat under these circumstances. Most important, however, is his ability to self-reflect and develop tools to address social silence in this context, as he was continuously doing in his practice.

Finally, a secondary form of social silence is much more structural in the context of refugees: the disengagement between social recognitions of histories of trauma, and the ways in which refugees and people seeking asylum are viewed in many societies. This point has underpinned many of these chapters, in particular Chapter 2 when considering the legacies and impacts of torture and torturous violence. However, it is well synopsized by Anne, a clinical psychologist, who reflects:

> 'You talk about refugee numbers and volumes, but you never, ever talk about what are these people coming with, like what have they been through and how does this affect them, and not even on a general level talking about refugees and what they need. You rarely hear discussions, I would say, on a sociable level, on what experience do they have and what kind of needs do they have because of that, and even less so with women.' (Interview, 2021)

This form of social silence perforates much further than practice or refugee sectors, but into the gaps in consciousness that pervade conversation, media and everyday lives. It is the rejection of glocalized realities, that histories from elsewhere can continue to affect people in the here and now. It is the silencing of histories of trauma or persecution which otherwise allows us as whole societies to overlook and silence refugee survivors in favour of social othering and misrepresentation (see Canning, 2018; McMahon and Sigona, 2018; Mayblin, 2019).

3. Institutional silencing: Institutions and organizations which adhere only to legal definitions of torture may have gaps in consciousness around sexually torturous violence beyond the narrow recognition of state violence and thus replicate silence around broader endemic and yet severe abuses, replicating a male-centric notion of torture

Combining points one and two, we can see that the ways in which torture is defined can lead to the inadvertent exclusion of survivors of torturous violence if and when their experiences do not conform to narrow legal dentitions, but do have the same impacts thereof. As we have already seen, this influences a gendered uptake in support, which for some organizations was at the closest 40 per cent women to 60 per cent men, and the widest 20 per cent women to 80 per cent men.

However, this is not to undermine the value of torture-specific organizational focus, but rather simply point out that these disparities exist. By recognizing this, organizations may consider moving towards broader definitions of what is torturous or – if not – help people to access other forms of support. Importantly, although social silence as discussed in the previous section perforates society systematically, institutional silence has the capacity to change more easily, since institutions and organizations often develop their own mandates and can influence whole sectors. This is an opportunity for influencing change, including supporting medical practitioners to recognize the plethora of implications histories of trauma may have when there are so many other issues at hand (van der Kolk, 2014) which they must also attend to. In relation to the gendered implications of this, Bodil, a director at a refugee advocacy organization, highlights, "a big problem [is] that many of the women have been abused in many ways and they don't get any kind of support or any kind of help when they arrive in Denmark. The doctors and the nurses, they don't ask a lot about these issues" (interview, 2018). However, this is also an issue which can be adjusted if institutional conditions shift to allow it.

4. Survivor self-silencing: Survivors may not wish to speak to their abuses due to a sense of shame or need to distance or dissociate from the violence

Moving towards the individual, and as has been a central point of this chapter thus far, is the ways in which survivors may regulate or avoid discussion or disclosure of torture, torturous violence, or sexualized torture and other violence. We have seen this in the oral histories of women in Chapter 5, pinpointed specifically by Antonia who eloquently asserted, "I don't want to, if I talk about my life, I will be sad when I get home today". This was a common consideration for practitioners also, who were often faced with a wall of silence but struggled to get past it. As Freja highlights, "if it's closer to your heart or closer to something that you've experienced, it's even more difficult … when it gets closer to something that would be something that you could experience or have experienced, obviously it's much more difficult" (interview, 2021). Understandably then, self-silence can be a mechanism for avoiding painful memories, or the sadness that they can induce. It may also be a means to reducing what Courtney Ahrens terms 'negative social reactions on the disclosure of rape' (2006. It is a reasonable and sometimes crucial means of self-support, so long as silence is not a manifestation of avoidance in ways which compound harm later.

There are various ways in which self-silence operates and as such can be difficult to address. For practitioners working to support people through claims for asylum, this is a difficult entity, in particular in addressing sexualized violence which may be relevant to gaining refugee status. Alan, a barrister representing refused applicants for asylum, considers that:

> 'I do work with people who are victims of sexual violence, I put them into two categories. I work with victims of sexual violence who tell me they're victims of sexual violence, but I also work with victims of sexual violence who don't tell me they're victims of sexual violence.' (Interview, 2018).

While self-silencing as a means of survival can be crucial for survivors, so too can disclosure if claims for refugee status are reliant on evidence of histories of persecution or violence, and subsequent potential for revictimization if the individual is returned. This is something which can be addressed, as we will discuss in the sections on spatial and temporal silencing. However, as the concluding chapter will highlight, access to support can be affected by wider structural issues relating to time constraints, space and trust building.

Although a highly individual experience, self-silencing is also intricately bound to the social, including for friends and family structures. Like torture and torturous violence, silence also wanders through lives, particularly manifest in cases of sexualized violence. Laura, a medical doctor, pinpoints this well:

> 'Also in terms of secrets in the family, secrets between husband and wife, between parents and children, and secrets both to protect the others, but also of course to protect themselves. Other impacts, well, there are also social impacts in terms of many people withdrawing, isolating themselves in their homes and only leaving the house if they have a medical appointment or if they have to go grocery shopping, for example. Sexual difficulties also; affected sexual life. I almost can't think of any way in which they're not affected.' (Interview, 2021)

Finally, and importantly, is the recognition that although a means of survival, self-silence may also impact on people gaining access to relevant support, rehabilitation techniques or other services. As Malin outlines:

> 'Even if they are not asking for it because it's very obvious that a lot of them, they're silently asking for it but they can't really speak up and say, "I need a therapist," or, "I need to talk to someone," they

suffer silently, so that's a problem. I think there is support to find for women in this situation but it's hard to make the connections.' (Interview, 2017)

As such, self-silence can impact obtaining support. However, as Malin highlights here, that can be addressed in part at least by practitioners. In the context of torturous and sexualized torturous violence, this can be done by recognizing that epistemological silence needs to be addressed if the structures around support for survivors are to adapt.

5. Practitioner self-silencing: Practitioners not specialized in working with the complexities of sexualized violence may avoid addressing it as a means to avoid, for example, retraumatization for the survivor, or a sense of discomfort for either party

This brings us to the other side of the same coin: practitioner self-silencing. Although silence may be deeply embedded in survivors' responses to violence, it is similarly so in practice, particularly practice which is not centred around sensitive subjects. As Tobias Kelly puts it, 'The issue is not so much that victims cannot voice their suffering, but that lawyers, doctors and other practitioners find it difficult to know when and where legally significant cruelty takes place. ... It is not the survivor's inability to speak; rather it is our inability to listen' (2012: 12).

With some interviewees, the desire to avoid seemingly awkward conversations was openly stated rather than alluded to in discourse. For example, Amalia – a detention custody officer – referred directly to the issue of awkwardness and sexualized violence, and the gendered implications of this:

Amalia:	We have some special people that are working with the women ... but not so much. And the women have some other problems than the men.
Victoria:	What like?
Amalia:	We have some women here in trafficking we can have, and it's very hard to talk to them. And many of them have been abused in some other ways. It's another problem.
Victoria:	What is it that makes it difficult to talk to women who are trafficked do you think?
Amalia:	I think you need some experience, I think. ... I can't understand how it is, I can't understand, and I don't want to blame them, so my attitude when I ask them thing or something that they. ... I think it's hard, I think it's very hard to talk to those women. I'd rather talk to the guys! (Interview, 2017)

This approach has been a common experience both when working with organizations and institutions who support (or, as in this case, control) refugees but are not developing tools to work with specific histories of violence. While it is of course not expected or advised every organization do this – given the complexity and expertise required for such strategies – we clearly see in this extract the implications for avoiding wanting to work with women due to their intersectional histories and disproportionate subjection to sexualized abuses.

This issue was reiterated by Pia, the director of a trauma and rehabilitation centre, who found that:

> '[M]edical doctors are not very good at identifying torture, whether it's sexual or not, just torture in general. They don't know how to look for the signs, they don't know how to ask, they don't refer, which has consequences for torture victims who are not allowed for example the Istanbul Convention, because no one really will assess the initial documentation or initiate the initial documentation.' (Interview, 2017)

This concern was corroborated by Anne, a psychologist, who thought that "medical staff within psychiatry or the medical healthcare sector, they also find it very, very difficult to ask, and how do you ask. I guess that we're afraid of asking because we don't know what to do with the answers" (interview, 2021). This should certainly not be taken as a blanket statement, but instead an example of an area that medical practitioners may benefit from support on learning and developing while studying, and for which more time should be structurally embedded, including during practice with people with complex needs or traumatic histories. This is something I have found in my own teaching also. Medical students can choose to study *Violence, Conflict and Forced Migration* as part of an intercalating year at undergraduate level. Recently, a student asked what relevance this could possibly have to her work as a medical practitioner in the future. Needless to say, by the end of academic year this question was answered: as discussed earlier, torture and torturous violence transcend the acts of violence, often with long-term consequences. These consequences manifest through health conditions, illness, chronic pain and other psychological, somatic and bodily pains. They are indeed an issue for medical practitioners, although (as some medical practitioners have told me) the time afforded to engage with such complex issues is seriously structurally affected by cuts to staffing, impacts on resources, and the often highly stressful nature of work in this sector more broadly.

Other interviewees drew out concerns for practices which actively avoided discussing some forms of violence even when it was within the practitioner's remit. Christian, for example, reflects:

'I had a supervisor whose practice was to talk about it [trauma] in every detail. That is sort of like the trauma-focused approach, to have very many details and the sensations and thoughts and feelings, but she has that very detailed, right up until the point that the penetration starts, and then she shies away from it, and I don't think that's wrong, really, but it's interesting that that's just the approach. Even though the client might want to talk about it or want to detail it, it's not really there, the practice.' (Interview, 2021)

Here we have a curious separation between trauma and sexualized trauma. This is perhaps a legacy of a phrase oft repeated by interviewees and practitioners in organizations, that sexualized violence is 'opening a can of worms' that is sometimes better avoided. The issue, however, lies in the ways in which this manifests, and who has the power to speak, direct conversation and – ultimately – the power to listen. To conclude this section, Anne considers the potential implications of this as a means to cyclically embed silencing: "[I]t's very, very difficult for most of our female patients. Why would you say, why would you talk about that if someone's not asking?" (interview, 2021).

6. Spatial silencing: The spatial set up of certain places are not conducive to trust-building or privacy that is inherently required to even begin to discuss sexualized violence of any form

Spatiality has extensive histories across the social, physical and psychological sciences. The concept has been studied and theorized through gendered uses of space (Valentine, 1992; 1996; Massey, 1994), cyberspace (Holloway and Valentine, 2000), global spatiality and its relationship to the local (Robertson, 2012), and space and constructions of age, youth and childhood (Massey, 1997 – and the list goes on. There is, as such, a plethora of ways in which one can interpret spatiality. In this point, however, the term *spatial* refers directly to the ways in which space is used or not used, engaged with or avoided. It is in one sense the physical space within which people live, move, work, create, engage and discuss. For the practitioners and survivors whose perspectives and experiences this chapter draws on, spatiality is rehabilitation clinics and centres, asylum centres, refugee camps, refugee reporting centres, immigration courts, social housing offices and doctors' surgeries. It is at the point at which some survivors wish to engage in therapy or support. For others, such as people seeking asylum, it is the spaces in which there exists a kind of structural coercion (see Canning [2020b] for further contexualization) which requires an applicant to disclose any and all histories which may be of relevance in the assessment of a claim for refugee status. These are very different contexts, but both are influenced by a kind of spatial silencing if and when spaces are not created that are conducive to either objective.

Given what we have explored in relation to torturous and sexualized violence in earlier chapters, it is clear that violence transcends various spaces, and the impacts can be pervasive at intersectional points of a survivor's life. As such, how space is constructed influences how and if people engage in such histories. This has been a fundamental concern for feminist researchers documenting violence, but also for practitioners working under duress in crisis situations, such as in camps, as well as hospitals and crisis centres. *Not* having adequate 'safe space' or privacy has significant impacts on disclosure. As Yüksel et al (2018) found when researching with Yazidi women who had fled the Islamic State offensive in Northern Iraq in 2014, 'It is also difficult to explain sexual assault in most situations, but it's even harder to explain it while living in camp conditions in a foreign country as a result of war and displacement' (2018: 129). Indeed, that is even in consideration of cases where there would be the infrastructure to do so. Considering that more people are living in camps globally than ever, and for longer periods of time, many such spaces do not have the capacity to do so, or to do so safely. This was similarly an issue I found in asylum centres in Denmark, including one which served as a safe space for survivors of trafficking, domestic abuse and torture, and which had no designated psychologist or support service. Likewise, in an interview at the deportation centre Sjælsmark, one Red Cross employee informed me that there were no resident psychologists at the centre to support migrants, even though she and her colleagues had repeatedly requested them (interview, 2017).

The issue of space and place was a recurring concern, not only for practitioners but for myself as a researcher. Space in detention centres, refugee organizations or deportation or asylum centres were seldom private spaces, making it difficult to discuss any forms of violence, let alone torture or torturous violence. This was even the case when trying to organize space away from public spaces, since people working in organizational capacities are also often seriously stretched in their remit and capacity (see Chapter 7 and Canning, 2021c). As Linnus, a lawyer working in immigration detention centres on asylum appeals, put it, the outcome can be that:

'When it comes to rape and violence overall, my impression is that they don't ask about it that much. You get an opportunity to talk about it, and describe it, but you don't have to go into details about it because it's … there is an understanding there from most case officers that this is not something that we can put any pressure on a person to talk about it.' (Interview, 2017)

Similarly, Miete highlights that:

> '[I]t's very, very little time to be able to establish trust, to be able to discuss difficult issues such as sexual violence, torture. So those reasons don't really come up if they do ever come up until very late in the asylum process, so that's a huge … *it's not a conducive environment to create trust*, to be able for people that have been subjected to torture violence to be able to talk about it and it's very rare that people are given a second interview.' (Interview, 2018; emphasis added)

This point brings me to the final aspect of spatial silencing. As Miete outlines, the environment that exists is critical to if or how people will be able to talk about sensitive issues, such as sexualized violence. When asylum claims are dependent on disclosure, as she refers to here in relation to a second interview, a window closes. Yet it is hardly surprising that anyone should not wish to disclose, particularly in open environments and/or without space to build up rapport or trust on one's own terms. As Amina, a psychologist, went on to state, "it very much depends on the trust. If there is a therapeutic ambience between the therapist and the client, then they're more likely to be open about talking about some of the things that they haven't told anybody before, but sometimes it's also whether there's a confidentiality" (interview, 2021).

7. Temporal silencing: Discussion and disclosure take time that is not always allowed for, or where the time to speak is not appropriate for the survivor

As with spatiality, temporality is a deeply debated and variously constructed entity. The multifarious nature of time has been studied by social scientists and physical scientists, as culturally specific and as an aspect of evolution (Hawking, 1989; Mead, 2002 [1932]; Durkheim, 2016 [1912]). Indeed, as Bhatia and I have argued elsewhere, time is an enigma, simultaneously something we may all seemingly understand, yet have little everyday conceptualization of (Bhatia and Canning, 2021: xv). However, we can probably agree one thing: time is complex.

For survivors of violence and trauma, the complexity of time can affect memory, experiences of the here and now, and the linearity of personal histories. This affects how people relay past experiences. Indeed, as Judith Herman highlighted, 'People who have survived atrocities often tell their stories in a highly emotional, contradictory, and fragmented manner which undermines their credibility and thereby serves the twin imperatives of truth-telling and secrecy' (Herman, 1992: 1). It stands to reason, then, that how people choose to – or even can – disclose or discuss torture, torturous or sexualized torturous violence is deeply personal. It can be dependent on the stage in their lives, an aspect of avoidance or dissociation, or one of emotional liberation through speaking through violence. For others, structures around them – such as criminal justice systems, truth commissions or asylum processes – temporally dictate if, when or how someone should discuss violence, trauma or atrocity.

Annika, a psychologist, reflects:

'Sometimes a few of them actually just blurt everything out in the beginning almost, like and like there's a need for just flowing out, but others it takes a long, long time, if it comes out even. And that I can notice more among the women. It might be because the women are more subjected to sexual violence and rape, generally speaking from my experience, but that can take a long time.' (Interview, 2017)

We can see here that, on one's own terms and given an environment that feels appropriate, some survivors can and will speak openly and cathartically. This reminds me of a fellow rape support phoneline volunteer some years ago who answered a call from an older woman. She had been subjected to rape many years earlier, and called the Rape Crisis hotline – not for counselling or referral – but to make sure she told someone before she died and could thus, for her, leave it behind. So for some survivors, catharsis is itself tied to temporality, when the time is right for her to speak.

For others, disclosure is part of a longer rehabilitative or support process, and this has been most commonly the case in my experience as a researcher and volunteer, and in speaking with practitioners who are at the forefront of psychological support and counselling. As Annika went on to state, and as discussed at the beginning of this chapter, this can be particularly complex for survivors of sexualized violence where stigma and shame require trust building: which takes *time*. As Becky, a refugee women's support worker, similarly reflects:

'I work with them, who have revealed to me after four or five months that they were raped or they were trafficked, and I'm a female and that's after meeting with them I don't know how many times. Maybe 12, 13, 14 appointments, and they'll be like, "Listen actually, I wanna tell you something," and there's that level of trust there.' (Interview, 2017)

Temporality is also an aspect which affects if and how survivors with refugee status access psychological or psychotraumatological support. Across various organizations, there is a pattern of people only accessing torture rehabilitation many years after gaining refugee status. There are three key contributors to this: firstly, that some organizations are reluctant to support people who are not secure in their status or citizenship. That is, there is debate as to whether the time is right to begin therapy or support if there is no guarantee that the person will still be in the same place over the period of time which is required. This is even though research evidences that any access to support has a positive influence on survivors. For example, in one assessment of 40 studies over a 30-year period, McFarlane and Kaplan found:

> In all, 36 of the 40 studies (90%) demonstrated significant improvements on at least one outcome indicator after an intervention. Most studies (60%) included participants who had high levels of posttraumatic stress symptomatology. Improvements in symptoms of posttraumatic stress, depression, anxiety, and somatic symptoms were found following a range of interventions. Little evidence was available with regard to the effect on treatment outcomes of the amount, type, or length of treatment, the influence of patient characteristics, maintenance of treatment effects, and treatment outcomes other than psychiatric symptomatology. (2012: 539)

In short, some support is better than no support. This was thoughtfully synopsized by Rikke, who argues:

> '[E]ven if you think people will be sent home next week, you are ethically ... you should intervene because these symptoms, I mean they're gonna have them when they go back as well. It's gonna help them, no matter where they are in their life, and it's not that the treatment necessarily is nice, because you're forcing people to deal with it, right? But you're providing coping strategies that even if you don't end up finishing the intervention they have something they can work on, continue working on.' (Interview, 2017)

Similarly, Freja considers that, 'one could still argue that no matter if they're sent back or not, giving them the rehabilitative work that we do will help them in any respect, so before we send them back, ensure that they can help rebuild society. It's not going to help, sending broken people back' (interview, 2021).

Interestingly, over the period of time in which research for this book has focused predominately on torture and torturous violence, this trend has shifted in some of the organizations I revisited which were now working with people seeking asylum. While it is difficult to pinpoint why, it may be reflective of the acute position felt with the increase of people directly fleeing conflict and persecution during and after the 2015/2016 refugee reception crisis.

Secondly, many survivors understandably wish to move on and rebuild without unearthing violent histories. Specifically in relation to gaining refugee status, especially after long processes of migration or lengthy periods stuck in bureaucratic asylum systems, some will experience a 'honeymoon period', where there is finally a light at the end of a long tunnel and life can move forward in a new place or space. This can later manifest, and as such accessing support becomes necessary long after the trauma.

This was discussed by many practitioners, in particular those working with survivors of torture or torturous violence specifically. Jens, a social worker specifically supporting traumatized refugees, reflects:

'We have a big group of patients who came here in the nineties, especially people from Bosnia and Balkan countries and everything got going, they had their children, the children starting school, they started working, they learned the language, they had stuff going on all the time and it worked out fine. But then 25, 30 years later the children move out or they're … a lot of car accidents are triggers for PTSD [post-traumatic stress disorder], so the PTSD might have been dormant for a long time and then they're re-traumatized.' (Interview, 2017)

Similarly, Marcus, a director at a torture rehabilitation centre, points out issues which arise:

'[I]f it takes 14 years or more for them to access the treatment, many of them have developed pretty chronic states where it's very difficult, even with our highly specialized treatment, to get them to a level of functioning where they are actually able to take on jobs or other forms of integrated life.' (Interview, 2016)

This was a common concern among practitioners, and also reiterates the issue raised in the previous section – that having someone to go to and space to do so is important and, as we can see, also related to time and temporality in one's life. This access is not the case for all, a concern Lotte conveyed:

'[W]e've found that that's been the case, 10, 15, 20 years, and then people are either hit by a car or somehow put into a new trauma that reinvigorates the old trauma, that they might succeed even for a long time. Some succeed for the rest of their lives no doubt.' (Interview, 2017)

Thirdly, again in relation to refugee survivors, it is clear that accessing organizational support is not only related to temporalities which are determined by survivors or even what is or is not available, but that wider systems affect if, when and how people can engage. As we will explore in much more depth in the concluding chapter, for refugee groups specifically, this relates to bureaucratic forms of bordering. According to Rajwinder, a member of the Queen's Counsel specializing in asylum appeals:

'[O]ne of the things that survivors of torture are often looking for is support that helps them get over their experiences, and if that support isn't really available to you until you've got your status, that may particularly delay your recovery if you've taken two years to get access to the counselling. So I think there are particular impacts, having to wait that long, and actually lots of torture survivors are at their most vulnerable when they first get here.' (Interview, 2017)

Temporal silencing, then, is not only based on the individual survivor or the organizations which work to provide support, but also bound to the structural – institutions, state facilitation of support and community and familial structures, all of which may change over time.

8. Protective silencing: Some survivors will avoid disclosing distressing accounts or histories to avoid causing emotional pain or harm to the person they are speaking with

Thus far we have considered ways in which people may silence or be silenced as a means to protect survivors from further harm or painful memories. However, protective silencing goes beyond protection of the self, but instead to those around who survivors do not want to cause distress to based on the traumatic nature of the atrocities or violence they have suffered. It can be an avoidance strategy for causing the listener harm. To reiterate Freja earlier, some things can seem to 'horrible' to discuss or put on to another person. This was coherently conveyed by Luna, who considers that:

'Most of the patients really just want to take care of not hurting the clinicians. Whether or not I'm a physical therapist or a psychotherapist or whatever, they just want to spare us the details because they're so gruesome. And just being open about it and talking about it, well, I hear this a lot, and I've heard very many gruesome stories from many people, puts me in the position to not only present myself as robust enough, if that is even a word in English, but also psychoeducating the patients that you're not the only one.' (Interview, 2021)

This draws out an interesting and important dynamic that is specific to torture, torturous and sexually torturous violence: silence as the modus operandi for protecting others. Interestingly, Luna goes on to consider the gendered nature of this, not only in the context of male patients, but in her position as a woman practitioner:

'I have to give the patient, especially the male patients, the impression that I can handle it, because many of them, they want to spare me the details in order for them to protect me, which they have been doing with everybody since they got out of prison or came into safety.' (Interview, 2021)

The latter of these points is not an irrelevance. Most of the practitioners I have interviewed in any of the projects for this book were women. In the most recent, only four out of 20 in-depth interviewees were men, which, as we saw earlier, was something Christian in particular considered deeply in his own practice. It reflects wider trends from the 1980s. Data from the 1986 American Psychological Association report, 'The changing face of American psychology', and the National Science Foundation show that 'the percentage of psychology PhDs awarded to men has fallen from nearly 70 percent in 1975 to less than 30 percent in 2008' (Willyard, 2011: 40). Similarly in the UK, psychology professions are pervasively female-dominated: 80 per cent of clinical psychologists and educational psychologists are women (Johnson et al, 2020). Although protective silencing is much broader than gender, it is nonetheless an interesting and important consideration when addressing or unpacking forms of silence, and one which exposes the deeply humane aspect of survival.

9. Preservation silencing: For some people, disclosure of certain forms of violence may have a negative effect on their relationships, community position or status, and as such silence becomes a form of self, family or community preservation

Building on from protective silence, preservation silence is an effort to maintain relationships, self-respect, community cohesion and one's own position or perspective of dignity (however one might see this inherently complex concept to be). The negative association of torture – that some things can be so *horrible*, as Freja said – can attach a kind of social trauma that supersedes how survivors are depicted or seen. This is not always the case, and indeed as Mookherjee showed in depth, can even encourage communities to consider survivors as just that: survivors rather than pitied victims or, worse, traitors (Mookherjee, 2010). Likewise, as many accounts from conflict and genocidal sexualized violence has exposed, the breaking of silence has itself allowed for a kind of ownership of narrative that allows for the preservation of difficult histories.

However, for many survivors, the threat or reality of stigmatization and shame, as well as blame, may be enough to induce a form of preservation silencing which partially or completely reduces the likelihood of disclosing histories of violence. For some, this silence pervades their intimate relationships, as Amina highlights: "I don't think any of the women that I have had so far have told their husbands what happened to them, and not even family members" (interview, 2021). This silence may be intricately linked to cultural and religious attributions of honour, in particular in relation to gendered honour. This works in complex ways: for women or girls, it is often tied to problematic sociocultural restraints on sexuality. As Klara addresses: 'Therapeutically, I think that sexual violence, also depending on your social context and your position in the social context, can be difficult to talk about because there is a lot of shame connected to these specific events' (interview, 2021). For men or boys, as we saw in depth in Chapter 4, it can be tied to notions of masculinity and unrealistic expectations around strength and survival, both notions which are tied to states and power where torture is concerned.

A final example of preservation silencing relates to that of those who have tortured or committed torturous or sexualized violence. Although a small group of practitioners working with families were also working with husbands who presented as perpetrators of domestic violence, including those working with individuals who had affiliations with violent states, armies or other paramilitary groups or indeed non-conflict-related 'gangs', there was very little discussion from perpetrators of violence. As Amina puts it, "in the last ten years that I've been working with this group of people, I haven't heard anybody say that they participated in any sexual act, and that's questioning as well".

This stands to reason: confronting our own harmful actions can cause us discomfort, with the potential to dissipate community status or familial relationships.

10. Capacity silencing: Reductions in support facilities, services and funding have significant effects on what services can be prioritized for provision, and if or how people with relevant or appropriate expertise can be employed. This affects how and what can be provided, often leading to prioritization of services needed for survival (such as food parcels, medical provision and clothing)

Capacity silencing is the simplest to conceptualize: many organizations involved in these studies were working to full capacity, often without predictable or sustained funds. As such, significant efforts were directed towards obtaining funds, an issue which diverts from the actual work required to support survivors of violence. This then affects if and how organizations can invest in supporting complex issues such as trauma, which take time and trust, and subsequently survivors of violence may be inadvertently silenced due to this lack of capacity. As Klara highlights in the context of sexualized violence, "talking about sexual exposure and sexual torture requires a higher level of trust, and requires doing trust in practice over a longer period of time before survivors feel safe enough to put it into words, because it can be loaded with big weights of shame" (interview, 2021).

Capacity is also affected by structural moves to Key Performance Indicators and increasing time restrictions on therapy, or even something as simple as seeing a medical doctor or General Practitioner. As Anne points out, "psychologists or nurses or doctors within the healthcare sector, have ten minutes to ask someone about their experiences of this" (interview, 2021). This then takes us back to the issues raised in the section on practitioner self-silencing, where debates are had about whether or not it is ethical to 'open a can of worms' if the practitioner does not have capacity to deal with the aftermath of doing so. Moreover, given complex traumata requires expertise to support, hiring, training and supporting practitioners who are qualified to do so is a feat in and of itself. Although I keep this point short here, it is a fundamental consideration in the following chapter when we come to discuss addressing and responding to torture, torturous violence and sexualized torture and torturous violence in the concluding chapter, particularly in emphasizing that without structurally embedded resources, including from funders, then capacity silencing will continue to manifest in organizations and institutions going forward.

The potential implications of unsilencing

The objective of this chapter has been to work towards 'unsilencing'. That is, to unpack and understand mechanisms and forms of silence around torture, torturous violence, sexual torture and sexualized torturous violence. To draw from the opening line from Darius Rejali, 'If we are to avoid past mistakes, then we must learn to speak intelligently about cruelty' (Rejali, 2011: 28). Understanding the multifarious nature of silence is therefore one feasible tool to do so.

This should not be taken to suggest that silence is equally distributed across time, all sectors, societies or individuals. Silence is not monolithic. Certainly, there are many examples where the voices of survivors have successfully led campaigns for justice, challenged silence, and brought realities of violence into the local, national and international spotlight. From the Comfort Women Justice Coalition to the International Criminal Tribunals for Rwanda and the Former Yugoslavia, from Freedom from Torture campaigns to the #MeToo movement, silence is perforated, shattered even, in ways that can be taken forward and reproduced institutionally and societally.

Silence can be a means to continue to function, for societies as well as for individuals, particularly in the aftermath of endemic violence or atrocities. As has been a central concern for many practitioners, ethics committees and scholars, retraumatization can have serious and negative effects, including symptoms which are reiterative of the trauma itself (Das and Kleinman,

2000), and this can happen in truth commissions. Indeed as Elizabeth Stanley expressly notes, 'Speaking out, then, brings about many potential benefits but it cannot be a process that is taken lightly' (2004: 19). Although not related to the justice objectives of truth commissions, one such example was raised by a person assessing asylum claims, whose role was to interview claimants and draw out personal histories. She reflects:

'One time I interviewed a girl and I understood that something had happened to her and after a while she was kind of, "I can't talk about it, I can't talk about it" and I told her, "Just so you know, I will never judge you by things that someone has done to you, and because this is not about you, I will never look at you in a different way, but we can take a break now and we can come back later and I will continue." And then in the end she told me, and it was just like she told me about this group rape and she turned around and threw up.' (Interview, 2017)

This is precisely a culmination of issues raised throughout this chapter. Silence can be temporal but functional, and disclosure requires trust, time and personal autonomy. However, some structures are built around coercive means to 'encourage' disclosure at points in a survivor's life which are not appropriate to the person, either to obtain support, or in this case obtain refugee status. This is a catch-22: some systems, including under the 1951 Refugee Convention, are so pervasively bureaucratic that disclosure, perceived victimhood and thus 'vulnerability' are intricately tied to tick-box events. In many cases, disclosing histories of torture specifically can be influential in determining whether someone can or should not be detained, as though detention in and of itself is not harmful (see Canning, 2017; Bhatia and Burnett, 2019).

The implications of *un*silencing have also been raised by both practitioners and researchers, in particular those who have concerns about the cultural limitations or implications of implementing highly Westernized concepts in conflict, post-conflict or in response to torturous regimes – itself an issue tied to neocoloniality of practice, health distribution and the socioeconomic and cultural dominance which is tied to globalized inequalities of healthcare distribution.

Drawing back to temporal silencing, although the evidence outlined suggests that accessing support even for short periods of time can be helpful for survivors, there remained some disagreements on the ethics of this in the context of asylum and the (very real) potential of deportation from host states. As Marcus, introduced earlier, raises in relation to asylum:

'[T]hat phase where they're still in a very insecure situation, it's definitely … it can be counterproductive to start doing trauma work in that phase. Because in doing trauma work, you're attacking also their strategies for survival, so you need to do it at least in a way where they will still be able to deal with their situation, because we don't know whether they'll be getting asylum or not.' (Interview, 2016)

This was – almost ironically – reiterated by Steffen, the governor of a closed detention centre, who notes, "we have one psychologist and she only works with coping mechanisms because we don't want to start out in a psychological treatment and then the day after you are sent back to some country where you have started something up that you cannot. … That would be unethical" (interview, 2017). Here, despite research to the contrary, ethical considerations lay not in the potential for the state to forcibly remove a detainee, but to start treatment that cannot be guaranteed to continue based on the structure of the state's border policies. This is not to say there are not legitimate concerns, and debates in this area are testimony to that. Rather, it is to emphasize that while structures around borders, camps, poverty and other sociopolitical contributors to globalized inequalities of experience pervade, then the complexities and implications of unsilencing cannot be overlooked.

Finally, in some senses, unsilencing can be affecting of preservation silence. Klara, a child psychologist, raised precisely these concerns in the context of children's wellbeing and the perforation of space with histories of torture, in that there may be an issue if,

'one parent that's silencing and not talking about it, but another parent in families can also be unfiltered speech. That would be typical of a parent that has been exposed to extreme torture, that because they are suffering and dealing with ways of being with these experiences themselves, of talking about it, sometimes not very consciously, talking about in detailed accounts about what they have been exposed to, and that is also one thing we know affects the children very negatively. … Talking unfiltered about your exposure is also a risk factor in terms of living; keeping on your everyday life, being with these experiences.' (Interview, 2021)

Indeed, if and when those exposed to torture or other violences come to speak, wider recognition is required that the journey is not always taken on one's own, but may affect those around them – positively as well as negatively.

Conclusion

As we can see then, unsilencing is not uncomplicated, and should not be taken as such. There are various significant considerations which relate to cultural appropriation and appropriateness, Westernized cultural dominance of psychology and psychosocial interventions, as well as neocolonial approaches to migration and borders, which – for people seeking asylum – harbour further forms of bureaucratic harm. Many of these points will be followed up in the concluding chapter.

What we can also determine is that silence in and of itself is not a simplistic notion, but comes in many forms. Some of these may be protective of the self and others, some may be gradually corrosive to survivors or those around them.

In all, the key point of this chapter has been to expose these complexities and create nuanced ways to view and discuss forms and mechanisms of silencing which perforate society, practice and consciousness in relation to torture, torturous violence and sexualized violence, including sexualized torture. It is not an invitation to break down barriers without consideration of the consequences, but to explore ways in which the pervasiveness of silencing can exclude, undermine or overlook the realities of survivors among and around us, so that we might more adequately come to recognize and address the consequences of trauma, atrocity and violence.

7

Addressing and Responding to Torture and Torturous Violence

Introduction

This book has sought to provide a lens which transcends disciplines and perspectives, incorporating intersectional feminism, and a zemiological approach to do so. By now, you may with agree some of the objectives, or with disagree the overall ethos of transcending the definitional boundaries of torture that underpins the central argument. It is an intervention which aims to draw debate rather than situate narrow or polarizing views, and hopefully it does so.

However, while all these aspects have been important, so too is considering responses to survivors. In undertaking interviews, I asked all practitioners across all projects to outline examples of best practice in working with survivors of violence, torture or with refugees (some worked across all these, some with one or two), and to consider what changes could be made to facilitate them to undertake their roles as well as possible. Similarly, as well as observing clear gaps – sometimes voids – in support in asylum centres and immigration detention, I also often asked people seeking asylum what would best support them.

This chapter outlines some of these responses. It draws out key issues and barriers to support in the aftermath of torture, torturous violence, sexualized torture and sexualized torturous violence. It does not seek to provide psychological or therapeutic answers to these questions: that is the role of psychologists, counsellors and psychotraumatologists, and I am none of these. Moreover, there are a plethora of texts, and the Istanbul Protocol (2004), which do this, developed by people with the expertise to do so, and for this there is a suggested reading list at the end of the chapter.

It does, however, offer some perspectives from practitioners working in these fields, as well as those working in managerial roles, legal capacities and in first response positions, specifically, in this case, with people seeking asylum in Europe or living in border camps across continents. Throughout this final chapter, we will consider the strengths and limitations of definitions of torture in practice and explore how the implications of silencing of violence can be structural counteracted. We will then move to consider structural issues which impede individuals' access to support, including ways in which borders compound the impacts of earlier traumas, and practitioners' capacity to provide it.

Addressing social silence, increasing consciousness: societal gaps in the recognition of trajectories of violence

At the very beginning of this book we reflected on how we consciously or unconsciously perceive or discuss 'torture'. It is a word regularly used for banal experiences (long meetings, an extended session at the gym – the list goes on) and in representations in exceptionalized and extreme forms of violence (think *Game of Thrones*). As participants pointed out in the penultimate chapter, with the exception of practitioners in this specific area, and perhaps some survivors, it is much less common to use the term 'torture' in everyday discussion unless it is being used flippantly. As Freja states, "When you get to torture and you start to talk about it and you get to the second or third sentence of something that people have experienced, and people start to shut down, because it's so horrible that they can't deal with it, really" (interview, 2021). Anyone reading this book who works in or has been supported by sectors responding to violence may have experienced this: the uncomfortable moment when your own work or experience or research perforates social norms, and you find yourself with a person or group whose facial expressions and body language tells you this discussion is too uncomfortable. Whether it is a lecture theatre or a dinner party, how sensitized or desensitized to hearing or speaking about torture or other violence is relational to the space we are using, and whether those around us 'shut down' to the lived realities of violence.

To this end, I am not advocating that every space should be filled with discussions of torture or sexually torturous violence. We cannot know if all of those around us have lived free of violence, or if we have the potential to induce painful memories. Moreover, in my experience, the inability to separate violence from other everyday activities can make for very dark views of the world indeed.

However, there are three fundamental issues which do require us to speak more openly and directly about torture, torturous violence, sexualized torture and sexually torturous violence. Firstly, there are significant gaps in social consciousness around the complex histories of survivors, and this impacts on access to support for survivors more broadly. As Miete states:

'[T]here's very little awareness and knowledge about the difficulties that torture survivors have to be able to tell their story in the first place, but also to do it in a coherent, chronological way. It's difficult for everyone but especially for them, for anyone suffering from PTSD [post-traumatic stress disorder] or whatever and the same for women subjected to torture or some sort of sexual violence.' (Interview, 2018)

Secondly, these gaps can affect local organizations, non-governmental organizations (NGOs) and international non-governmental organizations (INGOs), and first response units in areas of acute crisis. For officials and institutions assessing claims for asylum, there can be a lack of awareness of the impacts of trauma on the chronology of memory (see Herman, 1992). Stories which have muddled timeframes are often seen as lacking in credibility and thus asylum is refused (see Montgomery and Foldsprang, 2005; Canning, 2014; 2017). Even organizations and institutions which do not specialize in such violence benefit from information, training and consciousness raising to ensure complexities of experience are understood even if not therapeutically addressed. I have spoken many times to volunteers, social workers and activists who have been deeply affected by personal narratives of violence but had little or no knowledge of the complexities or prevalence. This subsequently leaves gaps in if and how people working with survivors can respond, as the following conversation epitomizes:

Victoria: Does anybody ever disclose experiences of violence or torture to you as well?
Johan: Yeah. I have heard about torture and violence from people.
Victoria: And have you been given any training on how to respond?
Johan: Nope. But I am searching for it. (Interview, 2021)

Like Christian in the previous chapter, there have been many times when knowledge – some of which is crucial to the demographic that practitioners are working with – is sought, but not incorporated or readily accessible.

Finally, and drawing back to the core of the first half of this book, a less obvious form of silencing takes place through scholarship and research which cyclically disengages with addressing what is meant by 'torture', and instead takes its lead only from legal definitions. Drawing from Lois Presser's points on the exploration of narratives through what goes *unsaid*, rather than what is written or spoken, this has led to a plethora of knowledge which frames torture as something which is predominately experienced by men. In the publicly political sense – that is, torture for the extraction of information by or with approval from state officials, usually in some form of confinement – this is accurate. However in relation to domestic or interpersonal torturous violence, it is not.

This is not inconsequential. In some ways, this dominant definition plays into practice since organizational mandates are often dependent on narrow legal approaches, as has been highlighted in Chapters 1 and 3. As Anne synopsizes, "we reject people that need our help because that's not defined as torture or war experiences. So we're broad, but at the same time, we're narrow and I think we're missing a lot of patients, female patients mostly" (interview, 2021). However, by addressing this in practice – if not in law – there is significant scope to reduce these voids and gaps and more holistically encompass support for survivors of torturous violence. Pia outlines this in relation to the rehabilitation centre she directs, stating:

'People from Eritrea, Afghanistan, Syria, who just managed to leave their country before abuse but then, coming to Sweden, they suffered from very, very severe trauma symptoms, but due to experiences taking place on their way over. So now we changed our criteria and when referring to sexual violence this makes an enormous difference as well, or gender-based violence because a lot of women mainly are exposed to very severe sexual violence, gender-based violence, on their way over, because our new criteria are trauma related to war, torture and/or flight. So, this is an important difference.' (Interview, 2017)

In short, although torture and torturous violence, and sexualized torture and torturous violence, are disproportionately subject to mechanisms of social silencing, these can be challenged and, where and when appropriate (taking into particular account the significance of cultural sensitivities and the use of language – see for example Omowumi Babatunde, 2018) overcome through processes of consciousness raising. It is this element we move to now, to focus on the value of intersectional feminism as a tool to do so.

The significance of intersectional feminism in consciousness, practice and approach

Intersectional feminism offers us ways in which we can see multiple life experiences and trajectories and how structural and institutional inequalities can disproportionately affect people based on race and ethnicity, citizenship, gender and sex, sexuality and orientation, wealth and poverty, ability, illness and age (see Davis, 1975; hooks, 1984; Crenshaw, 1989; 1991). I would argue that these should not be taken as a list or tick-box in which to create a kind of hierarchal oppression Olympics, as is sometimes evident in equality and diversity discourses. Instead, intersectional feminism can support organizations and practitioners in recognizing structural violence and its impacts on survivors. We will explore, for example, how structural and institutional violence directly affects survivors who are seeking asylum later in this chapter, as well as the negative implications this holds for practitioners.

For now though, this point is really about emphasizing the value of feminist approaches. Similar to the examples given in Chapter 4 on being approached with an air of suspicion for centralizing sexualized violence and gender, so too have I worked with organizations which have side-lined feminist approaches as 'soft', or accepted that they had fewer women service users because – as one asylum support organization manager told me – it is too difficult to address endemic sexism in male-dominated spaces. The former in fact contradicts the latter: if feminist approaches are 'soft', why is addressing gendered and patriarchal violence so hard?

There are many times when it is clear that the lack of recognizing gendered intersectionality affects support, and has direct implications on whether or not organizations or individuals within them will respond to gender-specific needs. The first, and similar to the example of the asylum support organization mentioned earlier, is that some spaces are not open to demographics other than men. As Chapter 3 highlighted, this can in part relate back to the narrow mandates of organizations working with torture, where survivors that meet the criteria are much more likely to be men for political reasons, including those who have been subjected to sexual torture in confinement. Simultaneously, since this more easily fits torture narratives, it is less likely that male survivors – even of sexualized torture – access organizations which respond specifically to sexualized violence. For some, this was directly relevant to who they worked with, for example Anne comments that, "a lot of the men seeking help have had experiences of imprisonment or being detained, and then it's easier to apply our intake criteria on that" (interview, 2021), while Elliot, who worked in coordinating support for unaccompanied minors, remarks that: "We have all unaccompanied minors but we mostly come in contact with men, that's the main group, there's a big man majority" (interview, 2017).

I went on to interview some of Elliot's colleagues and a refugee woman who was setting up a women's space precisely because there was such a significant gap for unaccompanied girls. In a similar scenario, Per, the head of unit in an immigration detention centre, states:

'[W]hen we do have a person, whether it's a male or a female that we know, for example, has been traumatized, sexual violence, someone who has been captured, tortured, imprisoned, raped, who reacts strongly to male staff or female staff, then we try to take that into consideration, but we don't have a routine that no males [are allowed] in the female section.' (Interview, 2018)

Here we see a hybrid: a consciousness that there may be specific histories which require sensitive approaches, but not the implementation of a structural strategy which would facilitate a gender sensitive environment where people could feel safe (and I emphasize here, as an immigration detention abolitionist, these are minor reforms which do not replace the civil liberties that are taken from migrants in these spaces – see Canning, 2020c; 2021b).

At times, the deliberateness of excluding women and girls was upfront. Like Amalia in Chapter 6, the complexity of 'dealing' with gender-specific experiences can be a complexity too far. For example, Vera, a regional director of an international refugee response programme, comments: "I don't think that our organization here, as part of the [NGO name], I don't think we are the best to support those girls or women, I think that there's other organizations. ... Sometimes I think it's good with special women's organizations to support" (interview, 2017).

This point is worth unpacking. It is absolutely the case that specialist organizations are essential in ensuring that certain forms of trauma are responded to with expertise, for example, those which work with people fleeing domestic violence, with women seeking asylum, or with survivors of torture or torturous violence. To employ a phrase used by Morten, not every organization should be "an NGO supermarket" – promising to supply answers to every social issue imaginable. While these broad statutes have their own value, some experiences require deep and niche responses. However, in emphasizing the value of intersectional feminism as well as the recognition of broader forms of torturous violence, I am not advocating a dissolution of niche approaches – quite the opposite. Instead, I am advocating a reflexive and intersectional feminist-informed response to social issues which otherwise go side-lined. While Vera is right to say that there are organizations better placed to work with women, women still use the services the organization that she works for supplies. They attend language classes, come to coffee mornings and live in asylum centres. As such, by avoiding the points that intersectional feminism encourages us to confront, we run the risk of inadvertently marginalizing groups that make up the societies, communities and organizations we live and work with. By recognizing this, we have scope to collectively challenge mechanisms of exclusion.

Finally on this point, intersectional reflexivity also allows us to more fully consider how people see practitioners. Christian, the psychologist we have heard from throughout, was particularly conscious of his role as a male psychologist working with men survivors. Similarly, Laura, a medical doctor, reflects:

'Some men prefer to have a female interpreter when we talk about these things; some people prefer to have a male interpreter when we talk about these things. But I think there, what I do is, I again ask more openly about what they've been subjected to and then see how much they want to talk about, and it is definitely one of the things that the patients have more difficulty talking about.' (Interview, 2021)

For others, such as Johan, a nurse working in an immigration detention centre that otherwise lacked gendered recognitions of support requirements, this influenced how he approached women requiring medical examination:

'I think that it should be difficult for them too because it has been a man who abused and done this and I could believe that for these women they don't trust a man. As I told you before, therefore I always have a woman by my side or if the woman [says] "No, I don't want you to go near me", then I have to get a female nurse instead.' (Interview, 2018)

These excerpts demonstrate reflexivity in practice. In every sense, the point I am making is not about dissolving specialist organizations, but instead developing a gendered and intersectional consciousness which supports us to recognize the complexities of experience, violence and survival, and which can be resisted as a 'soft' approach or a 'step too far' out of (particularly male-dominated) organizations and institutions. The flip side of this takes us to institutionalized racism and sexism at worst, and intersectional insensitivity at best.

Intersectional feminism is rigorous in its endeavours to consider multiple perspectives and experiential epistemologies, while centralizing the structural issues which relate to demographics which disproportionately experience certain forms or violence in certain spaces. By recognizing the value of this, how we construct knowledge, research, rehabilitation and other responses need not be monolithic, but instead open up ways in which methodologies for exploration or support are inclusive and holistic. It is not a threat to men's access to torture support: rather, a way of complementing perspectives which support consciousness raising to encourage us to see ways in which structural issues can impact differentially, and even across a person's life trajectory.

Separating sexual experiences from experiences of sexualized violence and torture in language

As Chapters 4 and 6 outline, there is often a conflation between what is sexual, and what is violence. The infliction of sexualized violence can erode a person's sense of sexual self and autonomy, and the intimate nature inherent to it often impacts on sexual health. As we have also seen, it can call into question one's own sexual preferences or even orientation, particularly if the physiological reaction has been stimulation or orgasm. For men survivors of male violence, this can result in questioning if he is homosexual and – as some practitioners highlighted – negative feelings towards gay or Lesbian, Gay, Bixsexual, Trans, Intersex and non-Binary (LGBTQI) people more broadly. Similarly, gay or bisexual men may have their sense of sexual safety negatively affected towards other sexual relationships with men. For women, sexual relationships and one's own sense of sexual self can be affected in many forms, including avoiding (or trying to avoid) sex, increasing sexual contact (sometimes as a means to dissociate from negative experiences) or inducing retraumatization during sexual acts.

These are all understandable responses to unreasonable subjections to violence. It is at this juncture, then, that it is relevant to consider the two entities as separate even if connected. To reiterate Luna's point in Chapter 6, "It was violence in the same way that everything else was violence, and it had a purpose, which was breaking him down, which often brings us to the whole sexuality talk: what is sexuality? What is intimacy? What is pleasure within the body?" (interview, 2021).

These are conversations that can be had with survivors, but also among ourselves as researchers, practitioners and/or students. In workshops, lectures and training sessions, it is worth asking people – and again, ourselves – what is sexual? What is violence? How are they distinct and are there times where we, as individuals, do not see them as so? If the answer is no, then can or will we ever? There are many ways this can be taken forward, all of which should consider when it is or is not appropriate to use this form of unsilencing, and how it fits the cultural environment in which we are working at the time. For the second of these points, the issues raised about language in previous chapters also require thorough consideration. Words such as 'rape' might not be used even when the act is rape, and terms such as 'he did/had sex with me' are commonly used to convey this (see Taylor and Shrive [2021] for a fuller discussion on this).

Barriers to supporting refugee survivors: the compounding of trauma through border harms

The importance of creating a safe space for survivors of trauma, torture and sexual abuse is well established in psychosocial and feminist literatures (Patel and Mahtani, 2004: 33; Sjölund et al, 2009; Women's Resource Centre, 2010; Kinzie, 2011). As Herman argues, 'The first task of recovery [from traumatic experience] is to establish the survivor's safety. This task takes precedent over all others, for no therapeutic work can possibly succeed if safety has not been adequately secured' (1992: 159). This should arguably be taken literally, in that space and time should be allocated to the development of rapport and trust with survivors seeking support, as well as structurally in that safety should be secured to avoid further future abuses or returning to harm.

It goes without saying that there are many people who are being subjected to torture and torturous violence who are far from safe spaces. This transcends the spatial boundaries within which torture and torturous violence often take place – it is prisons and custody suites, but also people's homes, schools and other institutions, internally displaced person camps and closed detention centres. For some people, safety from an abuser or abusers is made practicably impossible, physically in terms of imprisonment or other forms of confinement, psychologically if not physically for those subject to abuse from coercive partners or institutional staff. For people whose subjections are ongoing, safety can mean life or death.

For people who have survived such violence and seek sanctuary elsewhere, notions of safety are severely impacted upon by lengthy asylum processes, indefinite detention in some areas, and months or years spent in border camps. The constant fear of forced deportation and repatriation are often at the forefront of asylum applicants' consciousness. Space is neither figuratively or literally provided in terms of a guarantee of safety, affecting people's temporality and capacity to deal with the past or plan for the future. As Luna synopsizes:

'[T]he first thing they need when they come here is a sense of safety. That's the most basic need they have. Food and clothing and a warm place to stay, obviously that's important, but the sense of safety and sense of progress. "Now we're safe, so we can move on from here and we can build a normal life." That constant threat about being sent back or being handed over to some refugee camp in other places around the world is harmful for the families and especially for the kids, because even though the kids are small and doesn't quite get the political … around being alive and they're here, they get the parents' insecurity and their anxiety for what's gonna happen now, so just give them a sense of safety for a longer period of time.' (Interview, 2021)

Subsequently, for people seeking asylum, even the most basic of needs cannot be met if border controls continue to infiltrate practically every aspect of one's life, as we'll soon see. This was a point Mahira, Faiza and Asma in particular emphasized in each oral history. No matter what they had already come through, the process was intent on making every aspect of their lives more difficult, with a very confusing and unclear endgame.

While this clearly differs for refugees (who may have some level of temporal protection through refugee status) permanent status has been reduced to the point of eradication in many countries. Instead, people often find themselves reapplying for status after, for example in Sweden, every 13 months. Furthermore, as one asylum support worker highlighted in the

British context, "when they get their status. ... In some ways it's a bit of anti-climax because a lot of harm has been done in that seeking asylum period to their health, their mental health, their wellbeing" (interview, 2017). Thus, survivors of torture and torturous violence are subject not only to physical border controls, but also the existential and psychological impacts of uncertainty and temporal stuckness which serve to inflict further forms of harm (see also Griffiths, 2014).

Support is impeded by broader structural architectures of bordering and asylum systems

Having written fairly extensively about the harms of asylum systems and processes, I do not wish to tread old ground or regurgitate what has already been said (including by many others – see Khosravi, 2018; Mayblin, 2019; McMahon and Sigona, 2018; Abdelhady et al, 2020; Bhatia, 2020). However, the extent of harms inflicted through the bureaucratic violence of asylum systems cannot be separated from the experiences of survivors and the impacts thereof. As such, it is worth reflecting on some considerations of how these processes play out in reality, and the multifarious ways in which they can impede rehabilitation, access to support, and addressing trauma for survivors of violence. To echo concerns from Mila:

'[W]hen you work with these clients, you're not just working with the trauma; you're working with immigration issues around coming to a new country, what that actually means, having given up so much in your country of origin: loss of family, loss of life, loss of work, loss of identity, loss of future, in a way.' (Interview, 2021)

Moreover, some aspects are so insidiously tied with bordering and threats of deportation (such as for people still in domestically abusive or torturous environments and relationships, and people who have been trafficked and subsequently abused) that any considerations for barriers to support cannot overlook the significance of these. This point is relevant across all facets of asylum processes, and is deeply embedded in the inherent isolation built into immigration detention and offshoring. Indeed, Natasha Tsangarides (2012) addressed the detention of torture survivors as 'a second torture'. Even in the case of survivors of sexual trafficking – which as we have seen in Chapter 4, can amount to torturous violence: "There's an active disincentive [to engage with authorities for protection] because the moment that they leave the exploitative situation they're actually breaking immigration laws themselves" (Irena, barrister, interview, 2018; see Jobe [2020] for further discussion on the complexity of this).

The ways in which bordering affects individuals also ricochet off practitioners, affecting the mechanisms of support developed to engage survivors. As Annika puts it in relation to psychological counselling:

'Many of the people I meet are also being taken down by the system, by the asylum process because it's often long and during that time you often don't work and if you do work you do underpaid jobs, so in that sense it takes a lot of time so the system, it's almost like the system slowly breaks you down bit by bit in quite a few cases.' (Interview, 2017)

This was reiterated through all the projects undertaken for this book, where the impacts of poverty and destitution were tied to the reduction in the right to work for people seeking asylum. As Amina echoes, this is compounded by reductions in length for the right to remain, something which has shifted on a global level, meaning people cannot gain a sense of temporal safety and security, which is exactly contradictory to what Herman emphasizes as a basic requirement for people to work through the impacts of trauma:

'Every second year they have to apply for a new one [permission for the right to remain], so the basic security is missing, and even the economic situation for the refugees, most of them are receiving money that only covers the rent, so they are not able to afford sending their children to football or even themselves participating in some kind of physical ... fitness or whatever, and in effect it's excluding them more from society.' (Amina, interview, 2021)

Similar issues arose in relation to family reunification, particularly in the aftermath of the refugee reception crisis of 2015/2016 in Europe. As more people arrived, more stringent measures were placed on bringing families across borders to safety – including women who were increasingly stuck at borders or 'left behind' (see Schuster et al, 2021). For some, including people I spoke to from Syria and Afghanistan, this was itself compounded with endless worry for family in areas affected by conflict and with escalating violence. Anne states:

'[Reductions in reunification] is a huge problem for conducting successful trauma treatment, because it's nearly impossible to focus on trauma, and that's what we're supposed to do, when everything else is ... when you worry about where to live and where your family's at and the economic situation. That's a huge problem, or barrier, or challenge.' (Interview, 2021)

More banal and everyday forms of control also impacted on how and if survivors of violence would engage with formal services which are intended to offer support. For example, women I spoke with who were living in an asylum centre space for 'vulnerable' and trafficked women were often cautious not to outwardly appear as though they were unwell or struggling, for fear that their children may be removed if they did not present as 'good' or capable mothers. Amina echoed similar points, that "women are also afraid that if somebody knows that they are not doing well mentally, maybe that will be a reason for them to remove their children. I think there is a lot of barriers coming out I haven't seen before" (interview, 2021). Even if and when this was not a risk, women often regulated their behaviour and appearance accordingly, even if it meant not accessing support. Again, this reiterates the importance of intersectional feminist approaches that take into account the more insidious ways in which gender is regulated through borders, and the implications this can have for survivors of violence and even those still in domestically violent circumstances.

Finally, some practitioners aligned the gap between social recognition of torture and torturous violence with anti-migrant sentiment and racism. For example, Laura considered that further public knowledge campaigns about torture may counteract narrative that facilitate social othering, as she considers, "if there was a better appreciation of our patients' difficulties, because it hurts to hear patients describe how they're being spat at on the street and just being treated poorly by other people who are ignorant, but that's something big, a big change" (interview, 2021). The misrepresentation of Muslims in particular was a concern for some practitioners, likely related to increases in Islamophobic laws and policies (for example, during the course of one project, Ghetto laws were introduced in Denmark which specifically targeted Black and migrant communities, and facial coverings for religious reasons were banned in 2018). Mila reflects on the implications of this on her clients, as well as how that impacts on her role as a White practitioner working with survivors of torture specifically:

'They live segregated and there's a very strong anti-Muslim, anti-difference rhetoric and that really affects my clients and it really upsets me. I feel really pissed-off, because I feel like the society here, it's super-un-inclusive, and really not accepting of a different person who has a different worldview and might be able to bring something else useful to the table, so it's just trying to fit people into the Danish box: "If you can't give us what we're used to, then you're not useful to us." I think that really affects my clients and that of course affects their engagement with treatment, when everything else seems to not go their way.' (Interview, 2021)

In summary then, if and how survivors can engage with support services is marred by restrictions and processes of bordering which are not only impacting for people seeking asylum generally, but for survivors of torture and torturous violence specifically.

Recognizing and addressing impacts on practitioners as well as survivors

Working with refugee groups can be a fundamentally complex vocation. Although roles in this sector vary considerably (such as lawyers, psychologists or advocacy and support workers), the lived experiences of people seeking asylum or living as refugees can impact on the people supporting them in a multitude of ways. Likewise, the working conditions of practitioners can be reflected in the standard of care or services that they are able to offer when supporting people with complex lives, refugees and survivors of violence and persecution in particular. This is made particularly difficult when the landscape of refugee rights becomes unstable and ever-changing, an outcome of internationalized constant, ever-tightening immigration and asylum laws in receiving states.

Vicarious trauma and compassion fatigue are two of the most cited problems in working in this area. The former relates to emotional or psychological distress based on hearing or responding to trauma experienced by others (Barrington and Shakespeare-Finch, 2013). The latter refers to the emotional implications which can develop for people working at the frontline of response to trauma or other social problems, but feel restricted in their ability to do so due to exhaustion or burnout (Ray et al, 2013).

Alongside the obvious cause for concern for the wellbeing and mental health of practitioners, this trend carries a potential secondary but serious issue. That is, if practitioners are increasingly negatively impacted by restrictions in policy and their ability to work well under changing conditions decreases, then this will negatively impact on the people seeking asylum who require their support or care. Given the already evident barriers in accessing legal, psychological or social support for this group, in particular for survivors of violence (Jobe, 2009; Baillot et al, 2014; Emejulu and Bassel, 2017; Baillot and Connelly, 2018), then compounding these difficulties likely means we are at the edge of a precipice in exercising and administering crucial forms of support for some of the people who most need them, an issue already arising in the context of the COVID-19 pandemic (Nisanci et al, 2020). Practitioners and those working in state and NGO sectors were increasingly affected by the wider political environment. As increasingly punitive measures were taken regarding the control of migrants to and within the case study countries, practitioners were less enabled to undertake their roles well. This compounded a sense of powerlessness, and diminished faith in the value of their roles.

Five key themes[1] emerged from coding and subsequent critical discourse analysis of interviews with practitioners which draw attention to key issues and barriers for support, namely:

1. Restrictive asylum law and policy negatively impacts on the role of practitioners.
2. Emotional and psychological issues in working with refugee groups are compounded by increasingly hostile sociolegal environments.
3. Practitioners report feelings of powerlessness, helplessness and a structural diminishment of their professional roles.
4. Roles are increasingly bureaucratized, and so practitioners report 'managing expectations' of clients rather than fulfilling their assigned role/profession.
5. Trust in state responses to migration is diminishing.

This phenomenon creates a cyclical environment: sociopolitical hostilities against migrant groups (broadly, but here people seeking asylum specifically) compound already difficult working conditions for practitioners in this area. In turn, impacts on practitioners have potential for negatively affecting the people they support, thus disempowering a group which is already recognized as being disproportionally affected by violence, conflict and previous trauma.

The implications of this are threefold. Firstly, practitioners can experience negative emotional impacts as the conditions under which their service user group live deteriorate: an issue inherent to increased hostilities for migrants. Secondly, people are experiencing a sense of deprofessionalization and powerlessness in their work. Lastly, practitioners who feel they are over-stretched or 'managing expectations' may be less able to engage with the complexities of refugee groups, even with the best will in the world. This in itself is disenfranchising for people working in this field.

Practitioner ideas for best supporting survivors: what would work in an ideal world?

As already mentioned at the outset of this chapter, all practitioners in all three projects were asked what would be beneficial for themselves or their organizations. In short, what tools would you require to undertake your role to the best of your ability? The most common request from practitioners in interviews as well as in ethnography and advocacy related to sustained funding, and so this point will be drawn out further in the next section. To be sure though, organizations are not all in the same position so the requirement for funding is not equally felt across small, medium or large organizations, and what finances can be spent on can be dependent on variable remits, meaning those at the coalface of responding to survivors may be more limited in capacity to offer or engage with additional needs in practice.

I have also asked many survivors of violence the same questions, including in ideation workshops and focus groups. These ranged from being able to access rehabilitation at all (many areas where research was undertaken had no specialist centres near) or having the personal capacity to call a rape counselling or support service, to having childcare to be able to connect with people and build support networks and friendships, and money to travel (including to places of worship).

For people who were seeking asylum, these structural problems superseded longer-term considerations for support. As I discussed in *Gendered Harm and Structural Violence in the British Asylum System* (Canning, 2017), some of my projects, including originally my PhD, were focused on the impacts of conflict-related sexualized violence on survivors seeking asylum. However, this focus was dwarfed at times by the sheer number of issues that the process of seeking asylum caused, often deflating any capacity to meaningfully engage in trauma support. This was linked also to the threat of dispersal, a policy which allows for people seeking asylum in the UK (as the case study example in the book, but relevant in many other areas) to be moved around the country at little notice, subsequently cutting access to services and support.

As you can imagine, there are many examples that could be drawn from. However, the most commonly cited are listed in Table 7.1, with some excerpts from practitioners that highlight the points made succinctly. I focus specifically at this point on practitioner views as a means to emphasize what can be strategically addressed by structural means, so that provision is amplified. After all, a practitioner's working conditions are a service user's support conditions – the better they are for practitioners and organizations, the better provision there can be for survivors.

Reflecting on inequalities in wealth and finance distribution

Some of the concerns raised in addressing and responding to survivors draw from my own activist experiences, advocacy roles and ethnographic research with organizations and refugees over the past 15 years. Some relate to capacity and lack thereof, some to problematic gaps in organizations and institutions in supporting practitioners themselves. Other issues raised highlight structural problems and the consequences thereof.

This final point is a political one: it relates to the ways in which states prioritize finances and capital, in particular in the aftermath of the violence inflicted by the global financial crash of 2007/2008. Although differences exist in the socioeconomic environments of the projects, many organizations

Table 7.1: Recommendations from key practitioners

Requirements for improved conditions for practice	Views from practitioners
Funding	"It was always underfunded, it was always dependent on good grace and goodwill from community organizations and existing refuges and places that dealt with domestic violence and so on. So, in terms of women's issues as refugee and asylum seekers they were just expected to be absorbed into the existing organizations but what people didn't realize [was] that the existing organizations were only working to a minimum capacity because of their funding." (Cassandra, councillor and former Lord Mayor, 2017)
Time	"Relationship-building over time and giving people an embodied, felt experience that you can understand and recognize and contain their life and their perspective of life, and over time, I think trust allows people to share vulnerable information, because they feel recognized enough and have enough trust that the other person can carry the information they share." (Klara, 2021)
	"There are several issues but one is also that you don't have the proper time being a GP. 'OK, so have you been tortured?' 'Yes.' 'OK, so time's up.' So there is a structural and time-wise pressure on those common authority and clinical settings that do not really allow for the staff to actually consider those very, very hard and very, very delicate issues. There's no time." (Pia, 2017)
	"It would be nice also if we could have more doctors in our department, because in that way maybe we would have better time to do other things." (Laura, 2021)
Ability to work across contexts, institutions and disciplines	"Establishing meaningful connections between, for instance, the treatment context and the everyday life. I think this is where we, as a system often meet some barriers, because it can be in practice difficult to work across contexts." (Klara, 2021)
Tools to address silence around torture and torturous violence, and sexualized torture and torturous violence	"I try to draw on my own experience from other clients from the same region or the same city, and kind of suggest, 'This is something I've heard from others they have experienced. You don't have to talk about it right now if you don't want to.'" (Luna, 2021)

(continued)

Table 7.1: Recommendations from key practitioners (continued)

Requirements for improved conditions for practice	Views from practitioners
Flexibility in responding to forms of torture	"Having worked particularly in certain areas of the world, obviously, it's so context-related and so hard to say, 'We do this here because it makes sense here. We do something else here because it makes sense here'." (Freja, 2021)
	"We do try to design the therapy programme so that if they have a part-time job, for example, or part-time school, that we can still accommodate their treatment, at least in terms of the hours." (Laura, 2021)
Firm structures of support for practitioners	"You really need to have very firm structures of support around supervision and not overloading practitioners, not having too many clients, having breaks and making sure that there's a good environment for being able to work with this content, and there usually isn't that, a good environment for being able to work with this heavy content." (Mila, 2021)

I researched struggled hugely with finances, scrambling to stay open to provide even basic necessities for survivors of violence and/or people seeking asylum. Board meetings I attended in various organizations became less and less about the issue at hand, and more and more about the pressing need for funds, with Key Performance Indicators corrosively eroding the autonomy of practitioners and organizations themselves. Indeed, I witnessed the closure of many organizations – some I had written about in the report *Reimagining Refugee Rights* as examples of excellent practice (Canning, 2019a). As one manager of an HIV support organization that ran a specific group for LGBTQI people seeking asylum who were living with HIV put it, it had taken them 30 years to hone the practice of the organization, and in one swipe the very structure of it was being annihilated by financial cuts. Even some of the people I interviewed across these projects lost their jobs on the back of funding cuts.

Indeed, in Britain where I was mostly based, the infliction of so-called austerity measures – economic and structural violence by any other name (see Cooper and Whyte, 2017) – had devastating effects on camps, NGOs, INGOs and, as a consequence, individuals who relied on them. Domestic violence support groups, rape crisis organizations, women's shelters, refugee and asylum support communities and torture response practices often vied for the same (usually small) pots of money. Simultaneously, legal support and legal aid for refugees was reducing across most of Europe. Even in stating this, I am conscious that the countries within which this research was undertaken are still regions of comparative economic privilege and although this privilege is not equally experienced or distributed, stronger structures are in place for support provision than in many others.

It is a disgrace of our times that any survivors of violence are left without support in a world where more billionaires exist than ever, while more people are fleeing violence, conflict, poverty and persecution. In a chapter detailing journey and encampment on travelling to safety through Europe, Karam Yahya writes ironically that 'after travelling by foot, boat, taxi and truck … only spaceship remains as an unutilized method to enter the European territories' (2021: 27). As I was writing this conclusion, two billionaires were travelling into *space* – for a holiday. At the same time, the Royal National Lifeboat Institution was having to crowdfund to rescue refugees from the English Channel. The absurdity of it is boundless, and yet these wealth inequalities have very real consequences for survivors of violence, in all its forms, and as we have seen, the practitioners who work to support them.

Conclusion

The objective of *Torture and Torturous Violence* has been to highlight ways in which narrow legal definitions of torture can influence how we individually and collectively see and categorize forms of violence as torture. Narrow definitions can also prevent us from considering brutal forms of violence as torturous in nature, even when the techniques of abuse – physically and psychologically – are the same and have similar or identical impacts. It is a call for scholars working on narrow definitions to reflect more fully on what I have termed *orthodox legalism*, and take more seriously the *experiential epistemologies* that are addressed throughout.

With this said, the aim is not to argue that narrow definitions of torture should be abandoned altogether – as Green and Ward highlight, they facilitate one of the few ways by which we can meaningfully explore state violence and accountability (2004). Indeed, at the time of writing, accounts of state sanctioned or inflicted torture continue to perforate news and media – from the current coup in Myanmar, to the invasion of Ukraine, to the escalation in Taliban insurgencies across Afghanistan throughout the summer of 2021; from reports of torture and sexualized torture of imprisoned Uighur Muslims in China to reports of systematic rape of women and girls in Tigray by Ethiopian troops. Indeed, state violence remains endemic, and its consequences shattering.

Simultaneously, we are faced with systematic forms of violence which are torturous in nature, but seldom – if ever – presented as torture. We have explored these in depth in Chapters 3 and 4, hearing from women survivors of violence, and the trajectories thereof, in Chapter 5. To reiterate what is highlighted, women have described so-called 'false imprisonment', repeated strangulation (for some, to the point of passing out), scalding, rape and constant and unpredictable emotional and/or physical abuse including beating, cutting and death threats. Like torture, these violences are subject to processes of silencing, compounded for sexualized violence and sexually torturous violence, as the intimate nature and highly problematic social and cultural notions of honour attach specific forms of stigmatization and shame.

Finally – and crucially – this book has sought to highlight that, by recognizing the torturous nature of some violence, as well as unsilencing torture, torturous violence, sexualized torture and sexually torturous violence, we can collectively challenge the silence which often allows for cyclical abuses to continue, and that create barriers to support. By focusing also on the impacts on refugee and asylum-seeking survivors, we can begin to recognize that torture is not a problem 'elsewhere', but perforates time and space, the here and now. If and when we explore more experiences of violence from a torturous lens, we can most certainly dispel the myth that it is confined to areas of conflict or failed states, but may be present in marriages and partnerships, or institutions and schools. Indeed, torture and tortuous violence are issues for all of us, which benefit from collective recognition that its nature is pervasive, but never inevitable.

Suggested further reading
Responding to torture and survivors of trauma

Danish Institute Against Torture, DIGNITY online library, available at https://www.dignity.dk/en/dignitys-library/
Freedom from Torture research and submissions, available at https://www.freedomfromtorture.org/research-and-submissions
Institute of Recovery from Childhood Trauma, available at https://irct.org.uk/
International Justice Resource Center, available at https://ijrcenter.org/regional/african/committee-for-the-prevention-of-torture-in-africa/
International Rehabilitation Council for Trauma Victims, available at https://irct.org/
Victim Focus, available at https://www.victimfocus.org.uk/

Undertaking research in sensitive topics

DSCOUT, researching sensitive topics, available at https://dscout.com/people-nerds/conducing-research-sensitive-topics
Sexual Violence Research Initiative resources, available at https://www.svri.org/documents/our-resources
UCL research integrity, sensitive research, available at https://www.ucl.ac.uk/research/integrity/sensitive-research

Model toolkits for understanding asylum processes

Information on Refugees in Denmark, available at https://refugees.dk/

Refugee Council, available at https://www.refugeecouncil.org.uk/ information/refugee-asylum-facts/the-truth-about-asylum/?gclid= EAIaIQobChMI4JaK37mr8gIVQuDtCh3YOQhCEAAYAiAAEgLj IPD_BwE

Right to Remain Toolkit, available at https://righttoremain.org.uk/toolkit/

Notes

Introduction

1   Thanks to Ignasi Bernat for the discussions and insights into ongoing research on the history of Catalan resistance.

2   Similar internationalized relations can also be seen between the upsurge in kneecapping in Palestine and Israel. In Northern Ireland, it is not uncommon to see the Israel flag in Loyalist areas, and the Palestine flag in Republican areas – reflections of their histories of affiliation between occupations and resistance.

Chapter 1

1   This argument will be revisited in relation to the power/powerlessness nexus in Chapter 3, specifically in relation to domestic violence, femicide and so-called false imprisonment.

2   Special Rapporteurs on Torture and Other Cruel, Inhuman or Degrading Treatment or Punishment have included: Peter Kooijmans (Netherlands, 1985–1993); Nigel S. Rodley (United Kingdom, 1993–2001); Theo van Boven (Netherlands, 2001–2004); Manfred Nowak (Austria, 2004–2010); Juan Méndez (Argentina, 2010–2016); Nils Melzer (Switzerland but based in United Kingdom, 2016–present) – see OHCHR (2021b). This is not to say that sexualized violence has not been centralized – Peter Kooijmans and Nigel Rodley did pioneering work in relation to pushing for the recognition of rape as torture, which has been since followed by others – this will be elaborated on in Chapter 4. It nonetheless remains an interesting demographic representation for this particular role.

3   By this I mean the patients/survivors Laura works with have already undergone various assessments to determine whether they are survivors of torture. See appendices in Pérez-Sales (2017) for examples of what these may look like.

4   Authors can present as experts in a subject without consulting those who are at the fore of their fields in practice, which I hoped to avoid.

5   Huge thanks to Anette Carnemalm for this important and insightful anecdote, which gives us all a lot to consider, and thanks to Linda Jolef for inviting me to hold the workshop in the first instance.

6   This is not to deflect from the fact that not everyone involved in torture is in agreement on torturing, and coercion of course exists in many contexts. However, even coercion is arguably a bureaucratic process based on decision-making.

Chapter 2

1   This included: Afghanistan, Albania, Algeria, Australia, Austria, Azerbaijan, Belgium, Bosnia-Herzegovina, Canada, Croatia, Cyprus, the Czech Republic, Denmark, Djibouti, Egypt, Ethiopia, Finland, Gambia, Georgia, Germany, Greece, Hong Kong, Iceland,

Indonesia, Iran, Ireland, Italy, Jordan, Kenya, Libya, Lithuania, Macedonia, Malawi, Malaysia, Mauritania, Morocco, Pakistan, Poland, Portugal, Romania, Saudi Arabia, Somalia, South Africa, Spain, Sri Lanka, Sweden, Syria, Thailand, Turkey, United Arab Emirates, United Kingdom, Uzbekistan, Yemen and Zimbabwe – further evidence of Rejali's claim that states that are recognized as political democracies are not only complicit but often at the fore of organized torture in detention (2007).

Chapter 3

1   At surface level, this contradicts my points on moving away from motivation, however this argument remains, since the goals identified by researchers and scholars are not always those related to the UNCAT's focus on intelligence or punishment.

2   This was not uncommon even in recent history. My own mother was advised she should go to one when unmarried and pregnant with my brother at 16 years of age in 1976.

3   The issue of corporate and third-party violations was also raised in my discussions with lawyers, in terms of accountability, and the shift from the narrow lens of the state. As the Danish Institute Against Torture outlines, 'there is no authoritative definition of the term "non-state actors" under international law'. This means that in its broadest sense, torture can include 'all private actors distinct from the state – including private individuals, private companies, armed groups, and de-facto regimes'. Importantly, *non-state actors are not party to international human rights treaties that stipulate obligations of states* (DIGNITY, 2012: 33). Although such people can be held to account under domestic criminal laws, if the state in which violations occur fails to prosecute or respond effectively to torture, the state itself can become accountable.

4   BVMN is an independent network of non-governmental organizations (NGOs) and associations mainly based in the Balkan regions and in Greece, which monitors human rights violations at the external borders of the European Union and advocates to stop the violence exerted against people on the move. See https://www.borderviolence.eu/about/

Chapter 4

1   This is meant in the broadest sense of patterns of detention and confinement but is not monolithic internationally, including for example the disproportionate confinement of women and girls in psychiatric institutions and maternity 'laundries' as will be discussed later.

2   As I have argued elsewhere, states and corporations working with states do not necessarily ease the impacts of violence in the lives of survivors of trafficking. See Canning (2020b) for further discussion on forms of corrosive control.

3   When I was a trustee director at a rape support centre, I was involved in the decision to support men survivors of sexualized abuse – some of whom were also perpetrators. Almost all of the hundreds of men who sought support were survivors of other men's violence, another indicator that a gendered lens is required for men's experience of (predominately) men's violence. We ensured practitioners could choose if they were happy to support men – which almost all did – and that counselling sessions took place away from the women's safe house.

4   I use the term 'cope' here to suggest survival, but do not include it uncritically or without acknowledgement to resistance and survival more broadly. For further discussion, see Jefferson (2014).

Chapter 5

[1]   Some of these excerpts have been published in part in *Race & Class* in relation to degrading border practices– see Canning (2019b).

[2]   At the height of Denmark's asylum applications, these estimations are fairly accurate. However, under the current social democratic administration, Prime Minister Mette Frederiksen has set an objective to reduce applications for asylum to 0 – a testament to the longer-term reduction and dissolution of refugee rights in Denmark.

Chapter 6

[1]   This is not to suggest that domestic violence was not relevant to the wider discussion, nor that both forms of violence are separate – far from it, since sexualized violence is often one element of domestic or interpersonal violence. Rather that there was an invisible barrier which effectively quashed the topic we had come to discuss specifically: rape and sexualized violence.

Chapter 7

[1]   These are drawn out in more depth in Canning (2021c).

References

Abdelhady, D., Gren, N. and Joormann, M. (2020) *Refugees and the Violence of Welfare Bureaucracies in Northern Europe*, Manchester: Manchester University Press.

Ahrens, C.E. (2006) Being silenced: The impact of negative social reactions on the disclosure of rape, *American Journal of Community Psychology*, 38(3–4): 263–274.

Al-Dayel, N., Anfinson, A. and Anfinson, G. (2021) Captivity, migration and power in Libya, *Journal of Human Trafficking*, Online First. https://doi.org/10.1080/23322705.2021.1908032

Aliverti, A. (2012) Making people criminal: The role of the criminal law in immigration enforcement, *Theoretical Criminology*, 16(4): 417–434.

Al-Nuaimi, M.A., Hamad, R.A. and Lafta, R.K. (2015) Effects of witnessing or exposure to community violence on mental health of Iraqi men, *Qatar Medical Journal*, 1: 1–9.

Amnesty International (2021) Croatia: Fresh evidence of police abuse and torture of migrants and asylum-seekers, 11 June. Available at: https://www.amnesty.org/en/latest/news/2020/06/croatia-fresh-evidence-of-police-abuse-and-torture-of-migrants-and-asylumseekers/ (last accessed 2 November 2021).

AP News (2021) Danish court increases sentence for both brothers in murder case, 28 October. Available at: https://apnews.com/article/europe-geo rge-floyd-race-and-ethnicity-racial-injustice-denmark-f7ba815723ce9432d 18348c903462f56 (last accessed 2 November 2021).

Arcel, L.T. (2003) Introduction, in Arcel, L.T., Popovic, S., Kucukalic, A. and Bravo-Mehmedbasic, A. (eds) *Treatment of Torture and Trauma Survivors in a Post-War Society*, Sarajevo: Association for Rehabilitation of Torture Victims.

Arendt, H. (1963) *Eichmann in Jerusalem: A Report on the Banality of Evil*, New York: Penguin.

Arendt, H. (1970) *On Violence*, Orlando: Harvest Books.

Arthur, C.D. (2021) I've been strip-frisked over 1,000 times in prison: I consider it sexual assault, *The Marshall Project*. Available at: https://www.themarshallproject.org/2021/02/04/i-ve-been-strip-frisked-over-1-000-times-in-prison-i-consider-it-sexual-assault (last accessed 24 August 2021).

Athey, S. (2011) The torture device: Debate and archetype, in Biswas, S. and Zalloua, Z. (eds) *Torture: Power, Democracy and the Human Body*, Seattle: University of Washington Press, pp 129–157.

Baillot, H. and Connelly, E. (2018) *Women Seeking Asylum: Safe from Violence in the UK?* UK: ASAP and Refugee Council. Available at: http://www.asaproject.org/uploads/Safe_from_violence_in_the_UK._ASAP-RC_repo rt_.pdf (last accessed 9 April 2020).

Baillot, H., Cowan, S. and Munro, V.E. (2014) Reason to disbelieve: Evaluating the rape claims of women seeking asylum in the UK, *International Journal of Law in Context*, 10(1): 105–139.

Barak, G. (2003) *Violence and Nonviolence: Pathways to Understanding*, London: SAGE.

Barrington, A.J. and Shakespeare-Finch, J. (2013) Working with refugee survivors of torture and trauma: An opportunity for vicarious post-traumatic growth, *Counselling Psychology Quarterly*, 26(1): 89–105.

Başoğlu, M. (2017) *Torture and its Definition in International Law*, Oxford: Oxford University Press.

Başoğlu, M., Jaranson, J.M., Mollica, R. and Kastrup, M. (2001) Torture and mental health, in Gerrity, E., Keane, T.M. and Tuma, F. (eds) *The Mental Health Consequences of Torture*, New York: Kluwer Academic, pp 35–62.

Başoğlu, M., Livanou, M. and Crnobaric, C. (2007) Torture vs other cruel, inhuman and degrading treatment, *Archives of General Psychiatry*, 64(3): 277–285.

Bastick, M., Grimm, K. and Kunz, R. (2007) *Sexual Violence in Armed Conflict: Global Overview and Implications for the Security Sector*, Geneva: Geneva Centre for the Democratic Control of Armed Forces.

BBC News (2020) Denmark murder: Brothers jailed over Bornholm island case, 1 December. Available at: https://www.bbc.co.uk/news/world-eur ope-55143044 (last accessed 2 November 2021).

Bhatia, M. (2020) The permission to be cruel: Street level bureaucrats and harms against people seeking asylum, *Critical Criminology*, 28: 277–292.

Bhatia, M. and Burnett, J. (2019) Torture and the UK's 'war on asylum': Medicalpower and the culture of disbelief, in Perocco, F. (ed) *Tortura e Migrazioni*, Venice: Sapere l'Euopa, pp 161–180.

Bhatia, M. and Canning, V. (2021) *Stealing Time: Migration, Temporality and State Violence*, Basingstoke: Palgrave Macmillan.

Biswas, S. and Zalloua, Z. (2011) *Torture: Power, Democracy and the Human Body*, Seattle: University of Washington Press.

Boochani, B. (2018) *No Friend but the Mountains: The True Story of an Illegally Imprisoned Refugee*, Sydney: Picador.

Boochani, B. and Tofighian, O. (2021) The weaponisation of time: Indefinite detention as torture, in Bhatia, M. and Canning, V. (eds) *Stealing Time: Migration, Temporality and State Violence*, Basingstoke: Palgrave Macmillan, pp 65–83.

Border Violence Monitoring Network (2020) *Annual Torture Report 2020.* Available at: https://www.borderviolence.eu/wp-content/uploads/Annual-Torture-Report-2020-BVMN.pdf (last accessed 2 November 2021).

Bosworth, M. and Turnbull, S. (2015) Immigration detention, punishment and the criminalisation of migration, in Pickering, S. and Ham, J. (eds) *The Routledge Handbook on Crime and International Migration*, Oxon: Routledge, pp 91–107.

Cakal, E. (2021) 'For such purposes as': Towards an embedded and embodied understanding of torture's purpose, *State Crime Journal*, 9(2): 152–168.

Canning, V. (2011a) Who's human? Developing sociological understandings of the rights of women raped in conflict, in Hynes, P., Lamb, M., Short, D. and Waites, M. (eds) *Sociology and Human Rights*, London: Routledge, pp 39–55.

Canning, V. (2011b) Women seeking sanctuary: Questioning state responses to violence against women in the asylum system, *Criminal Justice Matters*, 85.

Canning, V. (2014) International conflict, sexual violence and asylum policy: Merseyside as a case study, *Critical Social Policy*, 34(1): 23–45.

Canning, V. (2016) Unsilencing sexual torture: Responses to refugees and asylum seekers in Denmark, *British Journal of Criminology*, 56(3): 438–456.

Canning, V. (2017) *Gendered Harm and Structural Violence in the British Asylum System*, Oxon: Routledge.

Canning, V. (2018) Zemiology at the border, in Boukli, P. and Kotze, J. (eds) *Zemiology: Reconnecting Crime and Social Harm*, Basingstoke: Palgrave Macmillan, pp 183–203.

Canning, V. (2019a) Reimagining refugee rights: Addressing asylum harms in Britain, Denmark and Sweden, Migration and Mobilities Bristol. Available at: https://www.statewatch.org/media/documents/news/2019/mar/uk-dk-se-reimagining-refugee-rights-asylum-harms-3-19.pdf (last accessed 24 August 2021).

Canning, V. (2019b) Degradation by design: Women seeking asylum in northern Europe, *Race & Class*, 61(1). https://doi.org/10.1177/0306396819850986

Canning, V. (2020a) Bureaucratised banality: Asylum and immobility in Britain, Denmark and Sweden, in Abdelhady, D., Gren, N. and Joormann, M. (eds) *Refugees and the Violence of Welfare Bureaucracies in Northern Europe*, Manchester: Manchester University Press, pp 210–226.

Canning, V. (2020b) Corrosive control: State-corporate and gendered harm in bordered Britain, *Critical Criminology*, 28: 259–275.

Canning, V. (2020c) Keeping up with the *kladdkaka*: Kindness and coercion in Swedish immigration detention, *European Journal of Criminology*, 17(6): 259–275.

Canning, V. (2021a) Compounding trauma through temporal harm, in Bhatia, M. and Canning, V. (eds) *Stealing Time: Migration, Temporality and State Violence*, Basingstoke: Palgrave Macmillan, pp 105–127.

Canning, V. (2021b) 'Sensing and unease in immigration confinement: An abolitionist's perspective, in Herrity, K., Schmidt, B. and Warr, J. (eds) *Sensory Penalities*, Bingley: Emerald Publishing, pp 143–157.

Canning, V. (2021c) Managing expectations: Impacts of hostile immigration policies on practitioners in Britain, Denmark and Sweden, *Journal of Social Science*, 10(2): 65. https://doi.org/10.3390/socsci10020065

Canning, V. and Matthews, L. (2020) *Right to Remain Asylum Online Covid-Safe Navigation Board*. Available at: https://righttoremain.org.uk/asylum-navigation-board/ (last accessed 24 August 2021).

Canning, V. and Tombs, S. (2021) *From Social Harm to Zemiology*, Oxon: Routledge.

Canning, V., Martin, G. and Tombs, S. (2023) *The International Handbook of Activist Criminology*, Bingley: Emerald Publishing.

Centre for the Study of Violence and Reconciliation (2014) Torture in South Africa: The acts and the facts, September. Available at: https://www.csvr.org.za/pdf/Torture%20in%20South%20Africa.pdf (last accessed 24 August 2021).

Chenowyth, S. (2017) 'We keep it in our hearts': Sexual violence against men and boys in the Syria Crisis, *UNHCR Crisis Report*. Available at: https://www.refworld.org/docid/5a128e814.html (last accessed 24 August 2021).

Cohen, S. (2001) *States of Denial*, London: Polity.

Convention on the Elimination of all forms of Discrimination Against Women (1979) *General Recommendation No. 32 on the Gendered Dimension of Refugee Status, Asylum, Nationality and Statelessness of Women*. Available at: http://daccess-dds-ny.un.org/doc/UNDOC/GEN/N14/627/90/PDF/N1462790.pdf?OpenElement (last accessed 4th October 2022).

Cooper, V. and Whyte, D. (2017) *The Violence of Austerity*, London: Pluto Press.

Copelon, R. (1994) Intimate terror: Understanding domestic violence as torture, in Cook, R.J. (ed) *Human Rights of Women: National and International Perspectives*, Philadelphia: University of Pennsylvania Press, pp 116–152.

Copelon, R. (2004) Surfacing gender: Reengraving crimes against women in humanitarian law, in Dombrowski, N.A. (ed) *Women and War in the Twentieth Century: Enlisted With or Without Consent*, Abingdon: Routledge.

Copson, L. (2018) Beyond 'criminology vs zemiology': Reconciling crime with social harm, in Boukli, A. and Kotze, J. (eds) *Zemiology: Reconnecting Crime and Social Harm*, Basingstoke: Palgrave Macmillan, pp 33–57.

Council of Europe (2011) *Istanbul Convention*. Available at: https://www.coe. int/en/web/istanbul-convention/home? (last accessed 25 August 2021).

Council of Europe (2018) Council of Europe anti-torture committee visits Norway, *2018 News*. Available at: https://www.coe.int/en/web/cpt/-/ council-of-europe-anti-torture-committee-visits-norway (last accessed 23 June 2021).

Crenshaw, K. (1989) Demarginalizing the intersection of race and sex: A black feminist critique of antidiscrimination doctrine, feminist theory and antiracist politics, *University of Chicago Legal Forum*, 1: 139–167.

Crenshaw, K. (1991) Mapping the margins: Intersectionality, identity politics, and violence against women of color, *Stanford Law Review*, 43(6): 1241–1299.

Danner, M. (2011) Now that we've tortured, in Biswas, S. and Zalloua, Z. (eds) *Torture: Power, Democracy and the Human Body*, Seattle: University of Washington Press, pp 46–66.

Das, V. (2006) Life and Words: Violence and Descent into the Ordinary, Berkeley: University of California Press.

Das, V. and Kleinman, A. (2000) Introduction, in Das, V., Kleinman, A., Ramphele, M. and Reynolds, P. (eds), *Violence and Subjectivity*, Berkeley: University of California Press, pp 1–19.

Davis, A.Y. (1975) *Women, Race & Class*, London: Penguin.

Davis, L. (2017) The gendered dimensions of torture: Rape and other forms of gender-based violence as torture under international law, in Başoğlu, M. (ed) *Torture and its Definition in International Law*, Oxford: Oxford University Press, pp 315–371.

Dehghan, R. (2018) The health impact of (sexual) torture amongst Afghan, Iranian and Kurdish refugees: A literature review, *Torture*, 28(3): 77–91.

Dershowitz, A. (2004) Tortured reasoning, in Levinson, S. (ed) *Torture: A Collection*, Oxford: Oxford University Press, pp 257–281.

DIGNITY (nd) *Who We Are*. Available at: https://www.dignity.dk/en/ about-dignity/ (last accessed 16 June 2021).

DIGNITY (2012) *Field Manual on Rehabilitation*, Copenhagen: Danish Institute Against Torture.

Durkheim, E. (2016 [1912]) *The Elementary Forms of Religious Life*, Oxford: Oxford University Press.

Edinburgh, L., Pape-Blabolil, J., Harpin, S. and Saewyc, E. (2014) Multiple perpetrator rape among girls evaluated at a hospital-based Child Advocacy Center: Seven years of reviewed cases, *Child Abuse and Neglect*, 38(9): 1540–1551.

Edwards, A. (2006) The feminizing of torture under international human rights law, *Leiden Journal of International Law*, 19(2): 349–391.

Einolf, C.J. (2018a) Sexual torture among Arabic-speaking Shi'a Muslim men and women in Iraq: Barriers to healing and finding meaning, *Torture: Journal on Rehabilitation of Torture Victims and Prevention of Torture*, 28(3): 63–76.

Einolf, C.J. (2018b) Why do states use sexual torture against political prisoners? Evidence from Saddam Hussein's prisons, *Journal of Global Security Studies*, 3(4): 417–430.

El-Khoury, J., Haidar, R. and Barkil-Oteo, A. (2020) Psychological torture: Characteristics and impact on mental health, *International Journal of Social Psychiatry*, 67(5): 500–506.

Emejulu, A. and Bassel, L. (2017) Women of colour's anti-austerity activism, in Cooper, V. and Whyte, D. (eds) *The Violence of Austerity*, London: Pluto Press, pp 117–123.

Erdbrink, T. (2020) A Black man was tortured and killed in Denmark: The police insist it wasn't about race, *New York Times*, 30 June. Available at: https://www.nytimes.com/2020/06/30/world/europe/denmark-bornholm-race.html (last accessed 2 November 2021).

European Parliament (2016) *The Gender Dimension of Human Trafficking*. Available at: https://www.europarl.europa.eu/RegData/etudes/BRIE/2016/577950/EPRS_BRI(2016)577950_EN.pdf (last accessed 25 August 2021).

Fabri, M.R. (2011) Best, promising and emerging practices in the treatment of trauma: What can we apply in our work with torture survivors? *Torture: Journal on Rehabilitation of Torture Victims and Prevention of Torture*, 21(1): 27–38.

Fair, E. (2016) *Consequence: A Memoir*, New York: Henry Holt and Company.

Farmer, P.E., Nizeye, B., Stulac, S. and Keshavjee, S. (2006) Structural violence and clinical medicine, *PLoS Medicine*, 3(10): e449. https://doi.org/10.1371/journal.pmed.0030449

Farrell, M. (2013) *The Prohibition of Torture in Exceptional Circumstances*, Cambridge: Cambridge University Press.

Farrell, M. (2021) *Torture: The Marks of Civilisation*. International State Crime Initiative Seminar Series. Available at: https://www.youtube.com/watch?v=VPvI7IAwtuE (last accessed 25 August 2021).

Fitzpatrick, B. (2016) *Tactical Rape in War and Conflict: International Recognition and Response*, Bristol: Policy Press.

Freedom from Torture (nd) *What We Do*. Available at: https://www.freedomfromtorture.org/what-we-do (last accessed 16 June 2021).

Freedom from Torture (2016) *Proving Torture: Demanding the Impossible*. Available at: https://asylumineurope.org/wp-content/uploads/2016/11/resources_proving_torture.pdf (last accessed 25 June 2021).

Galtung, J. (1969) Violence, peace, and peace research, *Journal of Peace Research*, 6(3): 167–191.

Ghosn, F., Braithwaite, A. and Chu, T.S. (2019) Violence, displacement, contact, and attitudes toward hosting refugees, *Journal of Peace Research*, 56(1): 118–133.

Gidycz, C. and Koss, M. (1990) A comparison of group and individual sexual assault victims, *Psychology of Women Quarterly*, 14(3): 325–342.

Ginbar, Y. (2017) Making human rights sense of the torture definition, in Başoğlu, M. (ed) *Torture and its Definition in International Law*, Oxford: Oxford University Press, pp 273–308.

Gineste, C. and Savun, B. (2019) Introducing POSVAR: A dataset on refugee-related violence, *Journal of Peace Research*, 56(1): 134–145.

Green, P. and Ward, T. (2004) *State Crime: Governments, Violence and Corruption*, London: Pluto Press.

Greenberg, K.J. and Dratel, J.L. (2005) *The Torture Papers: The Road to Abu Ghraib*, Cambridge: Cambridge University Press.

Griffiths, M. (2014) Out of time: The temporal uncertainties of refused asylum seekers and immigration detainees, *Journal of Ethnic and Migration Studies*, 40(12): 1991–2009.

Guterres, A. (2019) Secretary-General's message on International Day in support of victims of torture, United Nations. Available at: https://www.un.org/sg/en/content/sg/statement/2019-06-26/secretary-generals-message-international-day-support-of-victims-of-torture (last accessed 4 August 2020).

Hawking. S. (1989) *A Brief History of Time*, New York: Bantam Press.

Herman, J.L. (1992) *Trauma and Recovery: From Domestic Abuse to Political Terror*, New York: Pandora.

Hiles, D. and Cermak, I. (2008) Narrative psychology, in Willig, C. and Stainton-Rogers, W. (eds) *The SAGE Handbook of Qualitative Research in Psychology*, London: SAGE, pp 53–65.

Hillyard, P. and Tombs, S. (2004) Introduction, in Hillyard, P., Tombs, S. and Gordon, D. (eds) *Beyond Criminology: Taking Harm Seriously*, London: Pluto Press, pp 1–10.

Hogan Lovells (2020) UN Torture Committee delivers preliminary judgement against Ireland, deciding to hear Magdalene Laundries case in full. Available at: https://www.hoganlovells.com/en/news/un-torture-committee-delivers-preliminary-judgment-against-ireland-deciding-to-hear-magdalene-laundries-case-in-full (last accessed 2 November 2021).

Holloway, S. L. and Valentine, G. (2000) Spatiality and the new social studies of childhood, *Sociology*, 34(4), 763–783.

hooks, b. (1984) Black women: Shaping feminist theory, in Bhavnani, K. (ed) *Feminism and 'Race'*, Oxford: Oxford University Press, pp 33–40.

Iliadou, E., (2021) 'Violence continuum': Border crossings, deaths and time in the island of Lesvos, in Bhatiah, M. and Canning, V. (eds), *Stealing Time: Migration, Temporalities and State Violence*, Basingstoke: Palgrave Macmillan, pp 197–221.

International Criminal Tribunal for Former Yugoslavia (1998) Celebici case: The judgement of the Trial Chamber. Zejnil Delalic acquitted, Zdravko Mucic sentenced to 7 years in prison, Hazim Delic sentenced to 20 years in prison, Esad Landzo sentenced to 15 years in prison. Available at: https://www.icty.org/en/press/celebici-case-judgement-trial-chamber-zejnil-delalic-acquitted-zdravko-mucic-sentenced-7-years (last accessed 24 August 2021).

IRCT (nd) *About the IRCT*. Available at: https://www.irct.org/who-we-are/about-the-irct (last accessed 16 June 2021).

Ireland, J.A. (2011) This fragile body: Susan Crile's *Abu Ghraib: Abuse of Power*, in Biswas, S. and Zalloua, Z. (eds) *Torture: Power, Democracy and the Human Body*, Seattle: University of Washington Press, pp 188–214.

Jefferson, A. (2014) 'Performances of victimhood, allegation, and disavowal, in Jensen, S. and Rønsbo, H. (eds) *Histories of Victimhood*, Philadelphia: University of Pennsylvania Press, pp 218–238.

Jensen, S. and Kelly, T. (2016) Missing torture amongst the poor, *openDemocracy*, 7 November. Available at: https://www.opendemocracy.net/en/openglobalrights-openpage/missing-torture-amongst-poor/ (last accessed 16 September 2022).

Jensen, S. and Rønsbo, H. (2014) *Histories of Victimhood*, Philadelphia: University of Pennsylvania Press.

Jobe, A. (2009) Accessing help and services: Trafficking survivor's experiences in the United Kingdom, in Dresdner, L. and Peterson, L. (eds) *(Re)Interpretations: The Shapes of Justice in Women's Experience*, Newcastle upon Tyne: Cambridge Scholars Press, pp 277–297.

Jobe, A. (2020) Telling the right story at the right time: Women seeking asylum with stories of trafficking into the sex industry, *Sociology*, 54(5): 936–952.

Johnson, J., Madill, A., Koutsopoulou, G.Z., Brown, C. and Harris, R. (2020) Tackling imbalance in psychology, *The Psychologist*, 33: 5–6.

Jones, D. (2014) Introduction, in United States Senate (ed), *The Senate Intelligence Committee Report on Torture*, London: Melville House, pp 1–6.

Jones, D. (2019) CIA torture not needed to get terror leads, *BBC Hardtalk*, 5 December. Available at: https://www.bbc.co.uk/programmes/p07x01d9 (last accessed 12 March 2021).

Jordan, J. (2012) Silencing rape, silencing women, in Brown, J. and Walklate, S. (eds) *Handbook on Sexual Violence*, Oxon: Routledge, pp 253–287.

Judiciary UK (2018) Regina vs Broadhurst: Sentencing remarks, 17 December. Available at: https://www.judiciary.uk/wp-content/uploads/2018/12/broadhurst-sentencing-remarks.pdf (last accessed 24 August 2021).

Kaldor, M. (2013) In defence of new wars, *Stability*, 2(1): 1–16.

Kastrup, M.C. and Arcel, L.T. (2004) Gender-specific treatment, in Wilson, J.P. and Drozdek, B. (eds) *Broken Spirits: The Treatment of Traumatised Asylum Seekers, Refugees and War and Torture Victims*, New York: Routledge, pp 547–573.

Kelly, J.T., Betancourt, T.S. and Mukwege, D. (2011) Experiences of female survivors of sexual violence in eastern Democratic Republic of the Congo: A mixed-methods study, *Conflict and Health*, 5(25): 1–8.

Kelly, L. (1988) *Surviving Sexual Violence*, Minnesota: University of Minnesota Press.

Kelly, L. (2014) *Changing the Discourses on Sexual Consent: Lessons from Research with Young People*, Centre for Crime, Criminalisation and Social Exclusion: Critical Research Seminar Series, Liverpool John Moores University, 12 March.

Kelly, T. (2012) *This Side of Silence: Human Rights, Torture, and the Recognition of Cruelty*, Pennsylvania: Pennsylvania University Press.

Khosravi, S. (2018) Stolen time, *New Statesman*, June/July: 33–34.

King, R.H. (2009) *From the Bottom of the Heap: The Autobiography of a Black Panther*, Oakland: PM Press.

Kinzie, J.D. (2011) Guidelines for psychiatric care of torture survivors, *Torture*, 21/1: 18–26.

Lee, M. (2010) *Trafficking and Global Crime Control*, London: SAGE.

Levinson, S. (2004) *Torture: A Collection*, Oxford: Oxford University Press.

MacKinnon, C.A. (2006) *Are Women Human? And Other International Dialogues*, Cambridge, MA: Harvard University Press.

Massey, D. (1994) *Space, Place and Gender*, Cambridge: Polity Press.

Massey, D. (1997) *Cool Places: The Spatial Construction of Youth Cultures*, Oxon: Routledge.

Mayblin, L. (2019) Imagining asylum, governing asylum seekers: Complexity reduction and policy making in the UK home office, *Migration Studies*, 7(1): 1–20.

McFarlane, C. and Kaplan, I. (2012) Evidence based psychological interventions for adult survivors of torture and trauma: A 30 year review, *Transcultural Psychiatry*, 49(3–4): 539–567.

McGlynn, C.M.S. (2008) Rape as 'Torture'? Catharine Mackinnon and questions of feminist strategy, *Feminist Legal Studies*, 16(1): 71–85.

McGregor, L. (2014) Applying the definition of torture to non-state actors: the case of trafficking in human beings, *Human Rights Quarterly*, 36(1): 210–241.

McMahon, S. and Sigona, N. (2018) Navigating the central Mediterranean in a time of 'crisis': Disentangling migration governance and migrant journeys, *Sociology*, 52(3): 497–515.

Mead, G.H. (2002 [1932]) *The Philosophy of the Present*, New York: Prometheus Books.

Monckton Smith, J. (2021) *In Control: Dangerous Relationships and How They End in Murder*, London: Bloomsbury.

Montesanti, S.R. and Thurston, W.E. (2015) Mapping the role of structural and interpersonal violence in the lives of women: Implications for public health interventions and policy, *BMC Women's Health*, 15: 1–13.

Montgomery, E. and Foldsprang, A. (2005) Predictors of authorities' decision to grant asylum in Denmark, *Journal of Refugee Studies*, 18(4): 454–467.

Mookherjee, N. (2010) *The Spectral Wound: Sexual Violence and Public Memories and the Bangladesh War of 1971*, New York: Duke University Press.

Moylan, C., Herrenkohl, T.I., Sousa, C., Tajima, E.A., Herremkohl, R.C. and Russo, M.J. (2010) The effects of child abuse and exposure to domestic violence on adolescent internalizing and externalizing behavior problems, *Journal of Family Violence*, 25(1): 53–63.

Nisanci, A., Rumeysa, K., Yusuf, A. and Ulviyenur, K. (2020) Working with refugees during Covid-19: Social worker voices from Turkey, *International Social Work*, 63(5): 685–690.

Nowak, M. (2006) What practices constitute torture, *Human Rights Quarterly*, 28(4): 809–841.

Nowak, M. and McArthur, E. (2006) The distinction between torture and cruel, inhuman or degrading treatment, *Torture*, 16(3): 147–151.

O'Connell Davidson, J. (2015) *Modern Slavery: The Margins of Freedom*, Basingstoke: Palgrave.

Office of the High Commissioner for Human Rights (OHCHR) (2021a) *UN High Commissioner for Human Rights*. Available at: https://www.ohchr.org/EN/AboutUs/Pages/HighCommissioner.aspx (last accessed 15 June 2021).

Office of the High Commissioner for Human Rights (OHCHR) (2021b) *Special Rapporteur on Torture and Other Cruel, Inhuman or Degrading Treatment or Punishment*. Available at: https://www.ohchr.org/en/issues/torture/srtort ure/pages/srtortureindex.aspx (last accessed 15 June 2021).

Oliver, K. (2007) *Women as Weapons of War: Iraq, Sex, and the Media*, Columbia: Columbia University Press.

Omowumi Babatunde, A. (2018) The efficacy of traditional cultural practices in the rehabilitation of victims of torture in Nigeria's Niger Delta, *Torture: Journal on Rehabilitation of Torture Victims and Prevention of Torture*, 28(3): 31–46.

Oosterveld, V. (2014) Sexual violence directed against men and boys in armed conflict or mass atrocity: Addressing a gendered harm in international criminal tribunals, *Law Publications at Western University*, 109: 107–126.

Open Society Justice Initiative (2013) Globalising torture: CIA secret detention and extraordinary rendition. Available at: https://www.justiceinitiative.org/publications/globalizing-torture-cia-secret-detention-and-extraordinary-rendition (last accessed 25 August 2021).

Patel, N. and Mahtani, A. (2004) Psychological approaches to rape as torture, in Peel, M. (ed) *Rape as a Method of Torture*, London: Freedom from Torture, pp 56–68.

Peel, M. (2004) *Rape as a Method of Torture*, London: Freedom from Torture.

Peel, M., Mahtani, A., Hinshelwood, G. and Forrest, D. (2000) The sexual abuse of men in detention in Sri Lanka, *The Lancet*, 355(10): 2069–2070.

Pemberton, S. (2015) *Harmful Societies*, Bristol: Policy Press.

Pérez-Sales, P. (2017) *Psychological Torture: Definition, Evaluation and Measurement*, Abingdon: Routledge.

Presser, L. (2019) The story of antisociality: Determining what goes unsaid in dominant narratives, in Fleetwood, J., Presser, L., Sandberg, S. and Ugelvik, T. (eds) *The Emerald Handbook of Narrative Criminology*, Bingley: Emerald, pp 409–424.

Ray, S.L., Wong, C., White, D. and Heaslip, K. (2013) Compassion satisfaction, compassion fatigue, work life conditions, and burnout among frontline mental health care professionals, *Traumatology*, 19(4): 255–267.

Rejali, D. (2007) *Torture and Democracy*, Princeton: Princeton University Press.

Rejali, D. (2011) Torture and democracy: What now?, in Biswas, S. and Zalloua, Z. (eds) *Torture: Power, Democracy and the Human Body*, Seattle: University of Washington Press, pp 25–45.

Rivera, J. (2020) What is a cavity search?, *Legal Match*. Available at: https://www.legalmatch.com/law-library/article/what-is-a-body-cavity-search.html (last accessed 24 August 2021).

Robertson, R. (2012) Globalisation or glocalisation?, *The Journal of International* Communication, 18(2): 191–208.

Rodley N. (2002) The definition(s) of torture in international law, *Current Legal Problems*, 55(1): 467–493.

Rutherford, A., Zwi, A., Grove, N.J. and Butchart, A. (2007) Violence: A priority for public health? *Journal of Epidemiology and Community Health*, 61(9), 764–770.

Saar, E. and Novak, V. (2005) *Inside the Wire: A Military Intelligence Soldier's Eyewitness Account of Life at Guantanamo*, New York: Penguin.

Şalcıoğlu, E. and Başoğlu, M. (2017) Domestic violence and torture: A theoretical and empirical comparison, in Başoğlu, M. (ed) *Torture and its Definition in International Law*, Oxford: Oxford University Press, pp 107–135.

Scarry, E. (1985) *The Body in Pain: The Making and Unmaking of the World*, Oxford: Oxford University Press.

Schuster, L., Hussaini, R., Mossaini, M., Rezaie, R. and Shinwari, M.R.K. (2021) My beloved will come today or tomorrow: Time and the 'left behind', in Bhatia, M. and Canning, V. (eds) *Stealing Time: Migration, Temporality and State Violence*, Basingstoke: Palgrave Macmillan, pp 1–25.

Sexual Violence Research Initiative Resources (nd) Available at: https://www.svri.org/documents/our-resources (last accessed 25 August 2021).

Shalev, S. (2009) *Supermax: Controlling Risk through Solitary Confinement*, London: Willan Publishing.

Shin, H. and Salter, M. (2022) Betrayed by my body: Survivor experiences of sexual arousal and psychological pleasure during sexual violence, *Journal of Gender-Based Violence*. Early View: 1–15.

Sivakumaran, S. (2005) Male/male rape and the taint of homosexuality, *Human Rights Quarterly*, 27(4): 1274–1306.

Sivakumaran, S. (2007) Sexual violence against men in armed conflict, *European Journal of International Law*, 18(2): 253–276.

Sjölund, B.H., Kastrup, M. and Montgomery, E. (2009) Rehabilitating torture survivors, *Journal of Rehabilitation Medicine*, 41(9): 698–698.

Slahi, M.O. (2015) *Guantánamo Diary*, Edinburgh: Canongate.

Smith, E. (2004a) *Right First Time? Home Office Asylum Interviewing and Reasons for Refusal Letters*, London: Freedom from Torture.

Smith, E. (2004b) A legal analysis of rape as torture, in Peel, M. (ed) *Rape as a Method of Torture*, London: Freedom from Torture, pp 22–45.

Stanley, E. (2004) Torture, silence and recognition, *Current Issues in Criminal Justice*, 16(1): 5–25.

Stanley, E. (2008) Torture and terror, in Anthony, T. and Cuneen, C. (eds) *The Critical Criminology Companion*, Toronto: Hawkins Press, pp 158–169.

Sternberg K., Baradaran L., Abbott C., Lamb M. and Guterman E. (2006) Type of violence, age, and gender differences in the effects of family violence on children's behavior problems: A mega-analysis, *Developmental Review*, 26(1), 89–112.

Stumpf, J. (2006) The crimmigration crisis: Immigrants, crime and sovereign power, *American University Law Review*, 52(2): 367–419.

Taylor, J. and Shrive, J. (2021) 'I thought it was just a part of life': Analysing the prevalence of violence committed against women in the UK since birth, *Victim Focus*. Available at: https://irp.cdn-website.com/f9ec73a4/files/uploaded/Key-Facts-Document-VAWG-VictimFocus-2021a.pdf (last accessed 11 August 2021).

Thompson, L. (1998) *The Wandering Womb: A Cultural History of Outrageous Beliefs About Women*, New York: Prometheus Books

Tsangarides, N. (2012) The second torture: The immigration detention of torture survivors, *Medical Justice*. Available at: http://www.medicaljustice. org.uk/wp-content/uploads/2016/03/the-second-torture-full-version.pdf (last accessed 25 August 2021).

UN High Commissioner for Human Rights (2004) *Istanbul Protocol Manual on the Effective Investigation and Documentation of Torture and Other Cruel, Inhuman or Degrading Treatment or Punishment*. Available at: https://www. ohchr.org/sites/default/files/documents/publications/training8rev1en.pdf (last accessed 21 June 2022).

UN High Commissioner for Human Rights (2020) Committee Against Torture decision adopted by the Committee under article 22 of the Convention, concerning communication No. 879/2018. Available at: https://digitallibrary.un.org/record/3965976 (last accessed 4 October 2022).

UN Women (nd) *Ending Violence Against Women*. Available at: https://www.unwomen.org/en/what-we-do/ending-violence-against-women (last accessed 12 December 2021).

UN Women (2021) *Global Database of Violence against Women*. Available at: https://evaw-global-database.unwomen.org/en (last accessed 25 August 2021).

United Nations (nd) *Beijing Declaration 1995*. Available at: https://www. un.org/womenwatch/daw/beijing/platform/declar.htm (last accessed 25 August 2021).

United Nations (1984) *United Nations Convention Against Torture and other Cruel, Inhuman or Degrading Treatment or Punishment*. Available at: www. un.org/documents/ga/res/39/a39r046.htm (last accessed 3 March 2015).

United Nations (2000) *Security Council Resolution 1325*. Available at: https://www.un.org/womenwatch/osagi/wps/ (last accessed 25 August 2021).

United Nations (2008) *Security Council Resolution 1820*. Available at: https://www.unwomen.org/en/docs/2008/6/un-security-council-resolut ion-1820 (last accessed 25 August 2021).

United Nations (2010) *Security Council Resolution 1960*. Available at: https:// peacemaker.un.org/node/1931 (last accessed 25 August 2021).

United Nations Office on Drugs and Crime (2018) *Global Study of Homicide: Gender Related Killing of Women and Girls*. Available at: https:// www.unodc.org/documents/data-and-analysis/GSH2018/GSH18 _Gender-related_killing_of_women_and_girls.pdf (last accessed 5 February 2021).

Ussher, J.M. (2011) *The Madness of Women: Myth and Experience*, Oxon: Routledge.

Valentine, G. (1992) Images of danger: Women's sources of information about the spatial distribution of male violence, *Area*, 24(1): 22–29.

Valentine, G. (1996) (Re)negotiating the heterosexual street: Lesbian production of space, in Duncan, N. (ed) *Bodyspace*, London: Routledge, pp 56–75.

Van der Kolk, B. (2014) *The Body Keeps the Score: Mind, Brain and Body in the Transformation of Trauma*, New York: Penguin.

Vogt, W. (2013) Crossing Mexico: Structural violence and the commodification of undocumented Central American migrants, *American Ethnologist*, 40(4): 764–780.

Walby, S. and Towers, J. (2018) Untangling the concept of coercive control: Theorizing domestic violent crime, *Criminology and Criminal Justice*, 18(1): 7–29.

Wilcox, L. (2011) Dying is not permitted: Sovereignty, biopower and force-feeding at Guantánamo Bay, in Biswas, S. and Zalloua, Z. (eds) *Torture: Power, Democracy and the Human Body*, Seattle: University of Washington Press, pp 101–129.

Willyard, C. (2011) Men: A growing minority? Women earning doctoral degrees in psychology outnumber men three to one. What does this mean for the future of the field?, *American Psychological Association*. Available at: https://www.apa.org/gradpsych/2011/01/cover-men (last accessed 3 August 2021).

Women's Resource Centre (2010) *Power & Prejudice: Combating Gender Inequality Through Women's Organisations*, London: Women's Resource Centre.

Wood, E.J. (2009) Armed groups and sexual violence: When is wartime rape rare? *Politics and Society*, 37(1): 131–160.

Woodfox, A. (2019) *Solitary: Unbroken by Four Decades in Solitary Confinement*, Melbourne: The Text Publishing Company.

World Health Organization (2002) 'Definition and typology of violence', *World Report on Violence and Health: Summary, 4*. Geneva: Office of Publications.

Yahya, K. (2021) Journey and encampment observations: Liminality and the protracted refugee situation, in Bhatia, M. and Canning, V. (eds) *Stealing Time: Migration, Temporality and State Violence*, Basingstoke: Palgrave Macmillan, pp 25–39.

Yardley, E. (2020) The killing of women in 'sex games gone wrong': An analysis of femicides in Great Britain 2000–2018, *Violence Against Women*, 27(11): 1841–1861.

Yüksel, S., Saner, S., Basterzi, A.D., Oglagu, Z. and Bülbül, I. (2018) Genocidal sexual assault on women and the role of culture in the rehabilitation process: Experiences from working with Yazidi women in Turkey. *Torture*, 28(3): 124–132.

Žižek, S. (2002) *Welcome to the Desert of the Real*, London: Verso.

Index

References to figures appear in *italic* type; those in **bold** type refer to tables. References to endnotes show both the page number and the note number (164n1).

9/11 1, 8, 39, 43, 84

A
abortion 61, 98, 102
Abu Ghraib 1, 31, 41, 42, 82, 88
acid 44, 45, 96
activism 1, 3, 6, 17, 26, 79, 83, 87, 102, 146, 158
Afghanistan 5, 8, 9, 44, 85, 88, 89, 147, 154, 164n1
Africa 22, 89, 103
aftermath 1, 3, 8, 23, 34, 43, 51, **52**, 54, 56, 57, 69, 89, 98, 140, 144, 154, 158
alcohol 42, 94, 95, 97
Algeria 42, 164n1
American Psychological Association 138
Amnesty International 71
Annual Torture Report 2020 71
anxiety 44, **52**, 97, 152
Arendt, Hannah 40, 42
armed group 20, 165n3
asphyxiation 64
asylum 1, 6, 7, 10, 12, 20, 33, 38, 49, 51, 55, 56, 66, 72, 73, 79, 85, 90–91, 101–109, 111–116, 126, 128, 131–136, 141, 142, 146, 152–158, **159**, 160, 162, 166n2
  centre 73, 74, 101–109, 131–133, 144, 149, 155
  law 156–157
atrocity 89, 143
Australia 66, 164n1

B
Bachelet Jeria, Michelle 23
beating 8, 16, **18**, 28, 31, 38–42, 44–47, 54, 64, 66, 70, 79, 89, 94, 102, 107, 111, 115, 116, 162
best practice 6, 7, 11, 144
biological science 32
biopolitics 32, 51
Black Lives Matter 69

Black and migrant communities 155
black site 8, 44
blindfold 48
body functions 16, 51, **52**
Bolivia 5
Boochani, Behrouz 35–36, 72, 117
border 7, 11, 23, 35–36, 43, 46, 67, 69, 71–72, 102, 103, 104, 115, 117, 136, 142–143, 152–156, 165n4, 166n1
  camp 142, 144, 152
  control 152–153
  restriction 7
Border Violence Monitoring Network (BVMN) 71, 165n4
  see also Annual Torture Report 2020
Bosnia 7, 34, 84, 91, 97, 136, 164n1
British Journal of Criminology 3
bureaucracy 31, 73, 135, 136, 141, 143, 153, 157, 164n6
burning 8, 44, 45, 49, **52**, 68, 69, 94, 107, 116, 162
Bush administration 1, 8
  see also war against terror

C
Cambodia 42
Canada 66, 164n1
captivity 14, 63
Catalan resistance 2, 164n1
cavity search 83–84, 95–96
Central America 22
Central Intelligence Agency (CIA) 9, 33, 41, 44
Cheney, Dick 8
Chile 23, 121
childcare 104, 158
children 16, 27, 44, 48, **52**, 56–57, 63, 66–68, 70–73, 76, 82, 91, 94, 105, 128, 136, 142, 154–155
China 42, 161
Christianity 112

citizenship 86, 105, 134, 147
civil unrest 5
clothing 109, 139, 152
coercive control 16, 61–63, 81, 117, 131, 152, 164n6
Communism 42
community 48, **52**, 60, 69, 98, 137
compassion 43, 156
concentration camp 32
  see also Holocaust
confinement 13, 24, 29, 31, 45, 47, 63, 66, 78, 86, 102, 114–117, 123, 146, 148, 152, 165n1
continuum 11, 19, 67, 77, 78, 83, 88, 98, 103, 118
Convention on the Elimination of All Forms of Discrimination against Women 61, 80
Copelon, Rhonda 3, 4, 75, 77
Corll, Dean 96
counselling 97, 104, 134, 137, 154, 158, 165n3
COVID-19 156
crapaudine 42
credibility 49, 133, 146
criminal justice 6, 30, 59, 64, 120, 134
criminology 4, 39, 83, 102, 123
cruel, inhuman or degrading treatment (CIDT) 17, **19**, 20, 63, 64, 71, 78, 115, 164n2

D
Dahmer, Jeffrey 96
Danish Institute Against Torture (DIGNITY) 1, 3, 6, 10, 13, *15*, 17–20, 23, 29, 51, **52**, 61, 77, 78, 101, 162, 165n3
  see also Field Manual on Rehabilitation
death 2, 14, 16, 32, 47, 49, 50, 54, 60, 61, 69, 72, 94, 95, 98, 111, 113, 115, 152, 162
  see also murder
degradation 32, 36, 50, 51, 54, 69, 81–84, 97, 119
Democratic Republic of Congo 5, 69, 89, 91, 97
Denmark 6, 16, **18**, 22, 68, 69, 72, 90, 104–110, 116, 127, 132, 155, 164n1, 166n2
  see also Danish Institute Against Torture, Sandholm
deportation 108–109, 114, 116, 132, 141, 152, 153
depression **52**, 97, 135
deprivation of liberty **18**, 61
Dershowitz, Alan 5, 8
detainee 17, 32–35, 82, 88, 89, 96, 123, 142
detention 2, 6, 11, 13, 17, 29, 30, 36, 41, 44–45, 48, 63, 64, 71, 72, 77, 80–89, 91, 95, 96, 111–117, 129, 141, 144, 149–153, 165n1

centre 13, 111–117, 132, 142, 148, 150, 152
dignity 65, 80, 138
disclosure 55, 79, 103, 125–128, 132–134, 138, 141
discrimination 4, 35, 60, 61, 80
domestic abuse *see* domestic violence
domestic violence 1, 5, 8, 21, 22, 51, 62–66, 70, 77, 78, 80, 83, 89, 98, 111, 117, 120, 132, 139, 149, **159**, 160, 164n1, 166
drowning 38
drugs 94, 117

E
Eagleton, Terry 123
Economic and Social Research Council 6
economics 141, 154, 158, 160, 161
education 98, 105, 110, 138
electrotorture 38, 42, 77, 89, 90, 124
emotional abuse 3–6, 36, 53, 62, 78, 103, 105, 111, 137, 156, 162
employment 31, 32, 98
encampment 12, 161
Enhanced Interrogation Techniques (EITs) 1, 9, 31, 33, 39, 123
epistemology 10, 11, 14, 20, 22, 26, 29, 37, 60, 101–117, 150, 161
  see also experiential epistemologies
Eritrea 147
Ethiopia 161, 164n1
ethnicity 147
European Commission of Human Rights 16, **18**
European Convention on Human Rights 4, 71
European Union 165n4
experiential epistemologies 10–14, 20, 26, 101–117, 150, 161

F
falanga 27, 45, 49
false imprisonment 3, 8, 11, 24, 63, 102, 116, 161, 164n1
family 8, 14, 44, 47, 51–57, 61, 63, 70, 72, 73, 79, 82–91, 94, 97, 100–108, 111, 117, 128, 138, 139, 153, 154
  reunification 105, 108, 154
far-right 69
fear **18**, 53, 79, 93, 102, 105, 115, 117, 152, 155
female genital mutilation (FGM) 61
feminism 3–8, 11, 12, 16–17, 19, 23, 31, 34, 51, 75–79, 83, 84, 98, 102, 119, 121, 132, 144, 147–155
Field Manual on Rehabilitation 51
Floyd, George 69
food **18**, 46, 48, 109, 139, 152
force-feeding 8, 32
Foucault, Michel 32

Frederiksen, Mette 166n2
freedom 9, 20, 63, 66, 68, 102, 114
Freedom from Torture 9, 20, 33, 49, 101, 140
friendship 51, **52**, 57, 65, 158
funding 66, 139, 157, **159**
  cuts 7, 160
future **18**, **52**, 55, 65, 110, 116, 130, 151–153

G
Gacy, John Wayne 96
Game of Thrones 45, 145
gender 3–8, 11, 14, 29, 34, 37, 60–64, 73–75, 80–83, 84–88, 93, 98, 99, 105, 111, 123, 125–129, 131, 137–139, 147–155, 158, 165n3
  see also transgender
General Assembly of the United Nations **18**
genitals 42, 46, 61, 77, 78, 82, 90, 95, 96, 124
  see also female genital mutilation
genocide 34, 69, 81, 87, 91, 138
global financial crash 158
Global North 62
glocalization 10, 43, 46, 50, 126
Greece 16, **18**, 71, 72, 164n1, 165n4
Guantanamo Bay 8, 9, 32, 82
guilt **52**, 53–54, 70, 99, 125
gun 2, 42, 44, 105, 115
Guterres, António 13

H
handcuffs 111–112
hanging 27, 31, 45, 54, 96
harassment 61, 102, 108, 116
healthcare 113, 130, 140, 141
heritage 57, 68
holistic 16, 29, 35, 40, 58, 91, 93, 147, 150
Holocaust 32, 42
  see also concentration camp
home 3, 16, 24, 30, 34, 56, 63, 66, 70, 77, 81, 83, 84, 102–108, 111–116, 127, 128, 135, 152
homicide *see* murder
homosexuality *see* LGBTQ
honour 78, 98, 125, 139, 162
human rights 4, 16, **18**, 19, 23, 67, 71, 80, 99, 165n3, 165n4
  violation 2, 60, 61, 99, 165n4
  see also European Commission on Human Rights
humiliation 17, **18**, 41, 51, 54, 63–66, 69–71, 75, 81, 82, 85, 91, 96, 97, 99, 119
Hussein, Saddam 89
hysteria 77, 78

I
illness 77, 130, 147

imprisonment 21–23, 63, 73, 74, 83, 89, 96, 102, 108, 148, 152, 161
  see also false imprisonment, prison
incest 23, 24, 68, 84
information extraction 19, 33, 123
inhuman treatment 1, 3, 13, 16–17, **18**, 23, **52**, 59, 61, 63, 71, 77, 78, 80, 81, 89, 114, 115, 164n1
injury 16, **18**, 60
insecurity 152
Inter-American Convention to Prevent and Punish Torture 4, 17, **18**
International Criminal Court 80
International Criminal Tribunal for Former Yugoslavia 35
international law 5, 6, 10, 17, 39, 64, 76, 165n3
International Rehabilitation Council for Torture Victims 20
interrogation 1, 8, 9, 14, 29–33, 37, 39, 44, 45, 73, 76, 83, 90, 96, 123
intervention 7, 12, 69, 111, 135, 143, 144
intimacy 65, 93, 151
Iran 8, 35, 42, 69, 82, 88, 90, 97
Iraq 5–9, 41–44, 69, 88, 89, 97, 132
  see also Hussein, Saddam
Ireland 1–8, 32, 44, 66, 69, 164n2
Islamic State 28, 132
isolation 45–46, **52**, 53, 56, 65, 109, 153
Istanbul
  Convention 23, 60, 61, 80, 130, 134
  Protocol 118, 144
Italy 71, 104, 115

J
Japan 42
Johansen, Phillip Mbuji 68–69
justice 3, 6, **18**, 25, 30, 38, 41, 59, 64, 120, 134, 140, 141
  see also criminal justice

K
Key Performance Indicator 140, 160
kneecapping 1, 2, 24, 164n2

L
language 56, 73, 84, 93, 120, 121, 136, 145–151
Latin America 42
legalist hybridity 10, 14, 20, 22–24, 101
LGBTQI 72, 91, 151, 160
liberalism 65
Liberation Tigers of Tamil Eelam 34
Libya 1, 2, 89
lived experience 28, 64, 101, 156
Liverpool John Moores University 6
Lord's Resistance Army 45
loss 36, 51–57, 153
love 45, 57, 63, 65, 108, 110

M

magazine 94
Magdalene Laundries 66
marriage 61, 66, 87, 105, 106, 110, 111, 162
masculinity 8, 91, 125, 126, 139
media 8, 69, 94, 125, 126, 161
medical examination 150
medical practitioner 31 32, 127, 130
medication *see* medicine
medicine 32, 39, 46, 111, 113, 127
memory 43, 46, 50–53, 69, 71, 97, 123, 127, 133, 137, 145, 146
mental health 64, 98, 116, 118, 153, 156
see also anxiety, depression
#MeToo 140
Middle East 45, 46, 88, 92
migrant *see* migration
migration 7, 10, 11, 26, 35, 62, 71, 111, 113–116, 130, 135, 143, 148, 150–157
see also refugee
mock execution 38, 44–49
monolithic 23, 24, 41, 51, 57, 121, 140, 150, 165n1
murder 47, 49, 50, 68, 69, 94, 116, 117
Muslim 82, 84, 89, 105, 112, 155, 161
Myanmar 8, 161
myth 79, 162

N

nationality 7, 86
neglect 21, 60
neocoloniality 141, 143
Netflix 39
New York Times 69, 84
New Zealand 66
non-governmental organization (NGO) 6, 29, 40, 146, 149, 156, 165n4
non-refoulement 9, 10, **18**, 61, 80
Northern Europe 1, 6, 9, 43
Northern Ireland 1, 2, 44, 69, 164n2
nudity 25, 70, 82, 89, 96

O

Obsessive-Compulsive Disorder (OCD) 114, 116
Office for Legal Counsel 16
Open Society Justice Initiative 41, 43
oppression 147
oral histories 7, 8, 20, 24, 68, 71, 101, 102, 114, 116, 125, 127, 152
orthodox legalism 10, 14, 20, 101, 161
Ottoman Empire 42
outsourcing 30, 33, 36, 71

P

Palestine 31, 164n2
Palestinian chair 41
pandemic *see* COVID-19
paramilitary 2, 70, 74, 79, 83, 86, 139
patriarchy 62, 86–88, 91, 100, 148

Pérez-Sales, Pau 14, 17, 19, 23, 36, 42, 46, 47, 95, 118, 164n3
perpetrator 8, 16, **18**, 20–27, 31, 34–35, 62, 65, 68–70, 81, 83, 88, 101–102, 114, 116, 121, 126, 139, 165n3
persecution 10, 23, 44, 49, 55–56, 62, 79, 86, 90, 105–107, 115, 116, 126, 128, 135, 156, 161
Pinochet, Augusto 121
pleasure 77, 78, 93, 151
police 13–17, 20, 23, 31, 67, 69, 71, 72, 81, 103, 106, 111, 113
and Crime Commissioner (PCC) 120
station 13, 113
post-traumatic stress disorder (PTSD) **52**, 53, 57, 98, 136, 146
poverty 98, 105, 106, 142, 147, 154, 161
powerlessness 16, **19**, 30, 36, 41, 54, 62, 66, 84–86, 89, 91, 157, 164n1
practitioner 3, 6, 10, 11, 14, 19, 22–32, 37, 38–40, 43, 44, 48, **52**, 58, 59, 66–68, 71, 74–79, 81, 87, 90, 91, 97–102, 119, 120, *122*, 124, 126–131, 136–141, 144–149, 151, 154–158, **159–160**, 165n3
pregnancy 66, 97–98, 105, 165n2
Presser, Lois 123, 146
prison 8, 13, 21–26, 31–36, 37, 45–48, 63, 69–75, 81–84, 87, 89–96, 102–108, 111–117, 123, 148, 152, 161
guard 23, 81, 90
see also imprisonment
prohibition 13, 17
prostitution 66, 85, 104, 106, 108, 116
psychiatric hospital 30, 106
psychologist 6, 11, 19, 21–27, 30–32, 41, 48, 50–54, 59, 69, 71, 78, 79, 80–84, 90, 102, 117, 120, 124–130, 138, 140–144, 149, 156
psychotraumatology 6, 11, 44, 55, 59, 69, 84, 102, 134, 144
punishment 3, 13, *15*, 16–17, **18**, 19, 23, 31, 36, 45, **52**, 61, 77, 115, 164n2, 165n1

R

racism 69, 81, 111, 150, 155
rape 1, 3, 4, 5, 77–89, 90, 92–98, 99, 107, 108, 116, 120, 127, 132, 134, 139, 141, 148, 151
conflict-related 1–8, 11, 31, 34, 44–45, 61, 64, 65, 70, 75, 158–161, 164n2
crisis organization 134, 160
multiple perpetrator 8, 31, 34, 93
support clinic 77, 165n3
see also sexualized violence
Red Cross 29, 132
refugee 7, 9, 11, 20, 33, 40, 43, 55, 73, 74, 79, 91, 97, 98, 101–109, 110, 113, 117, 121, 126, 130, 132–136, 141, 144, 149, 152–158, **159**, 160, 162, 163, 166n2

camp 72, 102, 131, 152
Convention 104, 106, 113, 115, 117, 141
rehabilitation 7, 19–22, 50, 51, 59, 67, 76, 90, 118, 125, 128–131, 134, 136, 147, 150, 153, 158
Reimagining Refugee Rights 160
Rejali, Darius 5, 9, 14, 28, 31–33, 40–42, 49, 50, 81, 90, 119, 124, 140, 165n1
religion 115, 139
repatriation 152
Rodley, Nigel 75, 78, 80, 81, 164n2
Rwanda 5, 34, 69, 80, 81, 91, 140
see also genocide

S
sadomasochism 94–95
safety 62, 64, 103, 104, 106, 110, 138, 151, 152, 154, 161
sanctuary 152
Sandholm 109
Saw 45
Scarry, Elaine 14, 45, 54, 65, 119
school 30, 34, 66, 98, 104, 136, 152, **160**, 162
Second World War 90
Senate Intelligence Committee Report on Torture 13, 33, 124
sensory deprivation 41, 49, 66, 82
sequelae 97
see also illness, injury
sex games 94, 95
see also sadomasochism
sexism 148, 150
sexualized violence 1–7, 11, 23, 25, 31, 34, 38, 53, 55, 61, 70, 75–80, 81–89, 91–99, 102, 119–121, *122*, 124–139, 143, 148, 150, 158, 162, 164n2, 166n1
against men and boys 88–93
see also rape
Sierra Leone 5
silencing 3–7, 11, 13, 32, 33, 38, 65, 93, 103, 119–121, *122*, 123–129, 131–140, 141, 142, 147, 151, 162
self- 120, 127–129, 140
see also unsilencing
sin 92
slavery 83, 104, 106
sleep **52**, 53, 95
deprivation **18**, 31, 42, 46
Slovenia 71
social harm 6, 41
soldier 30, 32, 45, 82, 93
somatic 53–55, 97, 130, 135
Soviet Union *see* USSR
spatiality 10, 29, 131, 133
Special Rapporteur on Torture and Other Cruel, Inhuman or Degrading Treatment or Punishment **19**, 21, 23, 78, 79, 164n2

Sri Lanka 34, 44
see also Liberation Tigers of Tamil Eelam
statehood 86
state official 2, 4, 13, 14, 21, 83, 101, 146
state violence 13, 14, 35, 65, 86, 95, 126, 161
sterilization 61
stigma 11, 99, 103, 119, 125
strangulation 3, 64, 162
starvation 48, 49, 66
suicide 111, 116
support network 158
surveillance 31
survivor 3, 6, 7, 9–12, 14–28, 33, 34, 37–40, 41–59, 62, 71–79, 81, 83, 84, 90–99, 101–118, 119, 120, *122*, 123–131, 140–149, 158–162, 164n3, 165n2
Sweden 6, 29, 108–109, 112, 113, 117, 147, 152
Swedish Red Cross Center for Persons Affected by War and Trauma 29
Syria 5, 7, 20, 42, 44, 86–90, 97, 98, 147, 154, 164n1

T
taboo 82, 119
Taliban 161
teeth 47, 85
television 45, 94, 112, 114
temporality 29, 36, 41, 48, 54, 57, 65, 71, 100, 117–120, *122*, 133–136, 153, 154
terrorism 1, 4, 5, 8, 9, 21, 31
therapist 21, 45, 48, 128, 129, 133, 137
toilet 46, 48, **52**
torturer 20, 22, 31–37, 53, 54, 63, 65, 73, 82
lone 31–32
third party 37
threat 8, 16, 45–48, 60, 65–79, 80, 83, 94, 98, 102, 105, 111–115, 117, 138, 150, 152–158
to kill 8, 162
trafficking 1, 11, 24, 68, 85, 86, 102
transgender 62, 72, 106–108, 116, 129, 132, 153, 165n2
see also LGBTQ
trauma 6, 7, 11, 19, 22–29, 35, 44, 51, **52**, 53–59, 63, 64–75, 84, 87, 98, 99, 117–129, 130, 134–141, 145–158, 162
traumata 67, 75, 140
True Blood 45
trust 25, 34, 50–56, 63, 79, 94, 102, 117, 125, 128, 131, 133 134, 139, 141, 150, 151, 157, **159**
Tunisia 44
Turkey 71–72, 164n1

U
Uganda 45
see also Lord's Resistance Army

Ukraine 161
United Nations 3, 4, 14, **18**, **52**, 61, 67, 77, 80, 94, 115, 117, **159**
  Convention Against Torture or Other Cruel, Inhuman or Degrading Treatment or Punishment (UNCAT) 1, 3, 4, 13, 14, 16, 19–21, **52**, 61, 69, 71, 74, 77, 78, 83–99, 115, 117, 165n1
  Office on Drugs and Crime 94, 115, 117
  Security Council Resolutions 5, 23, 75
  see also Guterres, António
United States 16, 42
unsilencing 6, 7, 119–137, 140–143, 151, 162
see also silencing
USSR 42

V
victim *15*, **18**, 20, 28, 33, 62, 65, 69, 73, 83, 94, 95–98, 128 130, 138, 140, 141
violence 1–7, 10–17, 19, 21, 26, 32–43, 48–54, 56–58, 59–70, 74, 75, 83–99, 100–108, 112, 120–123, 125–129, 130–142, 144–158, **159**, 160–162, 164n1, 165n3, 165n4, 166n1
  institutional 60, 148
  militarized 34
  multiple perpetrator 34
  organizational 32
  psychological 21, 28, 40, 49, 59, 61, 94, 102, 103, 115–117
  structural 34, 60, 72, 74, 93, 147, 158, 160
  see also sexualized violence
visa 106, 108–110, 112, 113
vulnerability 76, 82, 137, 141, 155, **159**

W
war 5, 8, 14, 23, 24, 29, 30, 34, 44, 45, 53, 67, 69–71, 79, 80–86, 87, 89–91, 97, 98, 132, 147
  against terror 8
  crime 79–80
waterboarding 8, 31, 38, 42
wealth 7, 105, 147, 158, 161
wellbeing 21, 33, 142, 153, 156
Whiteness 8
women 1–8, 11, 24, 26, 30, 32, 53, 60–67, 74, 76–80, 83, 85, 87–99, 101–109, 111–115, 120, 129–139, 146, 147, 148–151, 155, **159**, 160, 165n1
  see also feminism, Convention on the Elimination of All Forms of Discrimination against Women
workshop 6, 11, 29, 76, 151, 158, 164n5
World Health Assembly Resolution 60
World Health Organization (WHO) 60
World Report on Violence and Health (WRVH) 60

X
xenophobia 69

Y
Yugoslavia 5, 35, 80, 87, 140
  see also International Criminal Tribunal for Former Yugoslavia

Z
zemiology 6, 12, 41, 144
Zero Dark Thirty 45
Žižek, Slavoj 40
Zubaydah, Abu 9, 33